The Lewis and Clark
COLUMBIA RIVER
WATER TRAIL

The Lewis and Clark

COLUMBIA RIVER WATER TRAIL

A Guide for
Paddlers, Hikers, and
Other Explorers

KEITH G. HAY

with a foreword by Gary E. Moulton

TIMBER PRESS
Portland ~ Cambridge

All royalties from the sale of this book will be donated equally between the Oregon and Washington Chapters of the Lewis and Clark Trail Heritage Foundation.

Jacket front, clockwise from top: The Columbia River, just upstream from Cape Horn (Ellen Morris Bishop); Youngs River Falls (Ellen Morris Bishop); Astoria-Megler Bridge. Spine: Near Cape Disappointment, Fort Canby State Park (Ellen Morris Bishop).

Frontispiece: Entering the Blind Slough.

Published in 2004 by
Timber Press, Inc.
The Haseltine Building
133 SW Second Avenue, Suite 450
Portland, Oregon 97204, U.S.A.

Timber Press
2 Station Road
Swavesey
Cambridge CB4 5QJ, U.K.

Library of Congress Cataloging-in-Publication Data
Hay, Keith G.
    The Lewis and Clark Columbia River Water Trail : a guide for paddlers, hikers, and other explorers / Keith G. Hay ; with a foreword by Gary E. Moulton.
        p. cm.
    Includes bibliographical references and index.
    ISBN 0-88192-620-5 (flexi-bind)
    1. Outdoor recreation--Lewis and Clark Columbia River Water Trail (Or. and Wash.)--Guidebooks. 2. Lewis and Clark Columbia River Water Trail (Or. and Wash.)--Guidebooks. I. Title.

GV191.42.L49H39 2004
796.5'09795'4--dc22   2003056519

A catalog record for this book is also available from the British Library.

Printed through Colorcraft Ltd, Hong Kong

The Indian nations in this neighborhood pass altogether by water. They have no roads or pathes through the Countrey which we have observed, except across portages from one Creek to another.

CAPTAIN WILLIAM CLARK

Fort Clatsop, Oregon, December 29, 1805

CONTENTS

Color plates follow page 128

FOREWORD

WATER. The safest, swiftest, and most reliable means of travel in Lewis and Clark's time.

It was water that would lead the expedition party, the Corps of Discovery, to the Rocky Mountains, and it was water that would plunge them toward the Pacific. Two great rivers of the West beckoned the explorers and beguiled them with dreams of an easy portage over the mountains and a quick passage to the sea. It was not to be, and the ephemeral Northwest Passage soon became the stuff of legend from the heroic age of exploration.

But water remained. Now it calls to modern-day travelers who want to follow in the paddle strokes of Lewis and Clark. Thanks to Keith G. Hay and his many supporters, we have a reliable guide to a fascinating 146-mile stretch of the Columbia River from Bonneville Dam to the coast. With this handy guide, boaters, hikers, and land-side travelers can follow in detail the day-by-day route of Lewis and Clark in 1805 and 1806, get practical directions for driving, docking, hiking, and bicycling, and learn of native life and lore.

Let's get on the water again.

GARY E. MOULTON,
professor of history at the University of Nebraska, Lincoln,
and editor of the thirteen-volume *Journals of the Lewis & Clark Expedition*

ABOUT THIS BOOK

THIS WATER TRAIL PROJECT began as an outgrowth of a study by The Conservation Fund, a national nonprofit land conservation organization, to develop a "Pacific Greenway" between Portland, Oregon, and the coast. The study recommended two routes: an overland trail system and a "blueway" down the Columbia. I began working with Sam McKinney, former coordinator of the Oregon Historical Society's Columbia River Heritage Program, to expand his Columbia River Heritage Canoe Trail (between Clatskanie and the John Day River) to begin in Portland and end in Astoria. This blueway project, now named the Lewis and Clark Columbia River Water Trail, begins near Bonneville Dam and ends 146 free-flowing miles downstream, near Fort Clatsop in Oregon and Fort Canby in Washington. Although the water trail ends at these historic forts, the maps included in this book continue to the ocean on both sides of the river, and additional boating and historical information is provided. The extension upstream to Bonneville was suggested by Washington State Lewis and Clark Trail officials, who also recommended creating a future guide to the portion of the Lewis and Clark Water Trail that begins at the Washington-Idaho border and follows the Snake and Columbia Rivers down to Bonneville Dam. Development of the overland trail system to the coast has been thwarted, to date, by private property.

Every effort has been made to ensure that all information is current, historically correct, and geographically accurate. Lewis and Clark quotes have been taken from *The Journals of the Lewis & Clark Expedition* (Moulton 1989, 1990, 1991).

ACKNOWLEDGMENTS

Generous support from the following organizations has made this guidebook possible: The Conservation Fund, the Meyer Memorial Trust, the REI Foundation, the PacifiCorp Foundation, the Ralph L. Smith Foundation, the Oregon Parks Foundation, and the National Park Service Challenge Cost Share Program. This project was also made possible in part by a grant from the Lewis and Clark Bicentennial in Oregon, the statewide planning organization for the Lewis and Clark Bicentennial commemoration. The project has been a cooperative effort, with a wide variety of people in Oregon and Washington sharing their knowledge and contributing to the book's accuracy. One of the joys of such research has been the encounters with the many friendly and helpful people in the cities, towns, and rural areas of these two states.

First and foremost has been the extensive contribution made by Allen Wesselius of the Washington Chapter of the Lewis and Clark Trail Heritage Foundation. His expertise on journal quotes, the history behind names of cities, towns, and geographical features, and Lewis and Clark on the Columbia is gratefully acknowledged. Phil Jones, author of several books on canoeing, kayaking, and bicycling in northwest Oregon and the Columbia River Gorge, contributed immeasurably with format and information regarding access, paddling trips, and boating cautions and conditions. Jack Remington, retired trails coordinator for the Oregon Parks and Recreation Department, contributed to the sections on river safety, trail etiquette, and the lower Columbia. The late Irving Anderson, among the nation's foremost Lewis and Clark scholars, provided historical research, advice, and encouragement. Thanks to Barb Kubik, past president of the Lewis and Clark Trail Heritage Foundation and chair of the Washington State Governor's Lewis and Clark Trail Committee, for her generous time and expertise in meticulously reviewing the text for historical accuracy, cultural sensitivity, and readability. I would also like to thank Phyllis Reynolds for her contribution to and review of the list of plants described by Lewis and Clark. John Davenport, retired Oregon Department of Transportation cartographer, designed and produced the excellent maps for this book. Geologist Ellen Morris Bishop kindly supplied several beautiful photographs, including the one appearing on the cover.

I thank Andrew Emlen, Russ Greenberg, and Gary Lofgren for their contributions of the sections on the lower Columbia through the seasons, Puget Island and the Lewis and Clark National Wildlife Refuge, and Welch Island and boating cautions and conditions, respectively. For technical, historical, editorial, and river knowledge, a hearty thanks is also extended to Bob Kenyon and Rob Elliot of the Lower Columbia River Canoe Club; Larry Warnberg of the Willapa Bay Water Trail; Cindy and Steve Scherrer of Alder Creek Kayak Supply; Denny McEntire and Ben Colliander of Pacific Wave; Mary Monfort,

Garth Johnson, and Reed Waite of the Washington Water Trails Association; Tim Lehman, Steve Gordon, and other members of the Oregon Ocean Paddlers Association; Ted Kaye, former executive director of the Lewis and Clark Bicentennial in Oregon; Chet Orloff, director emeritus of the Oregon Historical Society; David Nicandri, executive director of the Washington Historical Society; Murray Hayes, past president of the Washington Chapter of the Lewis and Clark Trail Heritage Foundation; Martin Law, Randy Henry, and Dave Obern of the Oregon State Marine Board; Susan Saul, Alex Bourdeau, Charles Stenvall, and Virginia Parks of the U.S. Fish and Wildlife Service; Gail Wells and Patricia Benner of the College of Forestry, Oregon State University; Curt Peterson of the Department of Geology, Portland State University; Lehman Holder of the Cascade Pacific Council, Boy Scouts of America; Al LePage, executive director of the National Coast Trail Association; Nancy Bell Anderson of the Knappton Cove Heritage Center; Carolyn Glenn, David Campiche, Catherine Morrow, Mack Funk, and Chris Jacobsen of the Pacific County Friends of Lewis and Clark; David Getchell, president of the North American Water Trails; Mark Hamilton of Ball State University; Chris Hathaway of the Lower Columbia River Estuary Program; Mel Huie of Metro, Trails, and Greenspaces; Glen Kirkpatrick of the Oregon Department of Transportation; Martin Plamondon II of Washington State Governor's Lewis and Clark Trail Committee; Steve Wang of the Washington Parks and Recreation Department; Maria Thi-Mai and Pete Bond of the Oregon Parks and Recreation Department; Mark Gosselin of Vancouver, Washington; Brian Atwater of the U.S. Geological Survey; Robert Goodwin of the University of Washington Sea Grant Program; James Agee, professor of forest ecology at the University of Washington; Pam Anderson of the Washington Chapter of the Lewis and Clark Trail Heritage Foundation; Jim Sayce of Long Beach, Washington; Betty Siebenmorgen of Portland, Oregon; Bob Brown, president of the Columbia County Historical Society; Jerry and Mike Igo, Oregon botanists; Leslie Labbe of Portland; Patti Williams of the Army Corps of Engineers; Tom McAllister, president of the Oregon Geographic Names Board; Paul Benoit, director of community development, Astoria, Oregon; Anne LaBastille of West of the Wind Publications, Westport, New York; Jan Mitchell, president of the Clatsop County Lewis and Clark Bicentennial Association; Tanya Gross, assistant to the director of the Oregon Historical Society; and David Evans and Associates. Finally, I would like to thank Timber Press for their professional skills and advice.

INTRODUCTION

THERE IS NO BETTER WAY to learn about history than by experiencing firsthand the sights, smells, and sounds of the environment in which it was made. This guide to the Lewis and Clark Columbia River Water Trail has two main goals: to provide boaters and other travelers with the information needed to safely enjoy and protect this riverine environment, on both day and overnight explorations; and to blend useful logistical information with the historical, cultural, and environmental assets of this 146-mile water trail, paying particular attention to the 1805–1806 role of the Corps of Discovery.

So what exactly is a water trail? It is a stretch of river, or a fresh- or salt-water shoreline, that has been designated and mapped with the purpose of creating water paths to natural and cultural resources. In addition, a water trail provides linkage to other recreational trails and outdoor experiences, be they hiking, biking, or vehicle-based trails. It is a flexible and responsive tool for promoting a healthy economy and a high quality of life while preserving our natural and historical heritage. Aquatic trails are thus ribbons of discovery that tie us to the past and present spirit of the land.

During the time of Meriwether Lewis and William Clark, such trails were the principal means of transportation for native people on the Columbia. Various tribes built and decorated canoes, carefully chiseling and burning each one from a single tree trunk, usually of white cedar. Some canoes reached 50 feet in length and were capable of carrying up to thirty people. Lewis and Clark were fascinated by the skill of the intrepid native boatmen and the seaworthy canoes they paddled.

This guide was specifically designed for canoes, kayaks, and shallow-draft motorized boats, which are able to explore the unique landscapes of the lower Columbia—quiet, special places in which to appreciate history, wildlife, and beauty—from the water. With its updated highway and road systems, however, it serves the traveling motorist as well, and bicyclists and hikers should find the information equally useful.

More than 260 sites, including significant historical, cultural, geological, and ecological features, are noted and described, including twenty-five Lewis and Clark campsites and many village sites of the Chinookan-speaking people. The interesting history behind the geographical names given to the islands and shoreline communities are also explained. The latest information is given regarding launch sites, day use, overnight camping, transit moorages, boating facilities, boat rentals, and guided tours. Maps cover key points along the trail, Lewis and Clark campsites, and the actual water routes taken by the expedition as they traveled westward in 1805 and eastward in 1806.

Many historic locations along the route are fragile and subject to environmental degradation, are on private property, or are sacred to Native Americans, so as you follow the expedition's pathway and experience this great American adventure firsthand, do so carefully, with permission, and without leaving a trace of your visit. Acceptable use also precludes loud music that disturbs wildlife and people seeking the river's solitude and the sounds of nature.

The ship channel, with its busy traffic, and the fishing seasons (from the third week in April to November) are competing uses of the river and are best avoided. Anglers, however, are usually cordial and unobtrusive. In summer, boaters seeking tranquility should avoid areas where water-skiing and jet-skiing are allowed, visiting these places in fall, winter, or spring instead. Regardless how much time you have to spend on the Lewis and Clark Columbia River Water Trail, the trip should prove to be a memorable experience.

More detailed information on GPS navigation, safety, and etiquette can be found at the back of the book. Helpful addresses, phone numbers, and Web sites are also listed, and the bibliography includes many good sources for additional information on the Columbia River and the Lewis and Clark expedition.

THE COLUMBIA RIVER

THE NCH'I-WANA, OR "GREAT RIVER OF THE WEST," begins in the spectacular snowcapped mountains of southeastern British Columbia. Here it emerges as a modest, quiet spring of clear green water, 2 yards wide, flowing from a stretch of glacial silt lying some 2,619 feet above sea level in a valley between the Rockies to the east and the Selkirks to the west. The small spring is fed by the huge melting glaciers of the Columbia Ice Fields and flows into the deep, cold aquamarine Columbia Lake. From the lake, it courses almost straight north for 110 miles before the Caribou Mountains force it to plunge south along the western side of the Selkirks. Joined by countless other springs, streams, and rivers from its enormous watershed, the Columbia finally meets the Pacific after a journey of 1,270 miles, delivering an average daily flow of 150 billion gallons of fresh water to the sea.

The Columbia basin encompasses some 259,000 square miles, draining an area larger than France and England combined. The region comprises most of the Pacific Northwest, including nearly all of Washington, Oregon, Idaho, and Montana (west of the Rockies), and some sections of Wyoming, Nevada, and Utah. The basin's eleven major tributaries contribute an annual runoff second in volume only to the Mississippi River. In the last century some 250 dams have been built on the river's tributaries, and 14 on its main stem, creating the world's largest hydroelectric system. Its waters have transformed a desert into a breadbasket, and its navigation locks enable barges to transport products inland to Idaho. These benefits, however, have come at a devastating cost to salmon populations, preventing more than 95 percent of the salmon from returning to their ancestral spawning grounds.

The Columbia traverses ice fields, lush temperate rainforests, marshy wet-lands, near-desert grasslands, cattle and wheat lands, steep basalt canyons, and subalpine meadows before it reaches Astoria, Oregon. It is a river corridor filled with some of the nation's most colorful history, including the international struggles involving Spain, Russia, the United States, and Britain that resulted in the unification of our young nation from coast to coast. Its English name was bestowed by Captain Robert Gray, a private Boston trader who sailed an American ship across the treacherous bar at the mouth of the river on May 11, 1792. He laid anchor 6 miles upstream (in what is now called Grays Bay) and promptly named the river "Columbia's River," after his brig, the *Columbia Rediviva*. After trading with the Clatsop Indians for sea otter skins, Captain Gray departed on May 20, but those nine days gave the United States a claim to the "Oregon Country" and the land that eventually became the Pacific Northwest.

THE CORPS OF DISCOVERY

THE LEWIS AND CLARK EXPEDITION OF 1804–1806 stands, incomparably, as our nation's epic in documented exploration of the American West. Many historians consider it among the most successful and significant overland explorations in world history. Preparations for the expedition were meticulously made and President Thomas Jefferson's instructions carefully executed. The party traveled more than 8,000 miles through unmapped terrain over a period of two years, four months, and nine days. Only one man died, from apparent appendicitis.

Politically it secured the American purchase of the entire territory called Louisiana, established friendly relations with native Indian tribes from the Midwest to the Pacific, and strengthened American claims to the Oregon Country. Economically and ecologically it provided the first accurate knowledge of the geography, natural resources, and inhabitants of the western lands.

Jefferson, the master architect of the expedition, conceived the project long before the Louisiana Purchase. In fact, he had previously failed on five different occasions to persuade Congress to authorize expeditions of western exploration. In 1762 France ceded to Spain the interior of the continent west of the Mississippi River along with the city of New Orleans. This arrangement was temporary, however, and in 1800 Napoléon forced Spain to return the Louisiana Territory to France. Jefferson was at once alarmed. Dealing with a deteriorating and incompetent Spanish colonial administration was one thing, but dealing with Napoléon, Europe's most brilliant and effective military and political leader, was a different matter. Jefferson saw French control of New Orleans as an iron gate across the main artery of internal American commerce. He promptly sent James Monroe to join the U.S. minister in France, Robert Livingston, to make arrangements to secure American rights and interests in the Mississippi and the country eastward of it.

They found Napoléon deep in debt. He had also lost some fifty thousand troops in Saint Domingue (present-day Haiti) and was facing another war with

Thomas Jefferson by Charles Willson Peale, from life, 1791–1792. Courtesy of the Independence National Historical Park, Philadelphia.

the British. He needed money badly and startled the American negotiators by offering to sell the entire Louisiana Territory for $15 million (less than 3 cents an acre). Jefferson quickly consummated the bargain. This enormous 827,000-square-mile area doubled the size of the young nation of seventeen states. It included most of the lands drained by the western tributaries of the Mississippi River, from the Gulf of Mexico to present Canada and west to the Continental Divide.

The timing of the purchase and the expedition was fortuitous. Jefferson had actually planned the expedition long before Napoléon's offer and had proposed an appropriation of twenty-five hundred dollars for the journey in his address to Congress on January 18, 1803. Congress appropriated the money in March. On October 20, 1803, the Senate ratified the Louisiana Purchase by a vote of twenty-four to seven. France officially transferred the territory on December 20, and the United States took possession on December 30, 1803.

The primary objective was to find a practical water transportation link between the Louisiana Territory and the Oregon Country, something that Jefferson explained in a draft letter to Lewis dated June 20, 1803: "The object of your mission is to explore the Missouri river, & such principal stream of it, as by it's course and communication with the waters of the Pacific ocean, whether the Columbia, Oregon, Colorado or any other river, may offer the most direct & practicable water communication across this continent for the purposes of commerce." The president's vision included far more than geographic exploration, however, and his lengthy instructions to Lewis were highly specific and scientific. Lewis was to observe and, where practical, collect plant, animal, and mineral specimens, record weather data, study native cultures and languages, map geographic features, and record all important observations and events in daily journal entries. It was, in fact, the first government-sponsored scientific exploration in the United States.

The expedition members made their way through the vast trans-Mississippi West, living off its resources and adapting to its harsh conditions. On foot, on horseback, and by boat they pushed over massive mountain ranges, across endless plains, through dense forests, against powerful currents and raging waters, in summer heat, winter freezing, and heavy rain.

Lewis began the journey in Washington, D.C., on July 5, 1803. At Pittsburgh he gathered supplies of arms and military stores from the federal arsenals at Harpers Ferry and Philadelphia. These items were loaded aboard a specially designed keelboat, on which Lewis and eleven men departed down the Ohio River on August 30. Other men were recruited along the way, and at Clarksville, Ohio, Lewis was joined by his cocommander, William Clark. Camp Dubois, their winter quarters, was established along the Mississippi River, above St. Louis at Wood River, Illinois, opposite the mouth of the Missouri River.

On May 14, 1804, the party of forty-five departed Camp Dubois and headed up the Missouri River "under a gentle brease." The party included seven soldiers and nine French boatmen "engages" who would accompany the expedition as far as the Mandan villages in North Dakota. In April 1805, after wintering at Fort Mandan, some of these men would return with the keelboat to St. Louis loaded with specimens (including a live prairie dog), maps, and journals for President Jefferson. One of the French boatmen later settled in the Northwest and is buried in the cemetery at St. Paul, Oregon. The "permanent party" of thirty-three that would continue to the Pacific included Clark's slave, York, the French-Canadian fur trader and interpreter Toussaint Charbonneau, Charbonneau's Shoshoni "wife," Sacagawea, and their newborn son Jean Baptiste, who joined the party at Fort Mandan. Also accompanying the party throughout the trip was Lewis's Newfoundland dog, Seaman.

As they continued up the Missouri in the spring of 1805 in two pirogues and six dugout canoes, they encountered dangers as a matter of course, suffering hunger, fatigue, privation, and sickness. They encountered the Great Falls of the Missouri in mid-June and spent three weeks portaging the heavy canoes and equipment 18 miles around the falls. By August they reached the source of the Missouri and fortuitously found the band of Shoshoni Indians that were Sacagawea's people, led by her brother, Chief Cameahwait. This remarkable coincidence, together with Sacagawea's ability to speak Shoshoni, greatly enhanced their ability to trade for the horses needed to travel over the Continental Divide and through the Bitterroot Mountains. It was generally assumed that by going up the Missouri River to its source, a short portage of possibly 20 miles would bring them to the headwaters of the Columbia River, which would carry them to the sea. The expanse of the Rocky Mountains was not anticipated. Unfortunately they missed the headwaters of the Clark's Fork, which would have given

A Jefferson Peace Medal given to principal Indian chiefs was discovered in an Indian burial site on the Palouse River in southeast Washington in the 1960s.

them easy passage to the Columbia. Instead they forged some 200 miles through the snowy Bitterroots, following ancient Indian trails to reach the Clearwater River in Idaho, a tributary of the Snake. Here they left their horses with the Nez Perce Indians, made new dugout canoes, and proceeded down the Clearwater, Snake, and Columbia Rivers, reaching the Pacific Ocean in November 1805.

The northern shore of the Columbia estuary proved sparse of game, and the party encountered near-starvation along with wind-driven rains and raging sea-borne waves. After consulting local Indians and polling the party, the captains decided to cross the river to the southern side, where they were told game was plentiful. After an extensive survey, Lewis found a sheltered site for a winter camp near present-day Astoria, and Fort Clatsop was constructed in December. The winter months were to be some of the wettest in history; but, though rainy and dismal, the four-and-a-half-month stay was a busy time. The captains worked over their field notes and maps, entertained and bartered with the Clatsop Indians for food, and gained important geographic and ethnographic information. Hunting parties were sent out daily, and elk and deer skins were made into clothing and moccasins for the return trip. A detail of men was sent south to make salt by boiling seawater.

Unfortunately, the Corps' time on the Pacific Coast did not coincide with the trading season, and thus they made no contact with coastal trading vessels for a return passage by sea. The Corps then began their long journey home overland on March 23, 1806. Paddling upstream against the strong current of the Columbia, they traded their dugout canoes to the Indians for pack horses near The Dalles, Oregon. They returned to the Nez Perce villages and retrieved the horses left there, but were delayed nearly a month in recrossing the Bitterroots due to deep snow. By July they reached Travelers Rest Camp near Missoula, Montana, and split the party, with Lewis taking a small detachment to explore what would come to be known as the Blackfoot, Sun, and Marias Rivers. It was here they encountered the most serious Indian skirmish of the expedition, in which two Blackfoot Indians were killed. Clark, meanwhile, headed southeast to the Yellowstone River through Shoshoni and Crow tribal lands, following Indian trails pointed out by Sacagawea. Once again they made dugout canoes and explored the river downstream to its confluence with the Missouri, where they rejoined Captain Lewis and party. They continued down the Missouri to the Mandan villages, Charbonneau, Sacagawea, and Jean Baptiste returning to their community. The voyageurs made a rapid descent to St. Louis, arriving there on September 23, 1806.

Although every generation rediscovers the heroic saga of Lewis and Clark, only recently have Americans come to truly appreciate the enormous accomplishments of the young members of the Corps of Discovery and the remarkable endurance and invaluable contributions of Sacagawea, a teenage mother who experienced the same hardships, over the same thousands of miles of terrain, burdened with an infant son on her back.

The men's journals are among the treasures of America's written history. The expedition strengthened the nation's claim to the Pacific Northwest, set the stage for westward expansion, dispelled the dream of a northwest water passage to the Orient, and contributed the first major scientific knowledge of the flora, fauna, geology, ethnology, and geography of the West. It also embraced many of the most cherished principles of human endeavor: trust, respect, ingenuity, leadership, courage, foresight, discipline, diplomacy, friendship, integrity, patience, resourcefulness, and diversity. It did not involve aggression, intolerance, or the imposition of religious beliefs on other cultures. The expedition's values and meaning for the twenty-first century are manifest. Though the Lewis and Clark expedition did not make America, without it the United States might not exist in its present form.

LEWIS AND CLARK
ON THE COLUMBIA

THE PACIFIC NORTHWEST had been inhabited for thousands of years by Native Americans before the Great River of the West was "discovered" and explored by Euro-Americans. In 1775 Captain Bruno de Heceta, a Spanish explorer, sighted the Columbia estuary and concluded that it was the mouth of a great river. He named it the San Roque but did not enter it. Three years later British Captain James Cook missed the river's entrance as he sailed up the West Coast. Comte de La Pérouse, a French naval officer, did the same thing in 1785. In 1788 British sea captain John Meares found the mouth of the river but assumed it was a bay. It was not until May 1792, when Robert Gray crossed the bar, entered the river, and claimed sovereignty of its waters, that it became a recognized part of American history and geography. Vague rumors hinting of a mighty river somewhere in the unexplored Pacific Northwest persisted from stories of Spanish merchants and explorers who had sailed along the coast and speculated on the river's location. An important element of this search was the eternal pursuit by Europeans of a water route—a "Northwest Passage" between the river systems flowing east and west of the Continental Divide—that would allow for easier access to the Orient and its markets. This quest also generated nationalistic attempts to claim the route's discovery and control.

Americans' "Rights of Discovery" to the Columbia were established when Gray successfully entered the river and named it Columbia's River. It was an internationally accepted practice at the time to gain possession of land by simply arriving first and recording the discovery, despite the long habitation of the land by native people. Such territorial claims of a river also included the provision for sovereignty of "All Lands Drained." Further exploration, however, would be required to determine the bounds of this extended sovereignty.

President Jefferson's concerns for establishing American sovereignty of the Columbia River were well founded. In October 1792 (a mere five months after

Gray's voyage), British Captain George Vancouver's Northwest Expedition explored 100 miles up the river, rebuking American exploration of only its mouth. Vancouver, acting on Gray's information, remained off the mouth of the river in his sloop of war, *Discovery*, and sent Lieutenant William Broughton in an armed tender, *Chatham*, across the Columbia River bar. Broughton sailed up the river as far as Reed Island with provisions for one week and claimed the river for the British Crown. He named many geographic features along the way to emphasize British claims to the Northwest territory (and because they were the first recorded identifications, many of these names persist). The five-month difference between Gray's discovery and Vancouver's exploration resulted in the contested territorial claims between the United States and England, which continued through the mid-1800s.

Jefferson had reminded Lewis, "The object of your mission is single, the direct water communication from sea to sea." Lewis and Clark realized that Jefferson's dream, plus centuries of Euro-American hopes, had vanished when Lewis topped the "dividing range" at present Lemhi Pass. A vast mountain range of wilderness lay between the supposed headwaters of the Missouri and Columbia Rivers. Unfazed by this reality, the captains were determined to fulfill another of Jefferson's goals for the expedition: they would reach the mouth of the Columbia River.

Merchants from Spain, England, Russia, and America competed for the fur trade with the Indian nations along the Pacific Northwest coast. Establishing territorial claims to expand their empires was an important goal for all of these countries at the beginning of the nineteenth century. The American and British explorations of the Columbia River in 1792 compounded the question of territorial sovereignty. Jefferson had realized correctly that to establish his nation's claim for territory in the Columbia River drainage, the expedition needed to reach the mouth of the river.

Reaching the confluence of two large rivers, now known as the Snake and Columbia Rivers, the captains were faced with the realization that another of Jefferson's dreams could not be fulfilled. The Columbia River drained from the north. They would not discover the headwaters of the Great River of the West.

Setting out on the final 450 miles to the ocean, the expedition encountered treacherous rapids, including the formidable Celilo Falls and the Cascades of the Columbia, which required time-consuming portages. They soon entered the lower river and found a smooth current that aided their downriver journey. There was a sense of urgency, for winter was approaching. Traveling 30 to 35 miles a day, they had little time to visit the numerous Indian villages they passed, which then embraced the largest concentration of aboriginal inhabitants in North America. Such visits would be conducted on their eastbound return trip. The captains noted and named most of the tributaries and islands in the river (though unfortunately, over time, nearly all the colorful names they bestowed on the riverine geography have changed; see Geographical Features Named by Lewis and Clark). They had learned of Lieutenant Broughton's exploration of this stretch of the river from Vancouver's six-volume *Voyage of Discovery to the North Pacific Ocean*, published in 1801. Lewis was so excited that he copied from the book the charts of the course Broughton had sailed in reaching the landmark he had named Point Vancouver.

Their westbound route was largely along the northern side of the river. The weather was rapidly turning bad and supplies were getting low. Campsites for the evenings were made wherever the Corps could find suitable shelter from the wind, rain, and tidal influence. It is interesting to note that the men of the expedition were voyagers—riverboatmen—not mariners, although they used nautical terms. They were not mountain men, either; their orientation was to river courses, and they rarely applied their unusual names to mountainous features.

If "just passing through" describes the first seven days the party spent on the lower Columbia, the next ten days would have to be called "miserable mission." As the group approached the Columbia estuary, climatic conditions in November became severe, delaying them from reaching the ocean even though they could see its breakers crashing into the river's flow. Heavy rains inundated the explorers, and high tides, aggravated by gale-force winds, forced them to proceed carefully. Finally Lewis and three men set out overland to reach the Pacific Ocean, Lewis later recording November 14, 1805, as the day they reached the sea. At long last the storm subsided, allowing Clark to establish Station Camp on the northern shore of the Columbia River, where the party would spend the next ten cold and rainy days. It was not the intention of the captains to spend winter on the coast, but once again nature played a leading role in shaping the expedition's destiny. The storm delayed the return up the river, and vital information gained from the local Indians now gave new direction to the expedition's course.

To resolve the issue of where to establish winter quarters, the captains surveyed members of the party and gave each the opportunity to express an opinion. This tally of opinions at Station Camp was quite unique in military discipline and American history, and it remains controversial. Among those participating were York and Sacagawea. York's opinion was counted in the tally, but Sacagawea's was not. Clark simply noted after the count, referring to

Chinook lodge. Sketch by A. T. Agate, Wilkes Expedition, 1845. Courtesy of the Oregon Historical Society (4465).

Sacagawea by her nickname, "Janey in favour of a place where there is plenty of Potas [wapato roots]." Fifty years would pass before black males would vote in America, more than one hundred before women or Indians.

The captains decided to cross the river and winter on the southern shore, where they were told elk and other game were plentiful. They would have to return upriver to negotiate their dugouts through a maze of islands and mud-flats (now called the Lewis and Clark National Wildlife Refuge). From their camp (on today's Tongue Point), Lewis set out to explore the area for a suitable winter camp. It would take two weeks before he found such a location. Fort Clatsop was built in December to house the main contingent of the Corps of Discovery. Here they would reside for four months, waiting for the snow to recede in the Rocky Mountains before their journey home. They kept busy trading with local Clatsop Indians and making salt from seawater on the coast; hunting parties supplied food and pelts for clothing and moccasins; and the captains edited their maps and journals. Clark made two trips to the ocean, first to survey the coast for the saltmakers' camp and then with Sacagawea to view a beached whale.

The Chinookan people occupied both shores of the Columbia River for 185 miles from The Dalles to the Pacific and carried on an extensive trading network with other tribes and with English and Spanish trading vessels. As the captains soon found out, they were hard bargainers. In addition to food, baskets, hides, and fur, they possessed tobacco, axes, beads, knives, kettles, thimbles, and pots and pans. Slaves were also an important trade item, and the Chinooks were reported to have more slaves than any other tribe (Moulton 1990). At Fort Clatsop on February 28, 1806, Clark was offered a ten-year-old boy in exchange for a gun and a few beads.

Leaving their damp and isolated winter quarters in the unclaimed territory, later to become known as the Oregon Country, the men were eager to return to the river. The eastbound journey was slowed by the river's current, wind, and tide. Daily mileage was only 18 to 20 miles compared to the 30 to 35 miles achieved westbound. Their upriver course in March was mainly on the southern shore. Geographical knowledge, in combination with information provided by local Indians, indicated there was a large tributary draining a valley to the south. The captains were intent on locating it. The elusive confluence of this river was missed on the westbound exploration. Now the expedition had time to investigate, yet they missed the river's mouth again. Several days later, while camped upstream for hunting near today's Washougal, Washington, a local Indian offered to guide Clark back down the Columbia to the mouth of a river that had been obscured by islands. It was today's Willamette River, known to Lewis and Clark as the Multnomah. Clark explored it and camped near the present location of Portland's St. Johns Bridge, adding another dimension to America's knowledge of the unknown territory. Clark did not fully understand the information provided him by the Indians, however, and later marked his maps incorrectly, placing the river's origin near the location of the Great Salt Lake in Utah. Unfortunately, this led to a misconception in cartography for fifty years regarding the existence and length of the river.

Although the Lewis and Clark expedition did not discover the supposed Northwest Passage nor the headwaters of the Great River of the West, its exploration of the Columbia changed world history by helping establish the Oregon Country as a territory of the United States.

It is doubtful that the British-American border dispute of the mid–nineteenth century would have been resolved in America's favor without the influence of the expedition. Westward immigration increased American presence in the territory, and eventually the present boundary between Canada and the United States at the forty-ninth parallel was negotiated. Jefferson's dream had finally materialized—a United States of America that stretched from sea to sea.

THE LOWER COLUMBIA
1805–1806 and Today

Please do what you can to take care of the beautiful places. Hear the deep song of the land and sea. For if we lose this place, this sense of place, then we shall truly have nothing at all.

RACHEL CARSON

WHAT DID THE LOWER COLUMBIA RIVER corridor really look like when the expedition passed through the area in the autumn of 1805 and early spring of 1806? You must first remember that this once wild, untamed river, like all rivers over time, has undergone continuous, dynamic changes. The members of the Corps of Discovery saw the Columbia corridor at one moment in time. It had sustained lava flows, glaciation, floods, earthquakes, landslides, and fires, as well as Native American influences, long before these explorers arrived. It changed while they were here, and it continues to change today. The greatest alterations since the expedition, however, have been wrought not by nature but by modern technology. Thus, to picture the river as it was in 1805 and 1806, we must peel away the heavy layers of human progress that followed: the bridges, dams, docks, roads, and freeways, the rail, phone, and power lines, housing and industrial developments, and the cityscapes with their rows of riverfront townhouses. Erase the homes that peek out from the surrounding hillsides, and fill in the clearcuts with old growth. Remove the quaint river villages along the shorelines and the incessant traffic of recreational boaters, barges, and international container ships. With this accomplished, you can now begin to imagine the wild character of the river environment of yesteryear. Today we can create a virtual image of the historic Columbia with a computer, but for a true and accurate description we must read the explorers' journals and their firsthand accounts of the environment as it was prior to Western influence.

Unquestionably, one of the greatest impacts to the river's character, hydrology, and ecology has been the construction of eleven major dams on the lower Columbia. Bonneville Dam, for example, completed in 1938, was primarily responsible for changes in the downstream floodplains by deleting the mosaic of braided streams, marshes, and wetlands in what the captains called "the beautiful Columbian Valley" (the Portland-Vancouver metropolitan region) (Metropolitan Regional Services 1992). The resulting dam-induced metamorphosis also changed the shape and location of many islands and tamed the roaring spring floods. The annual flooding, however, brought enriching sediments to the floodplains and resulted in a dense understory of trees and shrubs along the shoreline. The expedition's hunters often had difficulty penetrating the lush foliage and fallen trees in the bottomlands. They were surrounded by willow, cottonwood, ash, pine, Oregon grape, Western red cedar, rhododendron, red alder, bulrush, nettle, brier, honeysuckle, vine maple, wapato, and patches of huckleberry, strawberry, elderberry, gooseberry, blackberry, and salal—a virtual supermarket for both man and wildlife. Interspersed were pashequaw, shanataque, and compound fern with its edible roots. In the stream bottoms, grass grew 16 inches high, and there were luxurious beds of watercress, cinquefoil, sandrush, and flowering pea (Moulton 1990). These same species can still be found, but in many areas the rich floodplains and their marshlands have been cleared, diked, and drained. By eliminating these wetlands we have also reduced populations of many kinds of trees, plants, and animals that were adapted to those habitats.

The explorers found an abundance of huge logs and woody debris lining the shores. The annual floods washed down large quantities of fallen trees and limbs from throughout the vast Columbia watershed. Firewood was no problem. Today dam construction has significantly reduced this phenomenon on the lower Columbia, and modern inhabitants routinely remove beached timber for their fireplaces.

The now relatively placid river bottoms permit humans to live on and farm the floodplains. Channelization and levees curb the river's natural tendency to meander, changing its hydrology and diminishing its biological vigor. These changes have, however, made navigation safer and simpler, even for oceangoing vessels. The mining of gravel beds and creation of new dredge-spoil islands and oxbow lakes have also permanently changed the river's appearance and biology.

Numerous tidal creeks and tributaries of the lower Columbia no longer exist, because of land drainage and development. Landslides, a common interaction of gravity, water, erosion, wind, clear-cutting, road building, and development in the Pacific Northwest, continue to trigger many types of landscape alterations along the river. These resulting variations in surface features, however, still aid in forming the rich diversity of habitats that are used today by many different plants and animals.

Historically the countryside of the lower Columbia was blanketed with stately stands of Western redcedar, Douglas and grand fir, cottonwood, spruce, white pine, oak, maple, hemlock, and alder. Many had grown to gigantic size and amazed the explorers, who had never seen such large trees before. Near Fort Clatsop, on February 1, 1806, Clark measured a Sitka spruce that was 27 feet in circumference at 6 feet above the ground. In the Vancouver area the captains described a fallen fir tree that was 318 feet in length. On February 5, 1806, Lewis noted that the Western hemlock "rises to the height of 160 to 180 feet very commonly and is from 4 to 6 feet in diameter, very streight round and regularly tapering."

The composition of the forests described by Lewis and Clark and familiar to us today began about five thousand years ago. The mix of species, however, has changed by as much as 50 percent over the last several thousand years due to climatic changes. Drier, warmer periods produce more fires that favor more drought-tolerant species like Douglas fir. Cooler periods and fewer fires favor moisture-loving trees like Western hemlock. Current warming trends assisted by human activities could change forest communities once again (Wells and Anzinger 2001).

Fire is the major natural influence that has shaped the forests of the Pacific Northwest. Changes in fire regimes are keyed to fluctuations in climate. Different regimes affect both forest species composition and forest structure—how big the trees get, how close together, and how much deadwood is present. Shifts in fire regimes occur in an ongoing, though irregular, pattern. Tree-ring analysis indicates a period of widespread fire from about 1400 to 1650, followed by a period of cooler weather, and another flush of fire through the 1800s continuing until the early twentieth century (Agee 1992).

Along the banks of the lower Columbia, the Corps of Discovery was rarely out of sight of an Indian village; some were small, some very large, and many were deserted. From The Dalles to the ocean there were more than fifty settlements, among the highest densities of native people in all of North America. A series of Old World epidemic diseases such as smallpox, diphtheria, typhus, cholera, and malaria had taken an immense toll in the 1770s and 1780s, and again from 1800 to 1801 (Ramenofsky 1987). Burial vaults (8-feet-square, elevated wooden structures) were frequently encountered filled with corpses wrapped in skins and containing prized possessions of the deceased. The captains were careful to respect these graves and left them untouched. The disease curse would strike again in the 1830s.

Despite the impacts made by humans and nature, the lower Columbia's major islands and riverine formations, formed over the centuries, are little changed since Clark sketched them. The headlands and other prominent geological features such as rock outcroppings and unique basalt flows along the river remain as described in the journals. Most importantly for boaters, the Great River of the West remains unimpeded for 146 miles on its journey to the sea from Bonneville Dam.

According to Japanese archives, and later confirmed by tree-ring records, on January 26, 1700, a major earthquake struck the West Coast and lowered the coastline abruptly, submerging coastal forests and leaving lasting scars on the geology of the lower Columbia. The resulting tsunami was undoubtedly disastrous to coastal native communities as well. Evidence of this Cascadia subduction zone—the Juan de Fuca plate pushing under the North American tectonic plate—can be observed on numerous beaches and cutbank formations (Atwater 1996). The stumps of giant red cedars killed by earthquakes can still be seen protruding through the tidal marsh in Seal Slough, Grays River, Washington (Peterson and Madin 1997). Buried spruce stumps are visible north of Knappa, Oregon.

After the expedition passed Rooster Rock and the Sandy River Delta, they left behind the steep and rugged Columbia River Gorge and entered a vast lowland the captains called the Columbia Valley. This land is still covered with dense forests of second- and third-growth fir, cedar, pine, alder, maple, and cottonwood. The extensive islands, sloughs, shallow lakes, and wetlands along the river continue to harbor a great variety of waterfowl. Seals, which were frequently mentioned in the explorer's journals, are also present.

Lewis and Clark would still recognize the river's course and the region's volcanic, snowcapped peaks, especially from vantage points within the Portland-Vancouver area, but they would notice a great void in the waters of the Columbia. Few subjects impressed the captains more, took up a greater part of their diaries, or were described in more detail than the lifecycle, harvest, and economic potential of the Pacific salmon. On October 17, 1805, Clark wrote of the fish that were dying after having spawned at the end of their migration up the river:

*This river is remarkably Clear and Crouded with Salmon in maney places,
I observe in assending great numbers of Salmon dead on the Shores, floating
on the water and in the Bottoms which can be seen at the debth of 20 feet. the
Cause of the emence numbers of dead Salmon I can't acount for . . . the Indians were drying Salmon . . . for the purpose of food and fuel, and I do not
think at all improbable that those people make use of Dried fish as fuel. The
number of dead Salmon on the Shores and floating in the river is incrediable
to Say and at this Season they have only to collect the fish Split them open
and dry them on their Scaffolds.* (Moulton 1990)

For the Indian nations along the Columbia, salmon was of critical impor-
tance to their culture, economy, diet, and religion. The Midwest plains tribes
lived on a bison economy, the Columbia River people on a salmon economy.
Salmon were so abundant that the tribes made little impact on their vast populations. It is estimated that between ten and sixteen million wild salmon
and steelhead migrated up the Columbia in 1805, compared to only half a
million today (Hawthorne 1992). Clark counted 107 stacks of baskets filled
with nearly 10,000 pounds of dried, pounded salmon in a single village below
Celilo Falls.

Over sixty-seven stocks of salmon are now extinct, and seventy-six others are
at risk. Salmon numbers have declined to the point that many populations of
all six salmonid species (coho, chinook, sockeye, pink, steelhead, and chum) are
federally listed as threatened or endangered in the Columbia River Basin. Since
the time of Lewis and Clark, salmon runs have decreased 97 percent. This is the
result of a combination of dams, overfishing, and the degeneration or loss of
spawning, rearing, migration, and riparian habitat and probably climatic
changes in the Pacific Ocean. Nearly 80 percent of the basin's historic salmon
and steelhead habitat now lies behind impassable dams. The Columbia—Snake
River watershed includes more than two hundred dams, making it the most
heavily dammed watershed in the nation.

The progressive decline and continuing extinction of salmon clearly indicate
that this historic ecosystem is in trouble. Once hailed as a national showcase for
the reclamation of a polluted river, the Columbia's major tributary, the
Willamette, is again among the ten most polluted rivers in the nation, with sections declared Federal Superfund Sites. Encouraging reports by federal officials
in recent years, however, indicate a recovery trend for fall chinook. In 2002
more fall chinook were counted passing Bonneville Dam than in any year since

Fishwheels, like these near Beacon Rock, operated on the Columbia for some fifty years before being outlawed in 1934 to protect salmon runs. Courtesy of the Oregon Historical Society (9597).

the dam was built in 1938. Two decades of recovery efforts have played a part, along with favorable weather cycles, ocean productivity, and other factors not well understood (Brinckman 2002).

Could a similar expedition following the same water trail live off the land today, utilizing native food sources? It is doubtful. Satellite photos of the Columbia, compared with Clark's original maps, show the river to be in about the same location it was during their time. A series of impounded, slackwater lakes, however, has replaced the free-flowing, wild river. Only a few hundred thousand salmon (compared to former millions) are now produced annually by wild stocks—less than 3 percent of their historical abundance. It would be unwise to drink from the waters of the Columbia or any of its tributaries today. Indian villages have been replaced by towns and industrial complexes. Fish and wildlife are still present, but many species remain dependent on state and federal hatcheries, refuges, and other protected areas. Other species of birds and mammals are rare enough to be threatened with extinction.

Lewis and Clark made note of many animal and plant species encountered along their route (see Animals and Plants Described by Lewis and Clark for a list of species found along the lower Columbia). They were the first Euro-Americans to observe and describe the pronghorn antelope, Columbian white-tailed deer, Columbian black-tailed deer, mountain beaver, Columbian ground squirrel, Oregon bobcat, chickaree (Douglas squirrel), and packrat (bushy-tailed wood rat). Other animals they encountered can no longer be seen here—the sea otter, the gray wolf, the California condor. The Oregon Department of Fish and Wildlife still lists the fisher, marten, Western gray squirrel, sage grouse, Lewis woodpecker (named after Captain Lewis), bufflehead duck, mountain quail, and northern pileated woodpecker as sensitive species, while the bald eagle is rapidly recovering from a serious decline.

Although many of the animals Lewis and Clark described are gone or in trouble, the environment along the Columbia is still productive for most marmots, beavers, mountain beavers, cottontail rabbits, raccoons, badgers, river otters, skunks, coyotes, bobcats, and chickarees. Species such as skunks, raccoons, and coyotes are so numerous as to be considered a nuisance. Surprisingly, the black bear, mountain lion, and pronghorn antelope are listed as common, as are the mink, packrat, cormorant, great blue heron, red-shafted flicker, and crow. And harbor seals can still be seen as far up the river as Camas, Washington.

Many stretches remain wild and inhabited by many of the same species of yesteryear. Waterfowl seek the river's marshes by the thousands in fall and winter. The endangered Columbian white-tailed deer can be seen bouncing through the brush on the river islands in the Julia Butler Hansen National Wildlife Refuge. The riverine scenery is still as beautiful in many regions as described in the journals. The hardships endured by the explorers can now be softened or eliminated altogether by taking advantage of shoreline facilities that make camping out unnecessary. The captains would have been very happy to stop in the many bed-and-breakfasts along the water trail, or to barter for sea kayaks in place of their heavy dugout canoes. But could they have met the rental costs with blue beads and fish hooks?

Although the lower Columbia is not the true wilderness it was for the Corps of Discovery, a boat trip along its shorelines or among its many islands offers ecotourism at its best. It also offers an opportunity to discover, perhaps for the first time, the rich variety of natural and human forces that shaped and continue to shape this historic river corridor. All the human-caused changes we see today have taken place since the time of the Lewis and Clark expedition. As American conservationist Aldo Leopold noted in *A Sand County Almanac*, "The life of every river sings its own song, but in most, the song is long since marred by the discords of misuse." As we ponder what was, what can be, and what will be, one thing is certain: saving what remains of this beautiful greenway corridor and its culture and history for the centuries to come will require an unprecedented kind of stewardship, vision, and bipartisan cooperation.

THE LOWER COLUMBIA
THROUGH THE SEASONS

WHETHER FALL, WINTER, SPRING, OR SUMMER, a visit to the Columbia is always rewarding. Few other rivers provide boaters and other visitors with such a year-round variety of historical and natural-history events in a lineal panorama of scenic beauty.

FALL

Every season offers a reason to go out and explore the lower Columbia, and this is especially true for September, when the weather is superb for boating and the leaves are beginning to show hints of autumn colors. September is also the time to start exploring the tributaries of the river, for this is when the chinook salmon begin their return to the waters of their birth. Upstream, where such water clears, a paddler may be rewarded by sights of fish dashing below, some weighing 40 pounds or more. Beavers are busy repairing their lodges and dams for winter. The crisp air and the sound of geese winging south means that soon it will be time to don a wetsuit or drysuit to catch the fall sights. The last week of October, when most recreational boaters have vanished, is generally the peak of fall color. Redosier dogwood, probably the most abundant shrub lining the sloughs, turns a brilliant scarlet and can be astonishingly beautiful set off against golden cottonwoods and a dark backdrop of spruce. On the steep basalt hillsides, vine and bigleaf maples offer their own red and yellow color schemes. October offers some of the most windless days of the year, and reflections on the river's surface double the effect. November brings the big storms, but it also brings swans. It is hard not to be awestruck by the large flocks of tundra swans flying low overhead, glowing white against a leaden sky. The tundra and trumpeter swans are the most imposing of a wealth of waterfowl that move into the estuary for winter. Ducks, geese, and swans in the Lewis and Clark National Wildlife Refuge reach peak numbers in February. The most abundant are greater scaup, a diving duck who spends summers nesting on Arctic tundra; in winter, dense rafts of over two thousand of these birds may form along the river.

WINTER

Many other animals are best seen in the dead of winter. Harbor seals and California sea lions travel upriver. Larger numbers of peregrine falcons and bald eagles move in to take advantage of the hordes of waterfowl. The best wildlife show the river has to offer greets those who come out during a strong February smelt run. These fish are small, but they are abundant and laden with oil. Thousands of gulls, dozens of bald eagles, and thirty or forty sea lions can be encountered on a casual day's paddle during the peak of the run. In March, south-facing cliffs announce spring with red-flowering currant and spring-gold. The rufous hummingbirds have already returned and are soon followed by tree swallows, violet-green swallows, and the familiar soaring forms of turkey vultures. Osprey return in April and begin snapping branches from dead trees to build their ponderous nests. March and April are a good time to get out along the cliffs for another reason: the accumulated waters of winter still pour forth from every seep, and waterfalls are at their most spectacular.

SPRING

By April most seals and sea lions have moved below Tongue Point, and most waterfowl have begun flying north. Loons, which have spent the winter here in unassuming hues of gray and white, begin to change to their famous breeding plumage before they, too, fly off. This includes not only the glossy black-and-white common loons but also the spectacular Pacific and red-throated loons, who take on the crisp colors they will wear on the tundra.

May and early June make up for loss of action on the water with the colors of wildflowers and neotropical birds. Cliffs bloom red, blue, and yellow with paintbrush, cliff larkspur, and stonecrop. Spruce swamps are host to recent tropical arrivals such as yellow warblers, western tanagers, and black-headed grosbeaks. The sound of their song enlivens every island. Colonies of nesting herons become noisy with the sound of chicks ready to go out on their own.

SUMMER

July and August bring strong afternoon winds and crowds of summer boaters. The water temperature of the river, which drops to a dangerous 40°F in January, may rise above 70°F in August. This forgiving temperature offers comfortable overnight camping opportunities in designated areas and the chance to swim and cool off. The best wildlife sights in summer are young animals. Families of otters dive and roll together, beavers and their kits can be seen swimming in the evenings, and osprey chicks test their wings and their fishing abilities, sometimes even plunging next to groups of boaters.

THE LEWIS AND CLARK
COLUMBIA RIVER
WATER TRAIL

FOR THE PURPOSES OF THIS GUIDEBOOK, the water trail has been divided into sixteen sections, called reaches. Each trail reach is described, with additional information given on boating cautions and conditions, river accesses, other facilities and points of interest, and suggested day and overnight trips. At Skamokawa the river begins its expansion into the great Columbia estuary, reaching a width of 10 miles at one point. Here, of necessity, the river trail is divided into the Southern Route, following the Oregon shoreline to Fort Clatsop, and the Northern Route, following the Washington shore to Fort Canby.

The Index Map provided encompasses the entire trail and indicates the boundaries of individual trail reaches. Each trail reach also includes its own map. In addition to plotting out important sites and geographical features, these maps include all known campsites used by the Corps of Discovery and the routes they took as they traveled along the Columbia. Although accurate, the maps included in this book do not display current navigational information (buoys, pilings, water depths, shoals, beacons, and the like) and should not be used for navigation. Please use the appropriate National Oceanic and Atmospheric Administration (NOAA) nautical charts and 7.5-minute U.S. Geological Survey (USGS) maps indicated for each trail reach. Excellent maps are also available on CD-ROM.

Be careful to distinguish between facilities on the northern shore (Washington) and southern shore (Oregon). Bridges are often few and far between, and a car shuttle from one shore to the other will often be lengthy and time-

Index Map of the Lewis and Clark Columbia River Water Trail. The 146-mile water trail is divided into sixteen reaches, beginning near Bonneville Dam and ending near Fort Clatsop in Oregon and Fort Canby in Washington. Trail Reaches 1–16 are described in detail, each with a corresponding map. Please note that trail reaches slightly overlap.

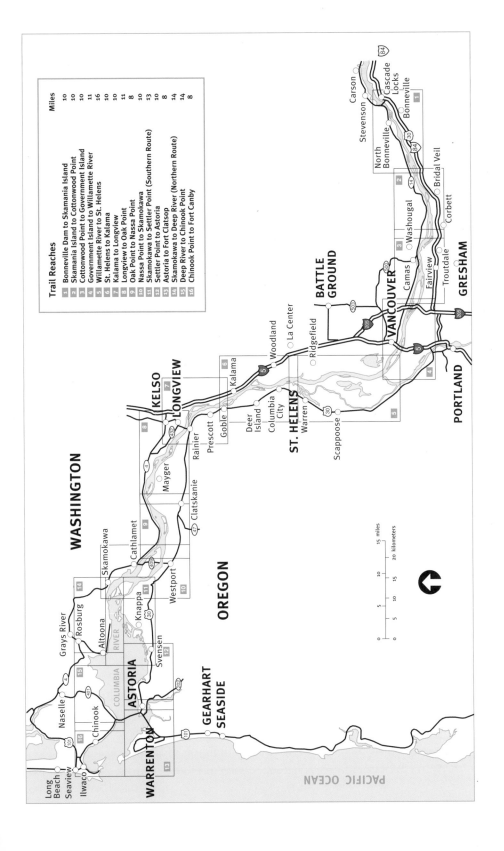

Trail Reaches

		Miles
1	Bonneville Dam to Skamania Island	10
2	Skamania Island to Cottonwood Point	10
3	Cottonwood Point to Government Island	10
4	Government Island to Willamette River	11
5	Willamette River to St. Helens	16
6	St. Helens to Kalama	10
7	Kalama to Longview	10
8	Longview to Oak Point	11
9	Oak Point to Nassa Point	8
10	Nassa Point to Skamokawa	10
11	Skamokawa to Settler Point (Southern Route)	13
12	Settler Point to Astoria	10
13	Astoria to Fort Clatsop	8
14	Skamokawa to Deep River (Northern Route)	14
15	Deep River to Chinook Point	14
16	Chinook Point to Fort Canby	8

consuming. On the Washington shore the Columbia is followed by Highway 14, the aptly named Lewis and Clark Highway. On the Oregon shore the highway is followed by Interstate 84 and Highway 30. All three highways are marked by mileposts, and the location of parks and other facilities are often described by reference to these mileposts. Rivermiles are also used to designate locations and are measured from the mouth of the river.

In general, private marinas are not listed, even though most such marinas are open to the public. These marinas are listed only if located in an area where public access is limited. For a list of marinas in Oregon, consult the *Oregon Boating Facilities Guide* and the *Oregon Marina Guide* (Oregon State Marine Board 1997, 2001). In Washington consult the publications of the Washington Interagency Committee for Outdoor Education (see Useful Contacts).

No specific water trail route has been designated, as each boater has his or her own time frame, level of experience, interests, equipment, and style. Weather and tide will also direct the wise boater to use appropriate routes. Boating is a personal adventure, and no one route can begin to reveal all the wonders of the lower Columbia. There are countless side trips to explore up creeks and inlets, in backwaters and sloughs, to interesting islands and historical landmarks. Remember, however, that canoeing and kayaking on a river such as the Columbia is inherently dangerous due to river current, wind, tide, cold weather and water, and other boat traffic. Boating safety is, thus, repeatedly stressed, and boaters assume all risks of using this guide.

Though the information in this guide is accurate, conditions often change, and no guarantee can be offered that the trips described are necessarily safe or suitable for all paddlers. Camping on the islands and wetlands of the lower Columbia can be a challenging proposition. One goal of this book is to establish a series of campsites that boaters may use when traveling from Bonneville Dam to Astoria or Ilwaco. Eventually the trail will encompass campsites located a day (or less) apart. A few campsites have been established and improved with fire rings, picnic tables, and toilets, but many more are needed. In some cases sites have merely been identified but not improved in any way. These sites are described as "primitive camping." Some are very primitive, almost to the point of nonexistence. Boaters intending to use primitive campsites will need to be prepared for the worst conditions, from dense underbrush to no vegetation at all on some islands. In addition, all campers should be very careful of tides, as some campsites may be underwater at high tide. No camping is permitted on any of the national wildlife refuges. The Lower Columbia River Water Trail Committee is a group formed to address campsite needs and other issues (see the back of the book for more information). The Northwest Discovery Water Trail for the upper Columbia (Bonneville Dam and above), including the Snake and Clearwater Rivers, is a similar initiative.

Every trip to the Columbia is a new experience and an opportunity to imagine what this awesome, untamed river may have looked like during the time of Lewis and Clark, with its many busy Indian villages, dugout canoes, dense old-growth forests, and abundant and diverse animals overhead, on land, and in the deep clear waters.

TRAIL REACH 1

Bonneville Dam to Skamania Island

DISTANCE   10 miles.

MAPS   USGS Bonneville Dam, Beacon Rock, Tanner Butte, and Multnomah Falls 7.5-minute NOAA Chart 18531.

In this initial reach of the water trail a dramatic transition can be seen as you leave the steep and timbered basalt walls of the Columbia River Gorge and enter the gradually widening floodplains of the lower Columbia and the metropolitan regions of Portland and Vancouver. The Corps of Discovery soon determined that it was also passing into a new geographical region: the dense rainforests of the Pacific Northwest. Below the huge concrete barrier of the Bonneville Dam, the river runs free again, passing the cottonwood-covered islands of Pierce and Ives and the majestic Beacon Rock—the andesite throat of an ancient volcano. Although often referred to as a monolith, Beacon Rock is not a solitary piece of rock but a collection of basalt columns, as clearly seen on its south face.

This trail reach boasts two Lewis and Clark campsites, one used as they headed west in 1805 and the other used on their hurried return journey in 1806. Several Upper Chinookan village and national historic sites, a national wildlife refuge, and several state parks are located here, as is the popular Bonneville Lock and Dam, situated on both sides of the Columbia. The water trailhead is also located here on the Washington side (see Plate 6).

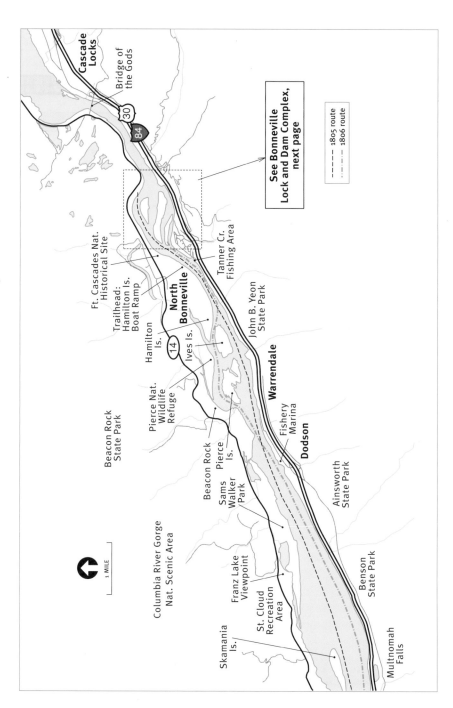

1 MILE

Cascade Locks

Bridge of the Gods

See Bonneville Lock and Dam Complex, next page

------- 1805 route
—··—··— 1806 route

Ft. Cascades Nat. Historical Site

Trailhead: Hamilton Is. Boat Ramp

Tanner Cr. Fishing Area

North Bonneville

Hamilton Is.

Ives Is.

John B. Yeon State Park

Pierce Nat. Wildlife Refuge

Warrendale

Fishery Marina

Dodson

Beacon Rock State Park

Beacon Rock

Pierce Is.

Sams Walker Park

Ainsworth State Park

Columbia River Gorge Nat. Scenic Area

Franz Lake Viewpoint

St. Cloud Recreation Area

Benson State Park

Skamania Is.

Multnomah Falls

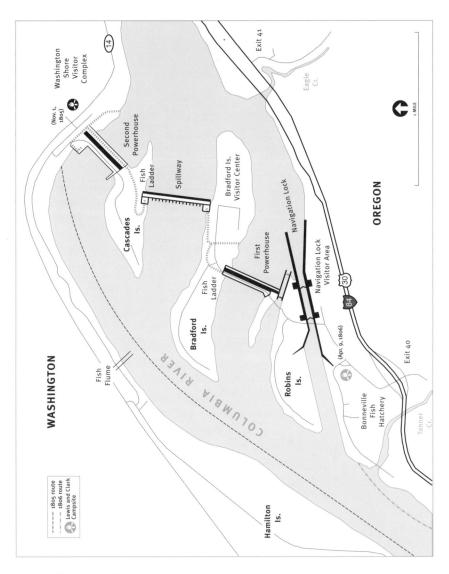

Bonneville Lock and Dam Complex

BOATING CAUTIONS AND CONDITIONS

At the Hamilton Island Boat Ramp, where the water trail begins, you will find numerous sport fishing boats anchored in midstream. They fish mainly for salmon and steelhead in fall and for sturgeon year-round. As you proceed downstream, keep an eye out for tugs and barges, which can quickly and quietly approach an unwary boater from either direction. Skippers of these commercial vessels have difficulty seeing small craft, so stay alert and get out of their way as soon as possible. Be sure to check tides and weather. If the weather is windy and nasty, do not venture out. Both currents and wind can be very strong in winter and spring, with winds blowing upstream against the current, causing rough water and whitecaps. Even in summer the wind blows upstream three days out of four and can create rough conditions. The river current is 2 to 3 miles per hour and the tidal current is 3 to 5 miles per hour, for a combined current of 5 to 8 miles per hour. Winds and waves come up quickly and in open water can be dangerous. Know where you are and where the nearest safe anchorage is, if and when needed.

RIVER ACCESSES

Hamilton Island Boat Ramp

FACILITIES	Boat ramp, toilets, parking.
ACTIVITIES	Picnicking.
RESTRICTIONS	Day use only. No upstream boating.

This boat ramp is the trailhead for the Lewis and Clark Columbia River Water Trail. To reach the ramp by car, turn south off Highway 14 at milepost 38.5 (just west of the Bonneville Lock and Dam Washington Shore Visitor Complex) and follow Dam Access Road about a mile to the boat ramp. From the water the Hamilton Island Boat Ramp is directly across from the mouth of Tanner Creek and navigational marker 94. West of the boat ramp is an extensive public-access area where small boats may be launched if the ramp is busy with other boaters. Hamilton Island was called Strawberry Island by Lewis and Clark because of its abundant growth of woodland strawberries. Today the strawberries, if any, are rare indeed.

Fort Cascades National Historic Site

FACILITIES   Steep concrete boat ramp, loading float, historic displays and
                  interpretive signs, historic 1.5-mile trail, toilets, parking.
ACTIVITIES   Hiking.
RESTRICTIONS   Day use only.

This site is located 1 mile west of the Bonneville Lock and Dam Washington Shore Visitor Complex on the Dam Access Road. The fort, built by the army in 1850, and the town of Cascades were important sites of mid–nineteenth-century settlement in the Pacific Northwest. Located below the Lower Cascades (now inundated by Bonneville Dam), the townsite of Cascades and the fort served as an important center for portage transportation around the falls. The Great Flood of 1894, the Columbia's highest recorded water level, destroyed the town and the abandoned fort. The site is now listed on the National Register of Historic Places. At either the Bonneville Lock and Dam Washington Shore Visitor Complex or the site you can obtain a free self-guiding brochure of the area, including its 1.5-mile interpretive trail. The trail follows the bed of the portage railroad as it was in 1836, passes the site of an early fishwheel, and leads to the Cascades Townsite and Fort Cascades Compound. This was a collection of civilian buildings and army tents, and a supply depot for the upriver portage. The compound was attacked by local Indian tribes in 1856. The buildings were burned and eleven civilians and five soldiers were killed. Fishwheels that scooped tons of migrating salmon operated in this area for fifty years. They were finally outlawed in 1934 to protect salmon populations. The site also offers a replica of a prehistoric Indian petroglyph found here and provides boat access to the Columbia.

Just northwest of Hamilton Island, the small community of North Bonneville, Washington, lies along Highway 14, 1.5 miles west of the Washington Shore Visitor Complex. The town was relocated here as a result of the construction of the second powerhouse. This is a good spot for last-minute grocery shopping and picnicking.

In 1805 four houses of the Wah-clallah tribe of the Shahala (Chinookan for "those upriver") nation were located at the site of Bonneville Dam's second powerhouse. When the expedition visited this site in October 1805, the village was largely unoccupied, as the Indians had gone downriver to collect roots. Those remaining were kind and gave Lewis and five men berries, nuts, and fish to eat, but Lewis could get nothing from them in the way of information. On the Corps' return trip, in April 1806, they encountered several hundred Chinooks here and were offered a mountain-goat headdress, which impressed Clark very much. After a major archeological data recovery, this Clahelehlah village site was destroyed in 1981 by the construction of the Bonneville Dam's second powerhouse, and the new town of North Bonneville was built at its present location.

Tanner Creek Fishing Area

FACILITIES	Bank access.
ACTIVITIES	Bank fishing.
RESTRICTIONS	Day use only. No upstream boating.

This public-access area is part of the Bonneville Lock and Dam on the Oregon shore. To reach the fishing area from Interstate 84, take exit 40, follow the signs to the Bonneville Fish Hatchery, and drive past the hatchery to the fishing area west of the mouth of Tanner Creek. No boat ramp is available, but canoes and kayaks may be hand-launched from the western end of the parking area. To find this fishing area from the water, look for navigational marker 94, directly across from the water trailhead at the Hamilton Island Boat Ramp. Boat traffic is not allowed upstream of this site except for traffic passing through the Bonneville Dam locks.

Beacon Rock State Park

FACILITIES	Boat ramp, dock, campsites (no hookups), group camping area, picnic sites, showers, toilets, facilities for people with disabilities, tables, stoves, kitchen shelters.
ACTIVITIES	Camping, hiking, swimming, fishing, picnicking, rock climbing, horseback riding, biking.
RESTRICTIONS	Fee for camping and boat launching.

To the north of Pierce Island stands the imposing Beacon Rock (see Plate 7), visible to road and river travelers for miles. The rock lies half a mile upstream from the launch site and mooring float. At its base is one of the river's most popular state parks. This large 4,482-acre park, with its nearly 10,000 feet of Columbia River shoreline, is located 35 miles east of Vancouver on Highway 14 at milepost 35. It includes grassy picnic areas and wooded primitive campsites. There are extensive hiking trails north of the highway on 2,445-foot Hamilton Mountain. The park consists of three main areas. The first is Beacon Rock itself, which includes a unique, easy trail that leads to the summit and provides a spectacular view of the Columbia River Gorge, from Wind Mountain in the east to Crown Point in the west. On the northern side of the highway is the second area, including a campground, access to 13 miles of fire road open to hiking and bicycle use, and an 8.5-mile loop trail to Hamilton Mountain. About half a mile west of the trail that leads to the top of the rock is Beacon Rock Moorage Road, which leads to the third main area of the park, consisting of a day-use picnic area, dock, and boat ramp. Phone 509-427-8265.

On November 2, 1805, Clark made note of "a remarkable high rock on Stard.side . . . about 800 feet high and 400 yds around, the Beaten Rock." As it turns out, he had a keen eye for estimating scale: Beacon Rock is actually 848 feet high. Geologically, Beacon Rock is the remains of a pipe (chimney) through which the lava of a volcano reached the surface. When the lava cooled it formed a dense gray rock and, through contraction in cooling, split into pillars or columns. At this location, 40 miles east of Portland, the expedition first noted the tidal action of the Pacific.

In 1805 Clark also wrote of the Chinookan village of Wah-clallah, located south of Beacon Rock. The people of this village named the rock Che-che-op-tin after a native princess who, as legend has it, died on the rock with her baby. Like many other Chinookan tribes, the people of Wah-clallah, often called Cascade Indians, were greatly affected by disease in the late nineteenth century, many of them dying. Most survivors eventually joined the Wascoes on the Warm Springs Reservation or Yakima Reservation. Prehistoric occupation in this area has a limited time frame, as all sites are situated on landforms created as a result of the Bonneville landslide that occurred around eight hundred years ago.

The first recorded owner of Beacon Rock was Phillip Ritz, a pioneer who came to Oregon in 1850. He sold it in 1870 to a Philadelphia banker named Jay Cooke, a backer of the Northern Pacific Railroad, who sold it to Charles Ladd in 1904. Ladd sold the rock to Henry J. Biddle in 1915 on the condition that the rock be preserved. Biddle's sole reason for buying the rock was to build a trail to its summit; he was attracted by the idea of building a trail "in perhaps the most difficult location in which a trail had ever been built" (Biddle 1924).

Biddle's trail would not result in the first climb to the summit, however. That honor went to Frank J. Smith and Charles Church of Portland, and George Purser of White Salmon, in 1901. In late 1915 Biddle hired Charles "Tin Can" Johnson, who had previously been employed as a construction foreman on Highway 30 (Columbia River Highway), to build the trail to the top of the rock. It was completed in April 1918, extending a length of 4,500 feet from the North Bank Highway (now Highway 14) to the top of the rock. The trail was 4 feet wide, with a maximum grade of 15 percent, and included fifty-two hairpin turns and twenty-two wooden bridges (the bridges were later replaced with steel). After the trail was complete, Biddle maintained it for public use, without charge.

In 1931 the Army Corps of Engineers began looking for a source of rock for building jetties at the mouth of the Columbia, and Beacon Rock was eyed as an excellent source. Samuel Boardman, head of the Oregon State Parks system, decided that Beacon Rock should be preserved. However, Roland Hartley, the governor of Washington, had already turned down a proposed gift of the rock to Washington for use as a park. So Boardman proposed to acquire the rock as an Oregon State Park within Washington. Biddle had since died, but his family was willing to sell the rock to Oregon for a dollar so long as it could be maintained as a park. Many people in Washington were outraged that Oregon would acquire a park in their state, and local Washington interests began lobbying the state to take action. Eventually Washington graciously accepted the gift, and Beacon Rock has been a Washington State Park ever since.

Fishery Marina

FACILITIES	Boat ramp, store, toilets, campsites with electrical hookups, commercial marina.
ACTIVITIES	Camping.
RESTRICTIONS	Open year-round. Fee.

The Fishery Marina, also known as Covert's Landing, lies just off Interstate 84 at the community of Dodson, 4 miles downstream from Bonneville Dam and 6 miles east of Multnomah Falls. From Interstate 84 take Ainsworth State Park exit 35 and proceed a third of a mile east. From the water the marina is located at rivermile 140.25. Phone 541-374-8577.

OTHER FACILITIES AND POINTS OF INTEREST

Bonneville Lock and Dam

FACILITIES	Observation deck, exhibits, theater, toilets.
ACTIVITIES	Touring fish ladders, fish viewing room, fish hatchery, hydropower plant, and navigation lock.
RESTRICTIONS	Open daily from 9:00 A.M. to 5:00 P.M.

At the eastern end of this trail reach is the Bonneville Lock and Dam Complex, among the most popular visitor attractions in the Columbia River Gorge

National Scenic Area). A national historic landmark, it covers nearly 100 acres on both sides of the Columbia and embraces an administration building, theater, spillway dam, navigation lock, two powerhouses, and a major fish hatchery. Bonneville Dam was originally built by the Army Corps of Engineers in the 1930s to provide employment during the Great Depression, and today it employs more than a hundred people to operate and maintain it.

The dam is named for the small railroad town of Bonneville, Oregon, which was lost in the dam's construction. The town, in turn, had been named for General Benjamin-Louis-Eulalie de Bonneville. Born in France, de Bonneville came to the United States with his family in 1803 at the age of seven. He graduated from the U.S. Military Academy at West Point in 1815 and in 1832 took leave from the army to explore the West and try his hand at the fur trade. Neither his explorations nor fur-trade ventures in the Northwest proved very successful. The army finally dismissed him for exceeding his leave, but his commission was later reinstated. He fought in the Mexican War of 1846–1848, and in 1852 he was given command of the Fourth Infantry Regiment at Vancouver Barracks. In

Bonneville Lock and Dam was constructed during the Great Depression and now produces enough electricity to supply the needs of about half a million homes per year.

1865 he received the rank of brigadier general, and later he became the subject of Washington Irving's popular book *The Adventures of Captain Bonneville*.

Construction of Bonneville Dam commenced in September 1933 and was completed in July 1938 at a cost of $83 million. It is the oldest dam on the Columbia River and was expanded in 1986 with the completion of the second powerhouse on the northern shore. It is operated by the Army Corps of Engineers. The dam complex can be reached on the Oregon side via exit 40 on Interstate 84 and on the Washington side via Highway 14 at milepost 40. Private vehicles are not allowed to cross the Columbia at the dam. The nearest public crossing is a toll bridge at Cascade Locks, exit 44, 3 miles to the east, called the Bridge of the Gods.

Visitors on both sides of the Bonneville Lock and Dam Complex may view the fish ladders, which extend from the river downstream of the dam to Lake Bonneville upstream. These ladders provide passageways for adult chinook, shad, and other fish to seasonally migrate upstream. Visitors can watch migrating fish swim past underwater windows at both the Washington Shore Visitor Complex and the Bradford Island Visitor Center. The Washington Shore Visitor Complex also offers a five-level facility with an observation deck, access to the powerhouse, and exhibits, including one on Lewis and Clark and others on fish species and the workings of a modern hydropower plant. From this center there is an outstanding panoramic view of the Columbia River Gorge.

Between seven thousand and one million migrating upstream adult salmon and steelhead, and from thirty to fifty million downstream fingerlings, pass through Bonneville Dam in an average year. The dam impounded a 48-mile-long reservoir, the first in a series of navigable lakes that constitute the Columbia—Snake Island Waterway, which runs 465 miles from the Pacific to Lewiston, Idaho. Power produced by the dam supplies energy to the Northwest and parts of California.

Lewis and Clark camped on the Washington shore, just upstream from the present location of Bonneville Dam, on November 1, 1805. The camp was made just below what the captains called the Great Shute (the Cascades of the Columbia). Their encampment followed a day of hard labor to make the portage around the 20-foot falls, which were preceded by 400 feet of swift water and followed by another set of rapids 1.5 miles downstream. This campsite, and the falls and cascades the explorers descended, have now been covered by the waters of Lake Bonneville.

On their return journey, unable to pass the rapids on the northern side of the river, the Corps sought a safe harbor in the narrow channel between what they called Brant Island (Bradford Island) and the southern shore. Their camp of

April 9, 1806, was made near the present site of the Bonneville Fish Hatchery. Clark wrote about the day they made camp here: "After purchaseing 2 dogs Crossed and into the Sluce of a large high Island seperated from the S.E. Side by a narrow chanel, in this chanel we found a good harbor and encamped on the lower Side. We Saw Some deer Sign and Collins to hunt in the mornig until the Canoes were toed above the rapids. Made 16 Miles to day. Evening wet & disagreeable."

The Bonneville Fish Hatchery is among the oldest hatcheries in Oregon and is operated by the Oregon Department of Fish and Wildlife. It is open daily without charge. Everything from eggs to full-grown salmon and trout can be seen in the raceways and in the crystal-clear ponds. A sturgeon-viewing pond includes an underwater observation area and is the home of Herman, a 400-pound, 10-foot, sixty-five-year-old white sturgeon.

Ives Island

FACILITIES	None.
ACTIVITIES	Informal camping.
RESTRICTIONS	Access by boat only.

This island is located west of Hamilton Island at rivermile 143. It is part of the Gifford Pinchot National Forest and is managed by the Columbia River Gorge National Scenic Area. Camping is permitted, but the island is heavily wooded and campsites may be difficult to find.

Pierce National Wildlife Refuge

FACILITIES	None.
ACTIVITIES	Viewing waterfowl.
RESTRICTIONS	Closed to the public, but group tours can be arranged.

This national wildlife refuge consists of the northern shore of the Columbia north of Pierce Island, at rivermile 142, just east of Beacon Rock State Park. It covers 336 acres and is one of five refuges in the Ridgefield National Wildlife Refuge Complex. It is largely comprised of tamegrass pastures, riverine wetlands, lowland hardwoods, and the Hardy Creek riparian corridor, which supports the last remaining chum salmon runs on the Columbia. The refuge provides habitat for a variety of waterfowl, including Canada geese, mallards, tundra swans, gadwalls, pintails, cinnamon teals, wood ducks, buffleheads, and mergansers. A great blue heron rookery can be seen in the cottonwoods on the island, and an elk herd also frequents the refuge. The refuge can be viewed from the trail that ascends Beacon Rock. Phone 509-427-5208.

Pierce Island

FACILITIES	None.
ACTIVITIES	Viewing native plants and wildlife.
RESTRICTIONS	Open from July 15 to February 15. No pets, camping, or fires.

Pierce Island, a 200-acre Nature Conservancy preserve located immediately east of Beacon Rock, is dedicated to protecting native riverine flora and fauna. The island is home to a variety of birds and mammals, including geese, ducks, ospreys, and beavers. The Nature Conservancy requests that this preserve not be treated as a park; visits should be brief and extra care taken to leave no trace. Geologically, Pierce Island is the most inland site of a convoluted cutbank showing liquefaction of the riverbed resulting from the earthquake of January 26, 1700.

John B. Yeon State Park

FACILITIES	Interpretive information, picnic tables, hiking trails, parking.
ACTIVITIES	Hiking, picnicking.
RESTRICTIONS	Day use only.

This state park consists primarily of a parking lot and the trailhead for a 1.75-mile hiking trail to Elowah Falls, which offers views of the Columbia Gorge. To reach the park from the west on Interstate 84, take Ainsworth State Park exit 35 and drive east on Frontage Road to the park. From the east take exit 37. This 284-acre Oregon State Park has its own captivating waterfalls. The captains, when descending this section of the Gorge, remarked about the beauty of the more than twenty waterfalls on the Oregon shore, some falling several hundred feet from the crest of the basalt escarpments. The falls resulted from the many floods that poured through the Gorge thirteen to fifty thousand years ago, when the glacial dams to the east broke, releasing the Ice Age waters, whose depths were estimated to be 600 to 1,000 feet deep. The floods changed the topography of the land and scoured the walls of the Gorge into their present form.

Sams Walker Park

FACILITIES	Trails, viewpoints, toilets, parking.
ACTIVITIES	Picnicking, hiking, wildlife viewing.
RESTRICTIONS	Day use only. Northwest Forest Pass required. Fee.

This Forest Service day-use area was completed in 1994 near the eastern end of the Franz Lake National Wildlife Refuge. It offers 1.75 miles of gravel paths through open meadows and deep woods. At three points the paths reach the shoreline of the Columbia River. From Highway 14 at milepost 32.85, turn south on Skamania Landing Road and drive about a quarter of a mile to the parking lot.

Ainsworth State Park

FACILITIES	Campground, picnic areas, showers, toilets.
ACTIVITIES	Camping, picnicking, hiking.
RESTRICTIONS	Campground open from mid-April to October. Fee for camping.

This state park consists of several small sites along Highway 30 (Columbia River Highway), including two picnic areas and a campground. Forty-five full hookup campsites are available. To reach the park, take exit 35 from Interstate 84, then drive west on Highway 30 a short distance to the campground. The two picnic areas are located a short distance west along the highway. The campground would be a good base camp for exploring the Columbia Gorge. Trails lead from the campground to the picnic areas and to Gorge Trail 400, a low-level trail that extends 35 miles from Angels Rest to Wyeth.

Franz Lake Viewpoint

FACILITIES	Viewing platform.
ACTIVITIES	Wildlife viewing.
RESTRICTIONS	Day use only.

The Franz Lake National Wildlife Refuge is generally closed to public entry, but this viewing platform at milepost 31.5 on Highway 14 gives a long-distance view of the refuge, with Horsetail Falls visible to the southeast, across the Columbia.

St. Cloud Recreation Area

FACILITIES	Trails, picnic tables, toilets, parking.
ACTIVITIES	Picnicking, hiking, wildlife viewing.
RESTRICTIONS	Day use only.

This recreation area located at milepost 29.9 on Highway 14 was constructed in 1994 near the western end of the Franz Lake National Wildlife Refuge. (The refuge itself is not open to the public.) From the paved parking lot, a half-mile loop trail leads to picnic sites along the shore of the Columbia, with views across the river to Multnomah Falls. Although no boat ramp is available, access to the river is possible via a quarter-mile portage on the loop trail.

SUGGESTED DAY AND OVERNIGHT TRIPS

Hamilton Island to Beacon Rock

DISTANCE	3 miles one way.
CAMPING	Beacon Rock State Park.

This day trip begins at the ramp at Hamilton Island and ends at the ramp at Beacon Rock State Park. Along the way it passes two large islands, Ives Island and Pierce Island. The channels behind these islands offer a chance to paddle away from the main channel of the Columbia. Behind the islands on the northern shore of the river is the Pierce National Wildlife Refuge, which is not open to the public. Pierce Island itself is a Nature Conservancy preserve and is open to the public from July 15 to February 15. No pets, camping, or fires are permitted. To avoid a car shuttle, launch at Beacon Rock State Park, paddle east around the two islands, and return to the park.

Beacon Rock to Dalton Point

DISTANCE	8 miles one way.
CAMPING	Beacon Rock State Park.

This day trip involves boating from the ramp beneath Beacon Rock on the Washington shore to the ramp at Dalton Point on the Oregon shore (see Trail Reach 2). A car shuttle will be needed to cross the river 3 miles above Beacon Rock at the Bridge of the Gods, a toll bridge. Just east of Dalton Point, the river is divided by Skamania Island. The shipping channel follows the main channel of the river south of the island, so you might prefer to use the northern channel.

TRAIL REACH 2

Skamania Island to Cottonwood Point

DISTANCE   10 miles.

MAPS   USGS Bridal Veil and Washougal 7.5-minute NOAA
Chart 18531.

In this scenic reach on the western edge of the Columbia Gorge, the river averages about a mile in width. The area is often windy and full of strong currents. The river can become very choppy, particularly if the wind is running in opposition to the downstream currents. Tidal action is also a factor, as is traffic from commercial tugs and barges. Before boating on this trail reach, be sure to check a tide table and a weather forecast. If wind and whitecaps are likely, make plans for another day.

This stretch contains some of the most spectacular waterfalls in the Gorge, including Multnomah Falls—the most famous and, at 620 feet, the highest falls in the area. Three-thousand-foot basalt cliffs line both sides of the river, the results of millions of years of erosion in which the river cut through the Cascade Range and carved out the Columbia Gorge.

The first island in Trail Reach 2 is Skamania Island, lying squarely in the middle of the river at rivermile 136. Like Ives Island, Skamania is managed by the Forest Service. Below Multnomah Falls is the tiny, midstream Phoca Rock and, on the Washington shore, the towering cliffs of Cape Horn. The cliffs here rise directly out of the water, leaving small caves at the water's edge. On the Oregon shore are seven state parks: Benson, Bridal Veil Falls, Shepperd's Dell, Guy W. Talbot, Crown Point, Rooster Rock, and Portland Women's Forum (phone 503-378-6305 for more information on any of these). Of these parks, only Rooster Rock offers river access. Massive landslides in this area thousands

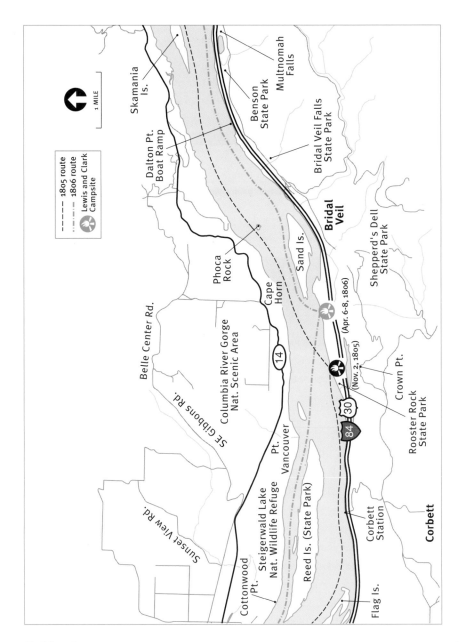

Trail Reach 2

Legend (within map):
- ----- 1805 route
- —·—· 1806 route
- 🌀 Lewis and Clark Campsite

1 MILE

Map labels:

Skamania Is.

Dalton Pt. Boat Ramp

Belle Center Rd.

Phoca Rock

Columbia River Gorge Nat. Scenic Area

Cape Horn

14

SE Gibbons Rd.

Sunset View Rd.

Pt. Vancouver

Cottonwood Pt.

Steigerwald Lake Nat. Wildlife Refuge

Reed Is. (State Park)

Flag Is.

Corbett Station

Corbett

Sand Is.

Bridal Veil

Shepperd's Dell State Park

(Apr. 6–8, 1806)

(Nov. 2, 1805)

Crown Pt.

Rooster Rock State Park

30

84

Bridal Veil Falls State Park

Benson State Park

Multnomah Falls

of years ago deposited the upright basalt formations now seen at Rooster Rock State Park and at Phoca Rock. Before the landslides, these rocks were part of the rim of the Gorge.

BOATING CAUTIONS AND CONDITIONS

This reach is influenced by the tide and can be very windy, often resulting in choppy water. Also watch for commercial tugs and barges. Just below Multnomah Falls, on the Oregon shore, boaters should be aware of Fashion Reef, which projects into the river. An unlighted buoy 74 and a lighted buoy 76 mark the safe route around the reef.

RIVER ACCESSES

Dalton Point Boat Ramp
FACILITIES	Boat ramp, toilets, parking.
ACTIVITIES	Launching only.
RESTRICTIONS	Fee for boat launching.

The Dalton Point Boat Ramp is located at rivermile 133.5, about 2 miles west of Multnomah Falls on Interstate 84. It can be reached only by westbound traffic on Interstate 84. Eastbound traffic on the interstate should continue east to Multnomah Falls and then return westbound 2 miles to Dalton Point.

Rooster Rock State Park
FACILITIES	Boat ramp, dock, toilets, facilities for people with disabilities, clothing-optional beach.
ACTIVITIES	Picnicking, fishing, boating, windsurfing, swimming.
RESTRICTIONS	Day use only. Fee.

Rooster Rock State Park, with its namesake basalt tower, is located east of Portland on Interstate 84 at exit 25. Here, at the base of Rooster Rock, the Corps of Discovery made camp on their way downriver. It was November 2, 1805. Clark noted how they "encamped under a high projecting rock on the Lard Side." Crown Point, 700 feet above, overlooks the campsite. The expedition observed great numbers of waterfowl and killed eighteen brant for dinner. They

Rooster Rock as it appeared in 1867. Photo by C. E. Watkins. Courtesy of the Oregon Historical Society (21095).

observed how the mountains here leave the river on each side and are thickly covered with pine species.

This park includes large parking lots for the many visitors who come for the sandy beaches, picnicking, and boating. Overnight camping is not allowed. The eastern end of the park features a loop hiking trail and a clothing-optional beach. The boat dock and launching ramp are located at the western end of the park in a small inlet beneath the rock. A pile jetty lies at the entrance to the inlet, which is about a quarter of a mile west of Rooster Rock itself. Late in summer, in dry years, the inlet is too shallow for boating, even for canoes or kayaks. Phone 503-695-2261.

Corbett Station

FACILITIES	Primitive boat ramp, limited parking.
ACTIVITIES	Launching only.
RESTRICTIONS	Ramp not maintained.

The Corbett Station Boat Ramp is located immediately north of Corbett exit 22 on Interstate 84, at rivermile 126.5. In the past it was maintained by the Oregon Department of Transportation, but the ramp was closed and gated in 1999. Paddlers may still park at the gate and carry their boats down the lengthy ramp, which is no longer maintained.

OTHER FACILITIES AND POINTS OF INTEREST

Skamania Island

FACILITIES	None.
ACTIVITIES	Informal camping.
RESTRICTIONS	None.

Skamania Island lies in the middle of the Columbia directly north of Benson State Park. Part of the Gifford Pinchot National Forest, it is managed by the Columbia River Gorge National Scenic Area. The island is heavily forested with cottonwood trees and has sandy beaches where dispersed camping is permitted. There are no facilities, trails, or formal campsites on the island.

Multnomah Falls

FACILITIES	Restaurant, gift shop, toilets.
ACTIVITIES	Hiking.
RESTRICTIONS	No camping.

Multnomah Falls is the most majestic of some two hundred waterfalls in the Columbia Gorge. The most popular tourist site in Oregon, it attracts more than two million visitors annually, perhaps partly because it is located just a few steps from a major interstate highway. The upper falls is 660 feet above sea level at the top, 117 at the base; and the lower falls is 103 feet above sea level at the top and 40 at the base. The total drop of the two falls is 620 feet. The bridge between the two falls lies at a height of 135 feet. The historic lodge is listed on the National Register of Historic Places.

Early explorers, including Lewis and Clark, did not apply specific names to the Columbia Gorge falls, usually referring to them as "numerous cascades." Most falls were named during the steamboat era on the river. No one seems to know who named the falls, but Multnomah was the name of a local Chinookan tribe. The word was first used by Lewis and Clark in their journals of November 3, 1805, referring to the Willamette River. A mile-long trail leads to the top of the falls and a grand view of the Columbia, the lodge, and the falls.

Benson State Park

FACILITIES	Picnic sites, toilets.
ACTIVITIES	Boating, swimming, fishing, picnicking.
RESTRICTIONS	Open spring, summer, and fall. Day use only. No camping. Fee.

Benson State Park lies along the Columbia 30 miles east of Portland on Interstate 84, with eastbound access only. The park is 3.5 miles west of Ainsworth State Park on Interstate 84 and 6 miles east of Rooster Rock State Park, stretching out on both sides of Multnomah Falls. This 272-acre park was named after Simon Benson, a pioneer lumberman, hotel owner, civic leader, and philanthropist. He purchased the property that includes the state park (circa 1910) and donated it to the city of Portland. He also purchased the popular bronze drinking fountains that are located on the streets of downtown Portland.

Bridal Veil Falls State Park

FACILITIES	Picnic sites, short hiking trails, toilets.
ACTIVITIES	Picnicking, hiking.
RESTRICTIONS	Day use only.

This park is located on Highway 30 (Columbia River Highway), 16 miles east of Troutdale. Take Interstate 84 to the Bridal Veil exit 28, and drive 1 mile west on Highway 30. The park is located on a basalt bluff above Interstate 84. A half-mile trail leads to the falls, and a shorter overlook trail leads to viewpoints on the bluffs.

Phoca Rock, meaning "seal rock," stands out in the river directly north of Bridal Veil Falls State Park (see Plate 8). The 30-foot basalt pillar was named by Captain Clark on November 2, 1805, because of the large number of harbor seals in the river and on the rock.

Shepperd's Dell State Park

FACILITIES	Hiking trail, viewpoint.
ACTIVITIES	Hiking.
RESTRICTIONS	Day use only. No drinking water.

Shepperd's Dell State Park is located on scenic Highway 30 (Columbia River Highway), 13 miles west of Troutdale. The 519-acre park overlooks the Columbia River and was donated to the public by George G. Shepperd. A short trail leads to a waterfall viewpoint. The trail also provides excellent views of the

Shepperd's Dell Bridge, a graceful concrete deck arch built in 1914. Designed by K. R. Billner under the supervision of Samuel Lancaster, it is considered to be among the most beautiful of the many fine bridges on Highway 30. There is no river access.

Sand Island

FACILITIES	Clothing-optional beaches.
ACTIVITIES	Boating.
RESTRICTIONS	No camping.

This island—one of several Sand Islands in the Columbia—is an undeveloped day-use unit of Rooster Rock State Park, which lies 2 miles west. It is partly forested with cottonwood trees and has extensive sandy beaches for easy access by boaters. From the Oregon shoreline its beaches are a quarter of a mile by boat.

Lying half a mile north on the Washington shore are the cliffs of Cape Horn, one of three points on the Columbia River christened Cape Horn by fur-trading canoe brigades in the early 1800s. Some say early voyageurs on the Columbia named it after the hazardous tip of South America, where strong headwinds also prevail. The steep 500-foot-high rock face of Cape Horn was a major obstacle to the construction of the Lewis and Clark Highway (Highway 14).

On their return journey, from April 6 to April 8, 1806, Lewis and Clark camped for three nights on the Oregon shore opposite the downriver tip of Sand Island and south of today's Shepperd's Dell State Park. (The eastern end of Rooster Rock State Park provides a view of the area.) It was a tough camping site. The wind and waves were so strong that the men had to unload their

Lying directly north of Sand Island are the shear basaltic cliffs of Cape Horn. Photo by C. E. Watkins, 1867. Courtesy of the Oregon Historical Society (21096).

canoes and haul them up the bank, and those that went hunting failed to return with any game. Clark commented on the loss of sight experienced by many Indians of the area, stating that the condition was more common among all nations inhabiting the river than among any other people he had observed. He attributed it to the reflection of sun on the water, to which Indians were constantly exposed in their occupation of fishing.

Crown Point State Park

FACILITIES	Interpretive center, gift shop, toilets.
ACTIVITIES	Viewing the western Columbia River Gorge.
RESTRICTIONS	Day use only.

Crown Point is a dramatic basalt viewpoint on the rim of the Columbia Gorge, towering 733 feet above the river. From here you have a 30-mile commanding view of the Columbia in both directions. The park is located on historic Highway 30 (Columbia River Highway), 11 miles east of Troutdale.

When engineer Samuel Lancaster designed the Columbia River Highway in the early part of the twentieth century, he selected Crown Point as the site for an observatory where the Gorge "could be viewed in silent communication with the infinite" and as a memorial to "the trials and hardships of those who had come into the Oregon Country" (Lancaster 1916). The domed, octagonal Vista House that now sits atop Crown Point was built in 1916 as a rest stop and observatory for the Columbia River Gorge. Crown Point is now a National Natural Landmark, and Vista House is listed in the National Register of Historic Places. Vista House is open March through October and features an observation deck, gift shop, information center, and exhibits on the area's history and geology and on the construction of the Columbia River Highway. Interpretive programs are often scheduled during the summer months.

Reed Island State Park

FACILITIES	Large sandy beaches, primitive campsites, vault toilet on western end.
ACTIVITIES	Camping.
RESTRICTIONS	Access by boat only.

This island is located in the Columbia River between rivermiles 124 and 127.5, just south of the Steigerwald Lake National Wildlife Refuge. To reach the island by canoe or kayak, boats may be hand-launched at Cottonwood Beach.

The nearest boat ramp is at the Port of Camas and Washougal, rivermile 121.5, about 2.5 miles west of Reed Island. On the Oregon shore, canoes and kayaks may be hand-launched directly south of Reed Island, at Corbett Station, rivermile 126.5. Ten primitive campsites are located on the southwestern side of the island. A trail leads from the campsites to the northern shore.

Point Vancouver juts out from the Washington shoreline just east of the upstream tip of Reed Island. This prominent landmark was named by Lieutenant William Broughton, under the command of Captain George Vancouver. It remains a reminder of how far up the Columbia River the British expedition explored in October 1792. In fact it was on Reed Island that Broughton claimed the region for England. When Lewis and Clark arrived here, they returned to country previously explored by Euro-Americans.

Steigerwald Lake National Wildlife Refuge

FACILITIES	None.
ACTIVITIES	Hiking, mountain biking, horseback riding, bird watching.
RESTRICTIONS	Closed to the public, but wildlife viewing is available around the perimeter.

Established to provide mitigation for wildlife habitat lost as a result of construction of the second powerhouse at Bonneville Dam, this refuge encompasses 1,288 acres of wetlands, riparian habitat, and agricultural pastures. A wide variety of wildlife inhabits the refuge, including bobcats, coyotes, red foxes, beavers, otters, black-tailed deer, minks, weasels, and 180 bird species.

The refuge is presently closed to the public. However, the dike between the refuge and the river is not part of the refuge, and a gravel road (closed to vehicles) runs along its top. The road, known as the Columbia River Dike Trail, is open to the public for hiking, mountain biking, and horseback riding. The dike trail begins at the intersection of Highway 14 and Fifteenth Street in Washougal. The trail travels east 1.5 miles through the new Captain William Clark Park at Cottonwood Beach, then continues east for another 2 miles past Steigerwald Lake to Point Vancouver near rivermile 127.75. The refuge is managed as part of the Ridgefield National Wildlife Refuge Complex. To arrange a group tour, phone 360-887-4106.

SUGGESTED DAY AND OVERNIGHT TRIPS

Dalton Point to Rooster Rock
DISTANCE   5 miles one way.
CAMPING   None.

A paddle route from Dalton Point to Rooster Rock can follow one of two routes. The first route is appropriate for more adventuresome paddlers. Leave from Dalton Point and head toward the Washington shore and the towering cliffs of Cape Horn, where small caves can be found at water level. The shipping lanes are very close to Cape Horn, so be careful when crossing them. Finally, head back to Rooster Rock. The second route involves simply following the southern shore of the Columbia, staying behind Sand Island as the route approaches Rooster Rock. If time permits, this trip could be extended an extra 2 miles to Corbett Station.

Rooster Rock to Captain William Clark Park at Cottonwood Beach
DISTANCE   5 miles one way.
CAMPING   Reed Island State Park.

From the boat ramp at Rooster Rock State Park, carefully cross the shipping lanes to Point Vancouver, and head west behind Reed Island to Cottonwood Beach, just northwest of the western end of Reed Island. Captain William Clark Park at Cottonwood Beach is part of Trail Reach 3.

Reed Island
DISTANCE   8 miles round-trip.
CAMPING   Reed Island.

Reed Island can be circumnavigated by launching at Cottonwood Beach and paddling a short distance east to the island. Or launch at Corbett Station on the Oregon shore. The island is 3 miles long. Because this trip involves paddling both directions past the island, carefully consider the tide, wind, and river current before departing.

TRAIL REACH 3

Cottonwood Point to Government Island

DISTANCE   10 miles.

MAPS   USGS Washougal, Camas, and Mount Tabor
            7.5-minute NOAA Chart 18531.

In this reach the river leaves the Columbia River Gorge and enters the Port-land-Vancouver metropolitan area. The mouth of the Sandy River, marked by Broughton Bluff rising above it, is usually considered the western end of the Gorge. It is also the western boundary of the Columbia River Gorge National Scenic Area. As the river leaves the Gorge, the surrounding terrain becomes much flatter and islands become more numerous, offering backwater channels and sloughs to explore, safely away from commercial boat traffic.

BOATING CAUTIONS AND CONDITIONS

Although this reach of the river leaves the narrow confines of the Gorge behind, wind can still present a problem, and the tidal current is present as always. This area is very popular with sailboats and powerboats, including many commercial tugs and barges.

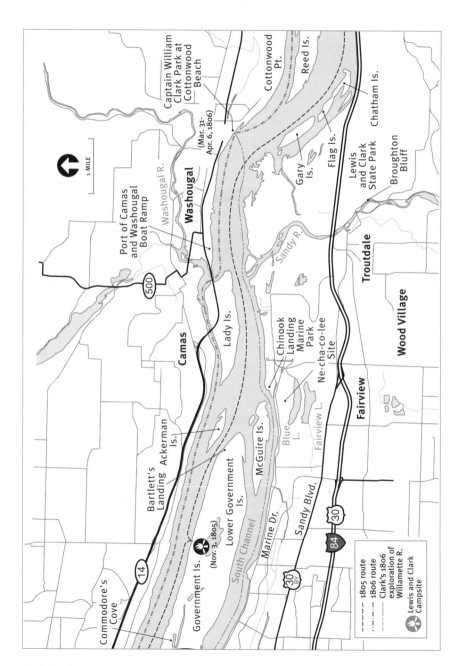

1 MILE

Commodore's Cove

14

Government Is.

(Nov. 3, 1805)

South Channel

Lower Government Is.

Marine Dr.

McGuire Is.

Sandy Blvd.

30 BY

84

30

Bartlett's Landing

Ackerman Is.

Lady Is.

Blue L.

Chinook Landing Marine Park

Fairview L.

Ne-cha-co-lee Site

Fairview

Wood Village

Camas

500

Port of Camas and Washougal Boat Ramp

Washougal R.

Washougal

(Mar. 31-Apr. 6, 1806)

Captain William Clark Park at Cottonwood Beach

Cottonwood Pt.

Reed Is.

Sandy R.

Gary Is.

Flag Is.

Lewis and Clark State Park

Chatham Is.

Broughton Bluff

Troutdale

- - - 1805 route

- · - · 1806 route

— — Clark's 1806 exploration of Willamette R.

Lewis and Clark Campsite

Trail Reach 3

RIVER ACCESSES

Captain William Clark Park at Cottonwood Beach

FACILITIES   Dock, sandy beach, 3-mile dike trail, nature trails, scenic viewing tower, historical interpretive exhibits, children's play area, volleyball courts, horseshoe pits, parking.

ACTIVITIES   Full-service camping, boating, swimming, fishing, picnicking.

RESTRICTIONS   Fee.

This Washougal city park, with its 600-foot public dock, is located at rivermile 122.75. From Highway 14 at milepost 16.1, turn south on Fifteenth Street to the park. The public beach is located slightly upriver at rivermile 123.4. At milepost 17.1, turn south on Thirty-second Street and follow it to a T-intersection with Index Street. Park here, then walk over the dike and about 200 yards to a sandy beach, where boats may be hand-launched. The same procedure may be followed using Thirty-fifth Street. Five parking areas for beach users are proposed along Index Street from Thirty-second to Thirty-fifth Street. To prevent flooding in this low-lying area, a 3-mile dike was built along the shoreline, 41 feet above mean sea level. The Columbia River Dike Trail was built atop the dike to provide an impressive pathway along the river for hikers and bicyclists. Steigerwald Lake National Wildlife Refuge lies east of the beach, and 3-mile-long Reed Island State Park lies just offshore from the wildlife refuge.

Lewis and Clark camped at Cottonwood Beach from March 31 to April 6, 1806, on their return journey from their winter camp near Astoria. The campsite is located near the junction of South Index and South Twenty-seventh Streets, across the Columbia River from the mouth of the original Sandy River channel (now blocked). The explorers camped here six nights to search for game on both sides of the river. Indians had told them that game was scarce up the Gorge, and it was too early for salmon to migrate up to this point; thus a supply of game meat was essential in order to proceed onward. Captain Clark used the stay at this camp as an opportunity to return downstream with an Indian guide to explore the Willamette River.

There are plans for development of additional park facilities in this area. Improvements will include expansion of the Steamboat Landing dock, scenic viewpoints, and historical interpretive stations, and the addition of a viewing tower, wildlife viewing blinds, picnic facilities (including group picnic shelters), camping facilities, RV hookups, toilets, a children's play area, and bike racks. Two day-docks are also planned—one for canoes and kayaks, another for

A group from the Lower Columbia River Water Trail Committee discusses improvements for the Cottonwood Beach area where the Corps of Discovery camped from March 31 to April 6, 1806, on their return journey.

motorized boats.

Port of Camas and Washougal Boat Ramp

FACILITIES	Boat ramp, dock.
ACTIVITIES	Picnicking, boating.
RESTRICTIONS	Day use only.

The popular Port of Camas and Washougal Boat Ramp (also known as Parker's Landing) is located at rivermile 121.5. From Highway 14 in Washougal, turn south on Second Street, right on Front Street, and follow Front Street half a mile to a large parking area and a boat ramp next to Parker's Landing Historical Park. This ramp is about a mile east of the upper end of Lady Island.

What Lewis and Clark referred to as the Seal River is now the Washougal, an Indian word meaning "rushing water." The city of Washougal, once an important steamboat landing, takes its name from the river. In a rough-draft map of Lady Island drawn in Clark's journal on November 2, 1805, it is labeled as Island of Fowl; however, the island was named White Brant Island on Clark's route map, and this is what Lewis called it on their return trip in 1806.

Formally known as La Camas by French-Canadian fur trappers in the nineteenth century, the name of the city of Camas derived from the camas, a native plant and valuable food source utilized by western Indians. The Indian word *Chamass* described the plant's bulb as "fruit" or "sweet." The low river-bottom plains supplied Native Americans with this important staple of their diet every spring.

Lewis and Clark State Park

FACILITIES	Boat ramp, picnic area, toilets.
ACTIVITIES	Picnicking, boating, rock climbing, swimming, fishing, hiking.
RESTRICTIONS	Day use only.

This state park lies at the foot of Broughton Bluff, just south of Interstate 84 exit 18 near Troutdale. The cliffs above the park are popular with local rock climbers. The boat ramp is on the Sandy River, across the road from the main park. Boats may be launched here and paddled 2 miles downstream to the Columbia, but the river current prevents paddling back to the park.

Chinook Landing Marine Park

FACILITIES	Boat ramp, picnic tables, toilets, parking.
ACTIVITIES	Boating, picnicking.
RESTRICTIONS	Day use only. Fee.

The popular boat ramp at this park is located adjacent to Blue Lake Regional Park on Marine Drive at the foot of NE 223rd Avenue in Fairview, north of Gresham, and is operated by Metro Parks. It provides ready access to Government Island. The 67-acre park has six launching lanes on the Columbia and is the largest public boating facility in Oregon. It also offers viewing areas and wetland and wildlife habitat. Phone 503-665-6918.

On April 2, 1806, Clark passed the small native village of Ne-cha-co-lee on his return trip downriver to locate the Willamette. The village was located near Blue Lake, south of the present-day Chinook Landing. His native guide lived here, and on Clark's return the next day, Clark visited the village and found one house 210-feet long divided into seven rooms. Five other houses remained of a large village. Clark remarked on the impact of a smallpox epidemic thirty years earlier, discussed local geography, and purchased five dogs.

OTHER FACILITIES AND POINTS OF INTEREST

Gary, Flag, and Chatham Islands

FACILITIES	None.
ACTIVITIES	Primitive camping.
RESTRICTIONS	None.

These three islands lie along the southern shore of the Columbia, just east of the Sandy River Delta. Metro Parks once maintained a public boat moorage at the eastern end of Flag Island, but it was washed away by the large flood of 1996. Bald eagles nest on Flag Island. Gary and Flag Islands, comprising 132 acres, are under the jurisdiction of Portland's Metro Parks Department, and boat access and no-facility camping are permitted. Phone 503-665-6918. Accessing these islands by motorized boat is not advised from August through September, when water levels are low.

The Sandy River Delta was created by lahars (mud flows) from Mount Hood, which surged down the Sandy River into the Columbia. The most recent flow, called the Old Maid Lahar, occurred in the late 1700s, just prior to the expedition's visit. The Sandy River was discovered by Lieutenant William Broughton in 1792 and named Barings River, after the English family of bankers and financiers. The name Quick Sand River, given by Lewis and Clark in 1805, was used for nearly fifty years until it was shortened by American pioneers in the mid-nineteenth century to Sandy River.

Government Island

FACILITIES	Campsites, boat moorage, toilets.
ACTIVITIES	Camping, picnicking.
RESTRICTIONS	Access by boat only. Interior of island closed to the public.

This large island, formerly owned by the Port of Portland, is now managed by Oregon State Parks. Three boating facilities are situated along its northern shore. From east to west, these include Bartlett's Landing, with moorage, toilets, and camping; Lower Government Island, or West Docks, also with moorage, toilets, and camping; and Commodore's Cove, a moorage under the Interstate 205 bridge, with no access to the island. The southern side of the island features a sandy beach. The interior is a wildlife refuge and is closed to public access. Phone 503-695-2261, extension 222, for more information.

On November 3, 1805, after passing the mouth of the Sandy River on their way down the Columbia, the Corps made camp on the northern side of Government Island. Lewis hunted waterfowl on a pond for the evening meal. While rounding the island, the party met Indians who reported having seen three sailing vessels at the mouth of the Columbia. Although this was encouraging news, no contact was ever made with American or European traders for fresh supplies.

Government Island was originally named Diamond Island by Lewis and Clark because of its shape. In 1850 the federal government reserved the island for a military installation, hence its present name.

SUGGESTED DAY AND OVERNIGHT TRIPS

Gary, Flag, and Chatham Islands

DISTANCE	7 miles one way.
CAMPING	Gary, Flag, and Chatham Islands.

To boat this trip, launch at Corbett Station (see Trail Reach 2) and head west past Gary, Flag, and Chatham Islands, all of which are publicly owned. The trip ends at the Port of Camas and Washougal Boat Ramp on the Washington shore. The Sandy River Delta, with its numerous channels and islands, could also be explored. For a somewhat longer trip, ending on the Oregon shore (but with a shorter car shuttle), finish at Chinook Landing.

Sandy River Delta

DISTANCE	3 miles one way.
CAMPING	Lewis and Clark State Park.

The Sandy River Delta can be explored by launching at Lewis and Clark State Park and proceeding 2 miles down the Sandy River to the Columbia. About a mile below the park the channel of the Sandy splits, offering several route choices. Because of the current, paddling back to the launching point is not possible. End the trip at the Port of Camas and Washougal Boat Ramp or, for a longer trip and a shorter car shuttle, at Chinook Landing.

TRAIL REACH 4

Government Island to Willamette River

DISTANCE   11 miles.

MAPS   USGS Mount Tabor, Portland, Vancouver, and Sauvie Island 7.5-minute NOAA Chart 18524.

This urbanized reach of the river flows between the large seaport cities of Portland, Oregon, and Vancouver, Washington.

The city of Vancouver, with a population of 140,000, has several waterfront parks and greenway paths. It is the oldest continuously occupied Euro-American settlement in Washington State. The location was selected by the British Hudson's Bay Company in 1825 for the headquarters of their extensive North American trading company. The impressive Fort Vancouver National Historic Site preserves its colorful past as a trading center and U.S. military post. The city—named for British Captain George Vancouver, who never visited or even laid eyes on the site—is the county seat of Clark County, named for William Clark. The county was originally also named for Vancouver, when it extended from the Columbia River to British Columbia. In 1853, five years after it was changed to Clark County, an *e* was inadvertently added, and the error was perpetuated until 1925, when *Clarke* was corrected to *Clark*.

Portland, with a current population of 1,900,000, was named in 1845 after a coin toss between its East Coast founders, Asa Lovejoy and Francis Pettygrove. If Lovejoy had won the toss, the city would now be known as Boston. Portland became the third post office in the Oregon Territory when it was established south of the strategic confluence of the Willamette River with the Columbia. Oregon's largest city, Portland is also a seaport and an important center of commerce in the Pacific Northwest. Dikes now protect the northern part of the city from floods, such as the Vanport Flood of 1948, which caused

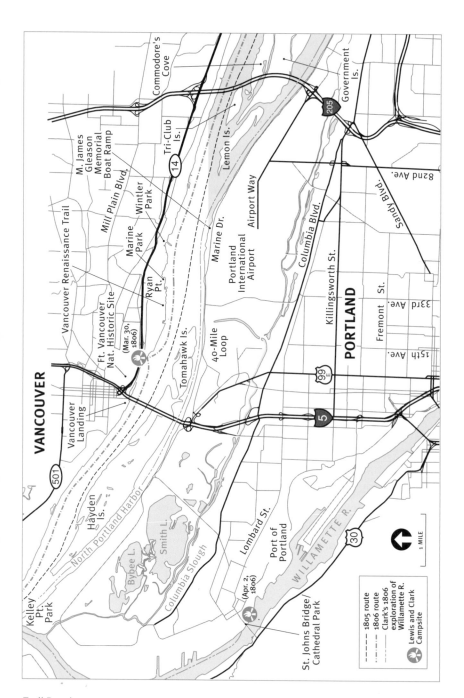

VANCOUVER

M. James
Gleason
Memorial
Boat Ramp

Mill Plain Blvd.

Vancouver Renaissance Trail

Wintler
Park

Marine
Park

Vancouver
Landing

Ft. Vancouver
Nat. Historic Site

(Mar. 30,
1806)

Ryan
Pt.

Hayden
Is.

Kelley
Pt.
Park

501

North Portland Harbor

Bybee L.

Smith L.

Columbia Slough

(Apr. 2,
1806)

Lombard St.

Port of
Portland

St. Johns Bridge/
Cathedral Park

WILLAMETTE R.

30

Commodore's
Cove

Tri-Club
Is.

14

Lemon Is.

Marine Dr.

Airport Way

Portland
International
Airport

Tomahawk Is.

40-Mile
Loop

Columbia Blvd.

Killingsworth St.

99
E

5

PORTLAND

Government
Is.

205

82nd Ave.

Sandy Blvd.

33rd Ave.

Fremont St.

15th Ave.

- - - - - 1805 route
- · - · - 1806 route
- · · - · · Clark's 1806
          exploration of
          Willamette R.
🌀 Lewis and Clark
   Campsite

1 MILE

Trail Reach 4

the river to crest at 40 feet above mean sea level and destroyed the city of Vanport. The city's beautiful waterfront park, named after the late governor Tom McCall, is linked to an extensive urban park and open-space greenway system. Portland is also home to the largest city park in the nation—the 5,000-acre Forest Park.

From the Portland-Vancouver area you can see some of the Pacific Northwest's most spectacular volcanic mountains, the results of intense friction between the Pacific and North American tectonic plates. Dominating the landscape 22 miles to the southeast is Mount Hood, the highest peak in Oregon at 11,235 feet (see Plate 10). It was named by Lieutenant Broughton (representing King George III) on October 29, 1792, in honor of Rear Admiral Samuel Hood of the British Admiralty. In Indian legend Mount Hood is known as Wy'east, named after a son of the Great Spirit. On October 25, 1804, Captain Clark observed the mountain from a point near The Dalles: "We called this Falls Mountain or Timm Mountain."

Looking directly south on a clear day you can see the peak of Mount Jefferson, the only mountain in the Pacific Northwest that has retained the name provided by Lewis and Clark. On March 30, 1806, in the vicinity of Sauvie Island, Clark wrote, "Discovered a high mountain SE. covered with snow which we call Mount Jefferson." The second highest peak in Oregon, at 10,497 feet, Mount Jefferson was named after the president.

Northeast of both Portland and Vancouver looms Mount St. Helens, at 8,365 feet (see Plate 11). Captain Vancouver, sailing off the Pacific Coast in 1792, named the mountain to honor the British Ambassador to Spain, Alleyne Fitzherbert, Baron St. Helens. In 1980 the peak lived up to its Indian name, Lawala Clough ("smoking mountain"), when it erupted, taking 1,300 feet off the top and blunting its perfect cone. Just east of Mount St. Helens is Mount Adams, 12,307 feet high, the second highest in Washington. Mount Rainier, the highest point in Washington at 14,410 feet, lies 90 miles slightly northeast. From the Portland area, Mount Rainier can often be seen over the left side of Mount St. Helens.

Lying between the two cities is Hayden Island, which is 5.5 miles long. In 1792 Lieutenant Broughton named this Menzies Island, after the Vancouver botanist Archibald Menzies. Lewis and Clark called it Image Canoe Island for the many large, beautifully crafted native canoes they observed on the shore. Gay Hayden, an Oregon pioneer and an early mayor of Vancouver, owned much of the island in the nineteenth century, and the island came to be named for him. The eastern end of the island is now heavily developed with shopping centers, hotels, and condominiums, while the western end is relatively unde-veloped. Another island located between Hayden Island and the northern shore was called Tomahawk Island, named by Lewis and Clark after a tomahawk pipe that was stolen and later recovered. This island later washed away, but in 1927 a new island formed at the eastern end of Hayden Island and was called Toma-hawk to perpetuate the name. The present Tomahawk and Hayden Islands have been consolidated by river silting and road construction.

BOATING CAUTIONS AND CONDITIONS

The Columbia River between Portland and Vancouver is a very busy water-way, with heavy recreational and commercial boating traffic, including barges, tugs, oceangoing freighters, Coast Guard vessels, sailboats, and cruise ships. Tomahawk Island has numerous marinas and most of them are locked between the docks and land.

RIVER ACCESSES

M. James Gleason Memorial Boat Ramp

FACILITIES	Boat ramp, river maps, river patrol office, toilets, parking.
ACTIVITIES	Launching only.
RESTRICTIONS	Day use only. Fee.

This Metro Parks boat ramp is located near the western end of the Portland International Airport, in the 4200 block of NE Marine Drive. East of the ramp is Broughton Beach, where picnicking is permitted. Phone 503-665-6918.

Near this site stood Ne-er-cha-ke-oo, a large Watlalas (Chinookan) village of twenty-four lodges thatched with straw and covered with bark, and one 50-foot wood-plank house. Visiting this village on November 4, 1805, Clark esti-mated a population of two hundred men of the Skil-lute nation, and fifty-two canoes.

Wintler Park

FACILITIES	Beach, picnic tables, toilets, parking.
ACTIVITIES	Picnicking.
RESTRICTIONS	Day use only.

This 15-acre Vancouver city park is located on the Columbia River about 3 miles east of Vancouver. From Highway 14, take exit 3 (Evergreen Boulevard to Riverside Drive). Turn right at the top of the exit and immediately turn left on Columbia Way, which leads to the park. Just before the park entrance is the east trailhead of the Tidewater Cove Trail, which leads west 1.5 miles to Marine Park and 4 miles to downtown Vancouver. Boats can be hand-launched from the beach.

Marine Park

FACILITIES	Boat ramps, docks, beach, picnic shelter, playground, viewing platform, interpretive displays, toilets, parking.
ACTIVITIES	Picnicking, viewing the river.
RESTRICTIONS	Day use only. Fee for boat launching.

This large Vancouver city park is located at Ryan Point, east of Vancouver at the site of a World War II Kaiser shipyard. From Highway 14 turn south, under the railroad tracks, onto Marine Park Way and follow it into the park. A paved road leads about half a mile west to the Henry J. Kaiser Shipyard Memorial and Interpretive Center, which includes a boat ramp, three-story viewing platform, and kiosk. A fee applies to all vehicles driving down to the boat ramp during summer. Adjacent to Marine Park is Vancouver's Marine Park Water Reclamation Facility, which includes a large interpretive center on sewage treatment and water quality.

Vancouver Landing

FACILITIES	Floating dock, concrete ramp, amphitheater, benches, parking.
ACTIVITIES	Launching only.
RESTRICTIONS	Day use only.

From Portland take the City Center exit off of Interstate 5 in Vancouver. Keep in the left lane, which turns into Sixth Street, and proceed three blocks to Columbia Street. Turn left, continue under the railroad overpass, and turn right into the large parking lot at the landing. This access point is located just behind the Red Lion Hotel at the Quay.

Columbia Slough

FACILITIES	Beach.
ACTIVITIES	Launching only.
RESTRICTIONS	Day use only.

From this beach launch site at Kelley Point Park, the Columbia may be reached by paddling west for a third of a mile, then paddling north on the Willamette for three quarters of a mile. The hand-launch site is on the left just inside the park entrance.

Cathedral Park

FACILITIES	Boat ramp, beach launching for paddlers, fishing pier, picnic facilities, amphitheater, hiking trails, summertime music events, history wall, potable water, toilets, parking.
ACTIVITIES	Picnicking, hiking, fishing, boating.
RESTRICTIONS	Day use only.

This well-developed urban neighborhood park is located under the eastern end of St. Johns Bridge and is accessible via North Alta Avenue from North Lombard Street or via North Pittsburg Avenue from North Willamette Boulevard. In addition to providing boating access to the Willamette River and park facilities, the area offers scenic views to the western end of Forest Park.

On April 2, 1806, while the rest of the expedition was camped at Cottonwood Beach near present-day Washougal, Captain Clark explored the Willamette River and camped just northeast of Cathedral Park near the Port of Portland's Terminal 4. Clark, seven other members of the Corps, and an Indian guide found a large, empty wooden house here—the temporary residence of Indians who lived near today's Oregon City. It was 30 by 40 feet, built of boards, covered with cedar bark, and full of possessions. It was also so infested with fleas that the men preferred to camp outside it. Today the nearby University of Portland has erected a statue on its campus commemorating Clark's river exploration of the Portland area. Recent analysis concludes that his turnaround point, however, was not at the campus site but lower downriver near St. Johns Bridge.

OTHER FACILITIES AND POINTS OF INTEREST

Lemon Island

FACILITIES	Campsites, fire rings, toilets.
ACTIVITIES	Camping, picnicking.
RESTRICTIONS	None.

This small island at the downstream end of Government Island was apparently labeled White Goose Island on Clark's route map and Twin Island on a rough-draft map. The island's configuration and location have changed considerably since Clark drew his maps, however. Camping is permitted on both the northern and southern sides.

Vancouver Renaissance Trail

FACILITIES	None.
ACTIVITIES	Hiking, biking.
RESTRICTIONS	Day use only.

This very beautiful and historic 5.5-mile trail lies along Vancouver's waterfront. It begins at Wintler and Marine Parks and ends near Interstate 5 at Vancouver Landing.

40-Mile Loop

FACILITIES	None.
ACTIVITIES	Hiking, biking.
RESTRICTIONS	Day use only.

The 40-Mile Loop was named in 1903 by famous landscape architect John Charles Olmstead, who was commissioned by the Portland Parks Board to prepare the master plan. The loop was intended to help beautify Portland for the Lewis and Clark Centennial Exposition of 1905. Today it stretches 160 miles throughout the city, linking parks and open spaces. It is among the oldest and most creative greenway projects in the nation, and it befits Olmstead's vision. As he pointed out in his 1903 report to the city of Portland, "A connected system of parks and parkways is manifestly far more complete and useful than a series of isolated parks." Building on Olmstead's original plans, Portland has put together an interconnected system of trails, parks, and greenways that encircle the metropolitan region and will link with the Vancouver Renaissance Trail and the Lewis and Clark Discovery Greenway.

Fort Vancouver National Historic Site

FACILITIES   Visitor center, replica of the fort.

ACTIVITIES   Touring the site, participating in living-history programs.

RESTRICTIONS   Day use only. Fee during summer months.

In 1825 the Hudson's Bay Company moved its headquarters upriver from Fort George (now Astoria) to the fertile plains on the northern shore of the Columbia. Naming the fort to honor Captain Vancouver was a pointed reminder that the British had been the first to explore beyond the mouth of the river and intended to control part of the Pacific Northwest. The site became an important administrative center for the vast British trading company, and later for the American military, after the international border dispute was resolved in 1846. It was the first regular army post in the Pacific Northwest. During the Civil War, Generals Ulysses S. Grant, Phil Sheridan, and George McClellan were stationed there, as was five-star General George Marshall in the 1930s.

River access at Fort Vancouver.

Lithograph of Fort Vancouver in 1854, twenty-nine years after it was founded by the Hudson's Bay Company. Courtesy of the Oregon Historical Society (CN008579).

Today Fort Vancouver is a national historic site. A replica of the large fort has been constructed, complete with several of the buildings that stood within it. At one time the fort's extensive agricultural practices extended 30 miles along the Columbia, involving some twenty-five different tribal and ethnic groups that resided in the employee village just west of the fort. The National Park Service recently completed a detailed management plan for the site to include numerous improvements for cultural preservation and interpretation. Included for improvement are the fort, village, orchard, and a canoe landing beach on the Columbia waterfront. The nearby Vancouver Barracks, Officers Row, and Pearson Air Museum are also must-see attractions. Tours and living-history programs are offered during summer months. The visitor center is located at 612 East Reserve Street. Phone 360-696-7655.

On March 30, 1806, the Corps spent the day paddling along the northern shore of the Columbia near present-day Vancouver. The Columbia River valley in this area contained one of the largest populations of Indians in North America at the time, and the expedition observed numerous Indian villages. That night, the explorers camped near what later became the locale of historic Fort Vancouver.

Kelley Point Park

FACILITIES	Beach, canoe launch, hiking trails, interpretive signs, toilets.
ACTIVITIES	Boating, picnicking, hiking, wildlife viewing.
RESTRICTIONS	Day use only.

This large city park at the confluence of the Willamette and Columbia Rivers does not provide any boat launching facilities on the Columbia, but canoes and kayaks may be launched just inside the entrance to Kelley Point Park at the parking area adjacent to the nearby Columbia Slough. To reach the park from Interstate 5, take exit 307 and drive west on Marine Drive. The canoe launch is on the left, just inside the entrance to the park.

The Willamette River is among the few American rivers flowing north and is wholly contained within Oregon, where it drains 12,000 square miles of territory. Lieutenant Broughton discovered it in 1792, naming it River Manning's, after a member of Captain Vancouver's expedition. The Indian name Wal-lant designated a place on the river near Oregon City. To Lewis and Clark, it was the Multnomah River. Controversy over the names and their spellings continued until 1841, when Charles Wilkes of the United States Naval Exploring Expedition standardized the present name and its spelling.

The Portland-Vancouver area was first called Wap-pa-too Valley by Clark, then changed to Columbia Valley by Lewis on the return trip in 1806. The first editor of the Lewis and Clark journals, Nicholas Biddle, named it the Columbian Valley. Neither Lewis nor Clark, incidentally, ever saw the Willamette Valley, which ends at the Willamette Falls, 26 miles upstream from the Columbia River. Portland hosted the 1905 Lewis and Clark Centennial Exposition, a celebration of the achievements of the Corps of Discovery. In addition to the large memorial to the expedition in Portland's Washington Park, a statue of Sacagawea, representing the women's rights movement of that era, stands nearby.

Portland in 1857. Note the tree stumps that led the city to be nicknamed "Stumptown." Photo by Lorenzo Lorain. Courtesy of the Oregon Historical Society (1502).

On April 7, 1806, Clark revealed his method of obtaining information about geographical features from native inhabitants: "I provaled on an old indian to mark the Multnomah R [Willamette River] down on the sand . . . He also lais down the Clark-a-mos [Clackamas River and] . . . Mount Jefferson which he lais down by raiseing the Sand as a very high mountain and covered with eternal snow." From this, Clark drew a remarkable map that included his estimated position of Mount Jefferson, together with the Clackamas River, Willamette Falls, and an array of numerous Willamette Valley geographical features that he personally never saw. This was a common occurrence, and it attests to both the Indians' willingness to generously share information and to Clark's expertise as a cartographer.

SUGGESTED DAY AND OVERNIGHT TRIPS

Marine Park to Caterpillar Island

DISTANCE   11 miles one way.

CAMPING   None.

Although the paddle trip from Marine Park, east of Vancouver, to Caterpillar Island, west of Vancouver, is 11 miles long, it goes quickly in spring when the current is strong and when the tide and wind are cooperating. This trip should last three to four hours. It covers portions of Trail Reach 4 and 5.

Tomahawk and Hayden Islands

DISTANCE   12 miles round-trip.

CAMPING   None.

From Tomahawk Island, tour downstream around Hayden Island and return. The southern side of Hayden Island is very scenic, with some wildlife. Watch for seagoing vessels on the northern side.

TRAIL REACH 5

Willamette River to St. Helens

DISTANCE   16 miles.

MAPS   USGS Sauvie Island and St. Helens 7.5-minute NOAA
            Chart 18524.

This 16-mile reach of the Columbia is unique: its west bank consists of Sauvie Island, which, at 16.5 miles long and 6.5 miles wide, is the largest island on the Columbia. Sauvie Island received its present name from Laurent Sauvé, a French-Canadian employee of the Hudson's Bay Company, who settled on the island to operate the Hudson's Bay dairy farm. Dairy farming became very popular, and milk was picked up by steamboats that ran daily from St. Helens to Portland; today, however, only one dairy remains in operation. Lewis and Clark called the island Wappato, the Indian name for the arrowhead root, *Sagittaria latifolia*, now commonly spelled *wapato*. Wapato grew abundantly in marshes and shallow lakes and was a staple of lower Columbian tribes. It still grows on the island and in ponds, lakes, and marshlands along the lower Columbia, although not as extensively as historically recorded. Some early maps show Sauvie Island labeled as Wyeth Island, after Nathaniel Wyeth, who built Fort Williams there between 1834 and 1835. The fort was named for one of Wyeth's partners and was an American commercial rival to the Hudson's Bay Company.

Lewis and Clark counted eight villages with about twenty-five hundred residents on and bordering Sauvie Island. Prehistoric sites have also been found here. One of the largest villages on the lower Columbia was located at Reeder's Beach, on the eastern shore of Sauvie Island, south of Willow Bar. From 1830 to 1835 a smallpox epidemic, in combination with other Old World diseases, devastated the Indians along the lower Columbia.

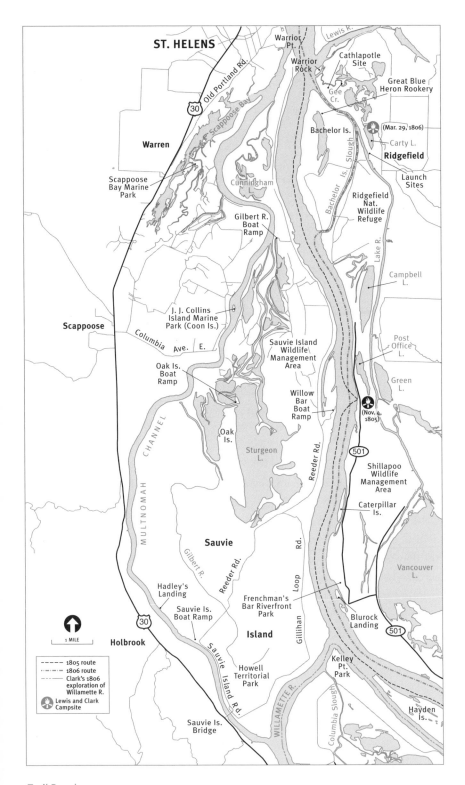

ST. HELENS

Warrior Pt.

Lewis R.

Warrior Rock

Cathlapotle Site

Great Blue Heron Rookery

Old Portland Rd.

30

Scappoose Bay

Gee Cr.

Bachelor Is.

(Mar. 29, 1806)

Carty L.

Warren

Bachelor Is. Slough

Ridgefield

Scappoose Bay Marine Park

Cunningham

Ridgefield Nat. Wildlife Refuge

Launch Sites

Gilbert R. Boat Ramp

Bachelor Is.

Lake R.

Campbell L.

J. J. Collins Island Marine Park (Coon Is.)

Scappoose

Columbia Ave. E.

Sauvie Island Wildlife Management Area

Post Office L.

Oak Is. Boat Ramp

Green L.

Willow Bar Boat Ramp

(Nov. 4, 1805)

Oak Is.

Sturgeon L.

Reeder Rd.

501

MULTNOMAH CHANNEL

Shillapoo Wildlife Management Area

Caterpillar Is.

Sauvie

Gilbert R.

Reeder Rd.

Rd.

Vancouver L.

Hadley's Landing

Sauvie Is. Boat Ramp

Loop

Frenchman's Bar Riverfront Park

Blurock Landing

30

Gillihan

Island

501

Holbrook

Sauvie Island Rd.

Howell Territorial Park

Kelley Pt. Park

WILLAMETTE R.

Columbia Slough

Hayden Is.

Sauvie Is. Bridge

1 MILE

- - - - - 1805 route
·-·-·- 1806 route
——— Clark's 1806 exploration of Willamette R.
⚑ Lewis and Clark Campsite

Wapato, seen here in the foreground, grows abundantly along the waterways of Sauvie Island and the lakes and sloughs of the lower Columbia.

Sauvie Island is so large that it contains its own rivers, sloughs, lakes, and islands. An improved half-mile nature trail wanders through dense habitat from the Multnomah Channel to near the Warrior Rock Lighthouse on the Columbia River. Planned additions will include viewing platforms, sculptures of indigenous wildlife, interpretive panels, and informational signs describing the flora and fauna that existed during the time of the expedition. A short trail can also be used to explore the area along the Multnomah Channel for wildlife, wildflowers, and wapato. It was from this island that Captain Clark sighted and named Mount Jefferson.

The northern end of Sauvie Island is managed by the Oregon Department of Fish and Wildlife as the 12,000-acre Sauvie Island Wildlife Management Area and is open to the public from April 15 to October 1. This area provides feeding and resting areas for a great variety of wildlife, including bald eagles, sandhill cranes, great blue herons, and black-tailed deer. Fall migration brings over 150,000 ducks and geese.

Warrior Point was named by Lieutenant William Broughton on October 28, 1792, when he anchored off the point and found himself surrounded by twenty-three canoes, each carrying three to twelve people attired in war garments and prepared for combat. The parties made peace and no bloodshed ensued. The 1853 Bybee House and Agricultural Museum are located at the Howell Territorial Park on Sauvie Island Road just north of the Sauvie Island Bridge. The park includes a permanent Lewis and Clark interpretive exhibit and a pavilion illustrating the colorful history of the island and its flora and fauna. Phone 503-665-6918. The Bybee House and museum are open only on weekends from June 2 to September 2. Phone 503-222-1741.

The 21-mile Multnomah Channel forms the western shore of Sauvie Island. Public ramps are located on the island side of the channel at rivermile 18 (Sauvie Island Boat Ramp) and rivermile 7 (Gilbert River Boat Ramp). Two public transient moorages are also located on the Multnomah Channel. At rivermile 17.5 Hadley's Landing offers a dock and access to trails through the adjacent wildlife area. Hiking trails lead to Sauvie Island Road, but the distance is much too long to portage a canoe or kayak. The other public moorage is the J. J. Collins Island Marine Park on Coon Island managed by the Oregon Marine Board at rivermile 8. Camping is permitted and a 1.5-mile nature trail permits exploration of the small island.

The Multnomah Channel, one of the Willamette's outlets to the Columbia, was not recognized by the early explorers as a drainage for the large valley between the Cascade and Coast Ranges. Lieutenant Broughton, in 1792, mistook the drainage for a river and called it Sir John Call. Lewis and Clark thought it was an inlet of the Columbia and called it Wappato Inlet. Among the many rivers and sloughs in this reach that offer quiet waters for exploration are the Gilbert River, Scappoose Bay, Bachelor Island Slough, Lake River, and Lewis River.

Across the Columbia from the northern end of Sauvie Island is the Ridgefield National Wildlife Refuge, a 4,627-acre refuge primarily devoted to waterfowl. The nearby town of Ridgefield began life as Shobert's Landing, but after Civil War veterans began to settle there the name was changed to Union Ridge as a statement of their loyalty. The name was changed to Ridgefield in 1890.

BOATING CAUTIONS AND CONDITIONS

Watch for heavy commercial traffic, including container ships and barges. Many wing dams made of piling fences can be found on both sides of the Columbia River near Frenchman's Bar Riverfront Park. Wing dams are rows of pilings constructed by the Army Corps of Engineers to divert the flow of water into the ship channel, resulting in a scouring action that helps keep sediments from building up in the channel. They are particularly dangerous because the river current flows through them. If a small boat passes close to a wing dam, the boat could be swept up against the dam, resulting in a capsize.

During periods of low water on Sauvie Island's Cunningham Slough and Gilbert River, you may encounter hazardous exposed brush and snags. At low tide many of the lakes on Sauvie Island become mudflats. During summer months Bachelor Island Slough can become shallow, so be aware. This slough has a sandy bottom, and a short portage is no problem. It is also a very scenic and peaceful area in summer. Another summer caution: on Lake River, jet-skis and powerboats can cause wakes.

RIVER ACCESSES

Blurock Landing
FACILITIES	Beach, bike path, parking.
ACTIVITIES	Biking.
RESTRICTIONS	Day use only.

This small park is located a mile south of Frenchman's Bar Riverfront Park, where Lower River Road (Highway 501) turns north near the mouth of a drainage canal from Vancouver Lake. It is also on the bike path from Vancouver Lake Park to Frenchman's Bar. The park consists of a parking lot and a short informal trail to a beach at the mouth of the drainage canal. To reach it from Interstate 5, take exit 1D in Vancouver and follow Fourth Plain Boulevard west (also Highway 501), where it eventually becomes West Twenty-sixth Street and then Lower River Road. Five miles from the freeway, turn left on Lower River Road, which follows a drainage canal to Blurock Landing.

Frenchman's Bar Riverfront Park
FACILITIES	Picnic tables, beach, short trails, playground, toilets.
ACTIVITIES	Picnicking.
RESTRICTIONS	Day use only. Fee for parking from May to September.

This large, popular Clark County park, also known as Hewlett Point, was named after Paul Haury, a French sailor who jumped ship in British Columbia and later bought land in the area west of Vancouver. The park was built in 1997 to serve the many people who were already using the site. It is located at 9612 NW Lower River Road. To reach the park from Interstate 5, follow the directions given for Blurock Landing (Frenchman's Bar is 1.25 miles further north, 6.75 miles from the freeway). Clark County has built a 2.5-mile paved trail to connect this park with Vancouver Lake Park to the east. The trail generally parallels Lower River Road.

Caterpillar Island

FACILITIES	Boat ramp, toilet, parking.
ACTIVITIES	Launching only.
RESTRICTIONS	Day use only. Permit required. Fee.

This long, narrow island lies just a few feet off the Washington shore northwest of Vancouver. A primitive boat ramp and limited parking can be found on the mainland near the northern end. The ramp, maintained by the Washington Department of Fish and Wildlife, is sometimes referred to as the Shillapoo Boat Ramp, for the nearby Shillapoo Wildlife Management Area. A Stewardship Access Decal is necessary to use it. To reach the ramp from Interstate 5, follow the driving instructions for Blurock Landing and continue north on Lower River Road (Highway 501) for 2.75 miles. The ramp is 8.25 miles from the freeway.

Willow Bar Boat Ramp

FACILITIES	Boat ramp, parking.
ACTIVITIES	Launching only.
RESTRICTIONS	Day use only. Permit required. Fee.

This boat ramp is maintained by the Oregon Department of Fish and Wildlife as part of the Sauvie Island Wildlife Management Area. A wildlife area permit is required and can be purchased at the store near the eastern end of the Sauvie Island Bridge and at other locations. Phone 503-621-3488. To reach the ramp, drive north on Sauvie Island Road 1.5 miles from the Sauvie Island Bridge, turn right on Reeder Road, and proceed 6 miles to the ramp entrance on the right.

Two additional no-facility access sites to the Columbia are available by proceeding north on Reeder Road. The first site, at the Rentenaar Road Junction (Fish and Wildlife check station), includes a parking lot but requires a Fish and Wildlife permit. It is located just downstream from the clothing-optional beach area. The second includes no designated parking, requires no permit, and is located near the southern shore of Cunningham Lake.

Gilbert River Boat Ramp

FACILITIES	Ramp and tie-up docks, toilet, parking.
ACTIVITIES	Nearby fishing.
RESTRICTIONS	Fee. Open 4:00 A.M. to 10:00 P.M.

This ramp is jointly managed by the Oregon Marine Board, Columbia County, and the Oregon Department of Fish and Wildlife. To reach this access site from Highway 30, cross the Sauvie Island Bridge, head north on Sauvie Island Road for 2 miles, and then turn right onto Reeder Road. Continue for 4 miles until you reach the next stop sign. At the stop sign, stay left, and continue for 7 more miles. About a mile after the pavement ends, you'll reach Dike Road. Turn left onto this road, which leads to Gilbert River Boat Ramp. Just 300 yards south of this site on Gilbert Road is a popular fishing pier that is accessible to people with disabilities.

Scappoose Bay Marine Park

FACILITIES	Boat ramp, campground, toilets, commercial marina, store, kayak shop, parking.
ACTIVITIES	Camping.
RESTRICTIONS	Fee.

The boat ramp at Scappoose Bay Marine Park is about a mile up Scappoose Bay from rivermile 2 of Multnomah Channel. It offers excellent access to Scappoose Bay, the northern Multnomah Channel, and the northern end of Sauvie Island. To reach the boat ramp from Portland, drive north on Highway 30 about 4 miles past the town of Scappoose, turn right on Bennett Road at milepost 25.8, take an immediate left on Old Portland Road, and follow that about half a mile to the boat ramp and marina. Phone 503-397-9734. Adjacent to the ramp is a commercial marina.

Ridgefield Launch Sites

FACILITIES	Boat ramps; nearby cafés, grocery, and boat rentals.
ACTIVITIES	Launching only.
RESTRICTIONS	No camping. Fee.

There are two launch sites at Ridgefield: the Ridgefield City Marina, which is open to the general public, and the Port of Ridgefield Boat Ramp, which is limited to canoes, kayaks, and other nonmotorized craft.

To reach the Ridgefield City Marina, drive north from Vancouver on Interstate 5 to exit 14, then turn west and follow NW 269th Street (Highway 501) for 3 miles, where it becomes Pioneer Street in Ridgefield. At the stoplight in Ridgefield, turn right onto Main Street, then left two blocks later onto Mill Street. A public parking lot and boat ramp are located at the foot of Mill Street. A fee is charged to use the ramp. Carry quarters to buy a ticket from the vending machine.

The Port of Ridgefield Boat Ramp is located at the foot of Division Street, two blocks north of the Ridgefield City Marina. A dock is also available. A user fee will eventually be imposed, but as of this writing a voluntary contribution box has been installed.

OTHER FACILITIES AND POINTS OF INTEREST

Ridgefield National Wildlife Refuge
FACILITIES   Hiking trails, wildlife viewing blinds, toilets, parking.
ACTIVITIES   Canoeing and kayaking, hiking, wildlife viewing.
RESTRICTIONS   Day use only.

The Ridgefield National Wildlife Refuge, founded in 1965, includes 5,150 acres of marshes, grasslands, and woodlands, all characterized by two types of management: natural and agricultural. The mild, rainy winter climate of the lower Columbia is an ideal environment for migrating and wintering waterfowl. Preservation of the natural Columbia River floodplain and cultivation of crops such as corn and barley provide food for waterfowl and create resting areas for the birds. The 2-mile Oaks-to-Wetlands Wildlife Trail follows the shoreline of the floodplain wetlands and passes through oak and Douglas fir woodlands. The refuge is also home to Cathlapotle, the best-preserved and largest Chinook Indian townsite on the Columbia River. Refuge headquarters are located at 301 North Third Street in Ridgefield. Interpretive tours are available by appointment. Phone 360-887-4106. The Discovery Center at the refuge will include interpretive features for paddlers.

The refuge consists of five adjacent units: Carty, River "S," Roth, Ridgeport Dairy, and Bachelor Island. The northernmost unit, Carty, offers hiking on the Oaks-to-Wetlands Wildlife Trail through a group of lakes. Boats may not be launched in this unit, but the lakes may be visited by canoes and kayaks launched at the Ridgefield City Marina. From the marina, paddle down the Lake River to Gee Creek, then up Gee Creek to the lakes. This trip is for the adventurous only, and should be considered only when water levels are high, as the creek is narrow and often blocked by logs. The southernmost unit, River "S," includes 4 miles of gravel roads for bird watching from the car or on foot. No boating is allowed. To reach the River "S" unit, turn south on Ninth Avenue in Ridgefield and follow it half a mile to the refuge entrance. South of here is the Roth unit, which is not accessible by car. Further south is the Ridgeport Dairy unit, located at the northern end of Lower River Road (Highway 501). This unit includes Post Office Lake, which lies just south of the northern end of Lower River Road, on a narrow strip of land between the Lake River (north of the mouth of Salmon Creek) and the Columbia. At the end of the road, near the southern end of Campbell Lake, is a residence for the staff of Ridgefield National Wildlife Refuge. Just south of Post Office Lake is the Shillapoo Wildlife Management Area, also located along Lower River Road. Highway 501 enters into this wildlife area.

On the morning of November 4, 1805, the Corps crossed the Columbia to the south bank to visit the various Indian encampments located in the valley where Portland is presently located. Trying to distance themselves from numerous and curious Indians, camp was made downriver in what is now the Shillapoo Wildlife Management Area. Clark wrote a vivid description the next morning, as fall rains continued:

We are all wet Cold and disagreeable. . . . Rain continues this morning, I {s}lept but very little last night for the noise Kept dureing the whole of the night by the Swans, Geese, white & Grey Brant Ducks &c. on a Small Sand Island close under the Lard. Side; they were emensely noumerous, and their noise horid.

A small village of the Skil-lute nation containing four houses was located here. Clark described the scene of November 4:

The Indians which we have passed today {in their boats were} of the Scilloot nation {going up to the falls}. They differ a little in their language from those near & about the long narrows. . . . Their dress differ but little, except they have more of the articles precured from the white traders, they all have flattened heads, both men and women, live principally on fish, and Wappatoe roots, they also kill some fiew Elk and Deer. . . . They are thievishly inclined as we have experienced.

Bachelor Island, the fifth unit within the refuge, is a large island located at the mouth of the Lake River. The Lake River originates from Lake Vancouver, draining the transition zone between the Columbia River and the uplands, a floodplain of marshes and small lakes. Bachelor Island Slough was used by Indians and fur-trading canoe brigades, especially when traveling upriver, to avoid the main current of the Columbia. Indian informants provided Lewis and Clark with this useful information on their journey home in 1806. Its mild climate and abundant wildlife made Bachelor Island attractive for native occupation long before recorded history. Lewis and Clark first called it Green Bryor Island when they traveled downriver in 1805, but changed it to Cathlapotle Island in 1806 to honor the nearby Cathlapotle people. The island was later named for three bachelors who once owned the island.

On March 29, 1806, the homeward-bound expedition had breakfast on Deer Island (see Trail Reach 6), passed the mouths of the Multnomah Channel and Lewis River, and arrived at the Cathlapotle townsite. Due to river movement over the last two hundred years, this ancient village now lies buried under some 20 feet of river silt south of the mouth of Lake River across from Bachelor Island. Lewis and Clark described the Cathlapotle village (then at the confluence of the Lewis, Lake, and Columbia Rivers) as extending a quarter of a mile along the shoreline and containing fourteen cedar-plank houses and nine hundred inhabitants. The Cathlapotles were an Upper Chinookan language group. Although they referred to their village as Nahpooitle, over time it has come to be known as Cathlapotle. The captains were surprised to find a number of large (3- to 4-foot) iron blades hanging by the heads of the Indians' beds. The blades, as it turned out, were used as weapons and had been traded to the Cathlapotles by English or Spanish traders on the coast.

Today an ongoing environmental and heritage education project conducted by the U.S. Fish and Wildlife Service, the Chinook nation, and Portland State University is providing a rich record of the daily life of the river's first inhabitants. Seasonal camps near the site of Cathlapotle indicate occupation spanning the last two thousand years. An interpretive center is planned for the area at the entrance to the Carty unit and will resemble a small village of Chinook longhouses. The old village site itself is not accessible to the public.

After leaving Cathlapotle in the afternoon of March 29, the expedition continued up the Lake River about a mile and, according to Clark, "encamped on a butiful grassy place, where the nativs make a portage of their canoes and wappato roots to and from a large pond [Carty Lake] at a short distance." The site of this camp is on the east bank of the Lake River, where it joins Bachelor Island Slough. The area, known as Wapato Portage, is a nationally significant archaeological site on the Ridgefield National Wildlife Refuge, dating back some twenty-three hundred years.

The Lewis River was not named for Meriwether Lewis. The explorers referred to it as the Cah-wah-na-hi-ooks River, an attempt to identify the drainage with the native population that resided on the river. The name Cah-wah-na-hi-ooks was a figurative form of the Chinookan term for "enemies." The modern name was given to the river for Adolphus L. Lewis (perhaps spelled "Lewes"), who homesteaded near its mouth. Lewis County, on the other hand, was named for Meriwether Lewis when it was created in 1845.

SUGGESTED DAY AND OVERNIGHT TRIPS

This trail reach offers an unusual assortment of boating opportunities, because several other rivers and sloughs join the Columbia here. At the southern end of this reach the Willamette joins the Columbia, and 3 miles up the Willamette the Multnomah Channel leaves the Willamette, only to rejoin the Columbia 21 miles to the north. At the northern end of this reach the Columbia is joined by the Lake River, Lewis River, and Multnomah Channel—all at once. The opportunities for exploring are countless. Though suggested trips are described, you may prefer to use your own imagination to discover the uniqueness of this area.

Bachelor Island

DISTANCE	10 miles round-trip.
CAMPING	None.

Bachelor Island, which is part of the Ridgefield National Wildlife Refuge, is accessible only by boat and is closed to public access during winter. During spring, summer, and fall, visitors are restricted to traveling by foot and must carry a permit. The island can be circumnavigated by launching at either the Ridgefield City Marina or the Port of Ridgefield Boat Ramp (for more information see Ridgefield Launch Sites). From either launch site, paddle north on the Lake River to Bachelor Island Slough, then turn south and follow the slough to the Columbia. Paddle north on the Columbia, where sandy beaches offer pleasant places to stop for lunch. Continue north on the Columbia, then turn southeast at the mouth of the Lake River, which leads back to Ridgefield. Kayaks may be rented in Ridgefield, a few blocks from the Ridgefield City Marina. The northern end of Bachelor Island features one of the largest great blue heron rookeries in the Pacific Northwest (see Plate 12).

Scappoose Bay

DISTANCE	1 to 5 miles round-trip.
CAMPING	Scappoose Bay Marine Park.

Large and intricate, Scappoose Bay can be explored from the public boat ramp at Scappoose Bay Marine Park. Because the bay is so intricate, the USGS topographic map will be very useful. A tide table should also be consulted when planning this trip. The bay can be very shallow at times, and boats can become stuck in mud that is exposed at low tide. If possible, plan to explore the shallow parts of the bay (particularly the southern reaches) only when the tide is high. If the tide starts to go out, head for deep water immediately.

Lewis River

DISTANCE	10 miles one way.
CAMPING	None.

The Lewis River flows into the Columbia just north of the mouth of the Lake River. Paddle down the Lewis River from the town of Woodland (see Trail Reach 6), then paddle up the Columbia for a short distance before turning up the Lake River to the final destination of the Ridgefield City Marina. In downtown Woodland, boats may be launched on the eastern side of the Lewis River, immediately north of the bridge. About 3 miles below Woodland the Lewis River is joined by the East Fork of the Lewis River. This area is heavily used by jet-skis and powerboats during summer.

Sauvie Island

DISTANCE	1 to 10 miles round-trip.
CAMPING	None.

The Sauvie Island region is among the most popular paddling areas in Oregon, featuring miles of sandy shores, winding tributary channels, wetlands, and wildlife. The interior of the northern end is an intricate network of lakes, rivers, sloughs, and islands. Boat access can be found at the Oak Island Boat Ramp on Sturgeon Lake, though the ramp is closed October 1 through April 15 and an Oregon Department of Fish and Wildlife permit is required. Access is also available at the Gilbert River Boat Ramp, located at the mouth of the Gilbert River. Boats can also be hand-launched at several sites. For more information see *Canoe and Kayak Routes of Northwest Oregon* (Jones 1997). Overnight camping is not permitted on Sauvie Island.

TRAIL REACH 6

St. Helens to Kalama

DISTANCE   10 miles.

MAPS   USGS St. Helens, Deer Island, and Kalama 7.5-minute
              NOAA Chart 18524.

This reach of the Columbia has only three public-access points: two at its southern end (St. Helens Courthouse Docks and Columbia City's Pixie Park) and one at its northern end (Port of Kalama Marina). Along the way are several large islands worth exploring. The largest, Deer Island, is no longer a true island; levees and dikes have closed off the ends of Deer Island Slough, which once separated the island from the Oregon mainland. Nonetheless, Deer Island has retained the name given it by Lewis and Clark, who reported seeing more than a hundred Columbian white-tailed deer there. The island was also identified as E-lal-lar, an anglicized version of the Upper Chinookan word for "deer." Deer Island is now under private ownership.

On March 28, 1806, Lewis and Clark made a hunting camp on the down-river end of Deer Island. They took advantage of the extended layover to dry their rain-soaked baggage and dugouts. The hunters killed seven deer but returned with only four—"the others," according to Clark, "haveing been eaten entirely by the Voultures except the Skin." It is believed these gluttonous "vultures" were the now-endangered California condor, huge birds with a wingspan of more than 9 feet. Clark also observed, "We have seen more waterfowl on this island than we have previously seen since leaving Ft. Clatsop . . . consisting of geese, ducks, large swan, and sandhill crains."

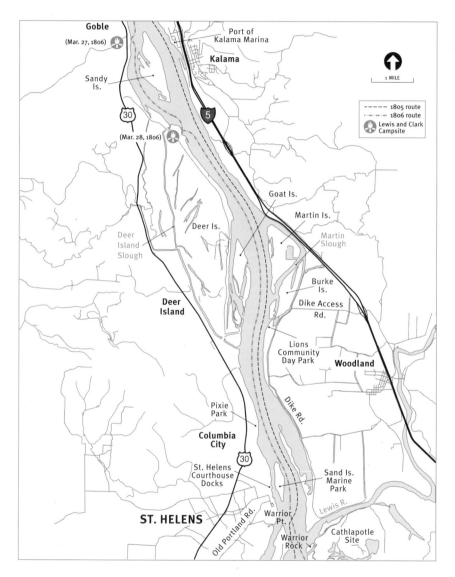

Goble
(Mar. 27, 1806) 🧍

Port of
Kalama Marina

Kalama

Sandy
Is.

1 MILE

– – – – 1805 route
–·–·– 1806 route
🧍 Lewis and Clark
Campsite

30

5

(Mar. 28, 1806) 🧍

Goat Is.

Martin Is.

Deer Is.

Deer
Island
Slough

Martin
Slough

Burke
Is.

Deer
Island

Dike Access
Rd.

Lions
Community
Day Park

Woodland

Pixie
Park

Dike Rd.

Columbia
City

30

St. Helens
Courthouse
Docks

Sand Is.
Marine
Park

ST. HELENS

Old Portland Rd.

Warrior
Pt.

Lewis R.

Warrior
Rock

Cathlapotle
Site

Trail Reach 6

BOATING CAUTIONS AND CONDITIONS

This reach of the river often experiences strong upstream winds. In addition, boaters should keep clear of numerous wing dams in the area.

RIVER ACCESSES

St. Helens Courthouse Docks

FACILITIES	Docks, picnic area, food, fuel, toilets, parking.
ACTIVITIES	Picnicking.
RESTRICTIONS	Day use only. Fee.

No publicly owned boat ramps are located in the city of St. Helens, but the city-owned public docks at the Columbia County Courthouse permit paddlers to hand-launch canoes and kayaks (see Plate 13). Phone 503-397-4162. To reach the park from Highway 30 in St. Helens, turn east on Columbia Boulevard, then right on First Street. Park in front of the courthouse and carry your boat down to the docks. The historic courthouse is at the foot of St. Helens Street in downtown St. Helens. A public park, Columbia View Park, is a block south of the courthouse. The national historic district of St. Helens and the Columbia County Historical Museum are located adjacent to the Courthouse Docks. The city of St. Helens was established as Plymouth in the 1840s by Captain H. M. Knighton, an early pioneer. The name was changed in 1850, apparently because of its proximity to Mount St. Helens.

Pixie Park

FACILITIES	Gravel beach.
ACTIVITIES	Launching only.
RESTRICTIONS	Day use only.

Pixie Park in Columbia City was named for a boat owned by longtime resident Harvey Jordan. In downtown Columbia City, turn east on First Street and follow it four blocks to the river and the park. A sidewalk leads to a small gravel beach, where canoes and kayaks may be launched. This beach can be rocky at times of low water.

Columbia City was founded in 1867 by Jacob and Joseph Caples, who hoped the site would become the terminus for the Willamette Valley Railroad, which ended in Portland instead. Today Columbia City is a tiny hamlet. The 1870 Caples home is a museum located at 1915 East First Street. Phone 503-397-5390.

Lions Community Day Park

FACILITIES	Beach.
ACTIVITIES	Launching only.
RESTRICTIONS	Day use only. Permit required.

Canoes and kayaks can be hand-launched from this primitive park, located northwest of Woodland on Dike Road. To reach it from Interstate 5, take exit 22 and follow Dike Access Road west 1.5 miles, turning south onto Dike Road and following it three-quarters of a mile to the park. A Stewardship Access Decal is necessary to use this park.

Port of Kalama Marina

FACILITIES	Boat ramp, 5-acre day-use park, RV park, campsites, playground, 2-mile walking path, showers, toilets.
ACTIVITIES	Camping.
RESTRICTIONS	Fee.

At the northern end of this 222-slip marina (sometimes called Kalama Boat Basin) is a public boat ramp. From Interstate 5 in Kalama, take either exit 27 or exit 30, cross under the freeway to the west, and follow the signs; the ramp is located at the northern end of the industrial peninsula that forms the boat basin. Canoes and kayaks may also be launched on a beach three-quarters of a mile south of the boat ramp, on the road from exit 27. Phone 360-673-2325.

The origin of the name Kalama is uncertain. One theory is that both the town and river were named after John Kalama, a Hudson's Bay Company agent of Hawaiian descent who established a fur-trading post at the mouth of the river. After arriving in the Northwest in the 1830s, Kalama married Mary Martin, the daughter of a Nisqually chief. Another theory has the town, which was founded in the late 1840s, named in 1871 after the Indian word for "pretty maiden."

There is nothing theoretical, however, about the fact that Elvis Presley spent the night of September 4, 1962, in Room 219 of the Kalama River Inn enroute to Seattle to film *It Happened at the World's Fair.*

OTHER FACILITIES AND POINTS OF INTEREST

Sand Island Marine Park

FACILITIES   Beach, boat docks, picnic tables, hiking trails, toilets.

ACTIVITIES   Camping, picnicking.

RESTRICTIONS   No automobile access.

Sand Island, owned by the city of St. Helens, offers moorage at two docks, with camping near both docks. The island, located directly across from the St. Helens Courthouse Docks, features nature trails and sandy beaches. A quarter-mile gravel trail leads to the southern end of the island, where a viewing platform and interpretive panels are scheduled to be installed. This viewpoint offers a commanding vista of Sauvie Island, Bachelor Island, the Multnomah Channel, Lewis River, Lake River, and the broad expanses of the Columbia. An interpretive exhibit planned for this spot will include an Indian canoe-carving village.

Martin, Burke, and Goat Islands

FACILITIES   Anchorage for powerboats and sailboats.

ACTIVITIES   Canoeing, kayaking.

RESTRICTIONS   None.

These three large islands lie in the Columbia just east of Deer Island. Goat Island is on the Oregon side of the river, nestled up against Deer Island, while Martin and Burke Islands lie on the Washington side and are clearly visible from Interstate 5. Recreational boaters frequently camp on or anchor in Martin Slough, behind Martin Island. If approaching from downriver, be aware of a long sandbar at the tip of the island. An interesting loop trip to these islands would involve launching from Lions Community Day Park northwest of Woodland. The sloughs behind the islands can also be explored while boating from Columbia City to Kalama.

Sandy Island

FACILITIES   None.

ACTIVITIES   Informal camping.

RESTRICTIONS   None.

This island just off Kalama has been officially designated a water trail campsite. It is marked by navigational markers 52 and 1. A sandy beach can be found on the southwestern side of the island. The best route past the island for catching scenic views and avoiding river traffic is on the western side.

SUGGESTED DAY AND OVERNIGHT TRIPS

Scappoose Bay to Columbia City

DISTANCE   5 miles one way.

CAMPING   None.

This short trip can easily be paddled in an afternoon. Beginning in Scappoose Bay (see Trail Reach 5), paddle past the St. Helens Courthouse Docks, and end at Pixie Park in Columbia City.

Only 5 miles long, this trip is a good introduction to paddling on the Columbia. The first half of the trip takes place on relatively protected waters (Scappoose Bay and Multnomah Channel), with only the second half experiencing the open waters of the Columbia. In the event of windy weather, consider exploring the bay.

St. Helens to Kalama

DISTANCE   10 miles one way.

CAMPING   Sandy Island.

This trip paddles the entire 10-mile distance from the Courthouse Docks in St. Helens to the Port of Kalama Marina. Unfortunately, they are on opposite sides of the river, and a lengthy car shuttle will be required, probably using the bridge at Longview (see Trail Reach 7). Nevertheless, this is a worthwhile trip, offering a chance to explore Martin, Burke, Goat, and Sandy Islands along the way.

Martin and Burke Islands

DISTANCE   10 miles round-trip.

CAMPING   Martin Island.

Launch from Dike Road access sites west of Woodland and explore the Martin Slough between Martin and Burke Islands. This is a very scenic route on the eastern side of the islands.

Sandy Island

DISTANCE   4 miles round-trip.

CAMPING   Sandy Island.

Launch at the Port of Kalama Marina, then cross the main channel of the Columbia to Sandy Island. Circumnavigate the island and camp overnight. Return to Kalama.

TRAIL REACH 7

Kalama to Longview

DISTANCE   10 miles.

MAPS   USGS Kalama and Rainier 7.5-minute NOAA Chart
           18524.

This 10-mile reach of the Columbia starts in the small town of Kalama and ends in the city of Longview. The Port of Kalama Marina, the first access point in this reach, is described under Trail Reach 6.

Just north of Kalama is the Kalama River, which joins the Columbia from the east. Lewis and Clark named this river Cath-la-haws Creek in 1806 on their return home. This was a perversion of the name given for a tribe of Native Americans that resided in the area. The best clue for the origin of the river's name comes from the journal of a member of the expedition, private Joseph Whitehouse, who recorded that Indians called the river Calanus.

Just downstream from Kalama on the Oregon shore is the tiny town of Goble, named for Daniel B. Goble, who made a claim on the site in 1853. He later sold the land to George S. Foster, who platted the town and named it for Goble. The river town was once the terminus for a ferry from Kalama on the Washington shore.

On March 27, 1806, returning upriver, the Corps spent a cold, wet evening near the present townsite of Goble on the southern shore of the Columbia opposite the mouth of the Kalama River. They were visited by a large canoe of eight men, from whom they obtained dried raspberries and salmonberries. Earlier they had visited two houses of the Skil-lute nation; the people were very hospitable and gave them smelt, sturgeon, wapato, and quamash.

Named after its founder, lumber baron R. A. Long, Longview was the first planned community in the Pacific Northwest. A glance at a map shows the

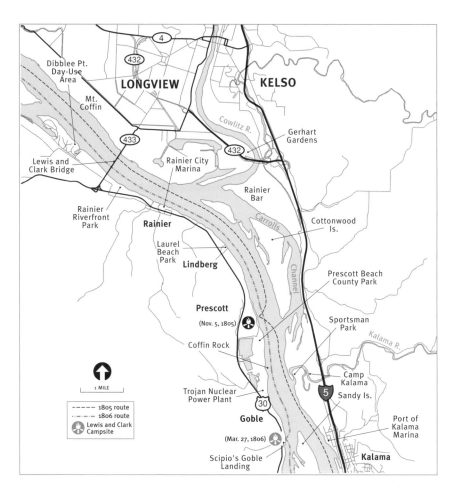

4

432

Dibblee Pt.
Day-Use
Area

LONGVIEW

KELSO

Mt.
Coffin

Cowlitz R.

433

Gerhart
Gardens

432

Lewis and
Clark Bridge

Rainier City
Marina

Rainier
Bar

Rainier
Riverfront
Park

Rainier

Carrolls

Cottonwood
Is.

Laurel
Beach
Park

Lindberg

Channel

Prescott Beach
County Park

Prescott

(Nov. 5, 1805)

Sportsman
Park

Kalama R.

Coffin Rock

Camp
Kalama

1 MILE

Trojan Nuclear
Power Plant

30

5

Sandy Is.

----- 1805 route
·—··—·· 1806 route

Lewis and Clark
Campsite

Goble

(Mar. 27, 1806)

Port of
Kalama
Marina

Scipio's Goble
Landing

Kalama

Trail Reach 7

careful planning that went into the layout of its street system. At the heart of the city is Lake Sacagawea, which forms a graceful crescent along Nichols Boulevard. Long founded the city in 1923 to support his large mill, which utilized the Columbia for transport of timber products. However, the town's more remote history began when the Hudson's Bay Company set up a warehouse on the river's delta in 1846. In 1849 Americans established claim to the land and named the resultant community Monticello, after Jefferson's home. Monticello's place in history stems from the 1852 pioneer meeting that petitioned Congress to create a Columbia Territory out of the Oregon Territory north of the Columbia River. Later Congress changed the name to Washington Territory to prevent confusion with the District of Columbia. Floods eventually washed away Monticello.

The Lewis and Clark Bridge (see Plate 14) spans the Columbia at Longview, a highway connection for Oregon and southwest Washington. It is the only highway bridge across the Columbia between the Portland-Vancouver area and Astoria.

Across the Cowlitz River from Longview is its sister city, Kelso, which was platted by Peter Crawford in 1847 and named after his home in Scotland. The Cowlitz is a large river rising from the glaciers of Mount Rainier. The mouth of it served as a water highway to the Cowlitz Valley, beginning with canoes and bateaux, the flat-bottomed, double-ended riverboats of the Hudson's Bay Company. The Cowlitz was referred to as Cow-e-lis-kee River in the journals of Lewis and Clark. Its name has been anglicized, after many various spelling attempts, but native tradition indicates that it means "capturing the medicine spirit," in reference to a custom of sending young males of the tribe upriver to communicate with guardian spirits. The Cowlitz County Historical Museum is located at the corner of Fourth and Allen in Kelso.

BOATING CAUTIONS AND CONDITIONS

When passing close to the Trojan Nuclear Power Plant expect major turbulence on the upstream end of its rocky ramparts. The shoreline along the Longview riverfront is a busy commercial ship-loading region with many ships moored in the river. In addition, this area experiences considerable jet-ski traffic.

RIVER ACCESSES

Scipio's Goble Landing

FACILITIES	Boat ramp, moorage, RV campgrounds, food, water, fuel, showers, toilets.
ACTIVITIES	RV camping.
RESTRICTIONS	Private property. Fee.

This full-service private launch site is located in the center of Goble. Camping is for RVs only. A fee is charged to launch. Phone 503-556-6510.

Sportsman Park

FACILITIES	Parking.
ACTIVITIES	Launching only.
RESTRICTIONS	None.

Hand-launching is allowed at this primitive access point located at the mouth of the Kalama River just off Interstate 5.

Camp Kalama

FACILITIES	Boat ramp, RV park, campground, fuel, showers, toilet, restaurant.
ACTIVITIES	Camping.
RESTRICTIONS	Fee for camping.

This full-service RV park and campground on the Kalama River can be reached from Interstate 5 at exit 32. Follow Kalama River Road, which doubles back on Frontage Road to Meeker Drive. Follow Meeker Drive a quarter of a mile to Camp Kalama. Boat launching is free. Phone 360-673-2456.

Prescott Beach County Park

FACILITIES	Beach, campsite, picnic area, playground, toilets.
ACTIVITIES	Camping, picnicking.
RESTRICTIONS	Day use only. Fee.

A sign at the entrance to this park says "no boat launching," but this refers to motorized boats on trailers; canoes and kayaks may be hand-launched on the sandy beaches. This 71-acre Columbia County park is located about 14 miles

Fishermen wait for a strike on the sandy beach near Laurel Beach Park.

north of St. Helens and 5 miles south of Rainier. To reach the park from Highway 30, turn east on Graham Road at milepost 43.1, just north of the Trojan Nuclear Power Plant, and follow it for a mile as it leads east, then north, to the park. You will pass through what remains of the old river community of Prescott, named around 1905 for the owners of a local sawmill. The park features newly installed Lewis and Clark interpretive panels and a great view of the Columbia.

On November 5, 1805, the expedition made a cold and disagreeable camp. Clark described the area "under a point of high ground, with thick pine trees" in the vicinity of Prescott Beach County Park. With the northern shore reportedly "bold and rockey," the party had crossed the river to find a suitable campsite: "We landed on the Lard. Side & camped a little below the mouth of a creek [Kalama River] on the Stard. Side a little below the mouth of which is an Old Village which is now abandaned."

Laurel Beach Park

FACILITIES	Beach, parking.
ACTIVITIES	Launching only.
RESTRICTIONS	Day use only.

This unimproved, nonmaintained Columbia County day-use park is located 1.5 miles south of Rainier on Highway 30. From milepost 45 on Highway 30, turn northeast on Laurelwood Road, bear left at the first fork, and turn right on Laurel Beach Road to the parking lot. Boats must be carried up a gangplank, across railroad tracks, and down a steep bank to the beach.

Rainier City Marina

FACILITIES	Boat ramp, dock, picnic area, toilets, parking, nearby cafés and grocery.
ACTIVITIES	Picnicking.
RESTRICTIONS	Fee. No camping.

The city of Rainier maintains a public boat ramp and dock at the foot of Third Street East in Rainier, two blocks off Highway 30. A metal sign designates

The well-maintained marina at Rainier lies in the heart of the city.

this ramp as access to the Lewis and Clark Columbia River Water Trail. Phone 503-556-7301.

Rainier Riverfront Park

FACILITIES   Beach, picnic area, hiking trails, playground, parking.
ACTIVITIES   Picnicking, hiking.
RESTRICTIONS   Day use only.

This small park is located at the western end of Rainier at the foot of Sixth Street West. Boats must be carried across a wide beach. Historical interpretive panels describe the area and the expedition's visit here. The Lewis and Clark Bridge is just downstream at Longview.

Gerhart Gardens

FACILITIES   Boat ramps, toilets, parking.
ACTIVITIES   Launching only.
RESTRICTIONS   Fee.

This large public park on the Cowlitz River in Longview includes two boat ramps and two large parking areas. To reach the park from Interstate 5, take exit 36, drive west on Highway 432 (also known as Willow Grove Connector) and turn right on Dike Road shortly after crossing the Cowlitz River. The Columbia is 1.5 miles downstream from the park.

OTHER FACILITIES AND POINTS OF INTEREST

Trojan Nuclear Power Plant

FACILITIES   Picnic areas, ponds, hiking trails, visitor center, toilets.
ACTIVITIES   Picnicking, hiking, paddling in ponds.
RESTRICTIONS   Day use only.

A portion of the grounds of this deactivated nuclear power plant are open to the public as a park, including large ponds and picnic areas. As a result of the events of September 11, 2001, however, security is a top priority and there is no access to the Columbia River. Additional portions of the grounds may eventually be opened to the public. The visitor center will become an interpretive center with exhibits on the history of the reactor and the Lewis and Clark expedition.

Coffin Rock juts out into the Columbia on the grounds of the power plant complex. The rock obtained its name from early explorers who found Indian burial grounds on the site. While the rock is inaccessible due to nuclear safety restrictions, information on the site and artifacts are on exhibit at the power plant's visitor center.

Cottonwood Island

FACILITIES	None.
ACTIVITIES	Primitive camping.
RESTRICTIONS	None.

Cottonwood Island is a large island southeast of Longview, immediately upstream from the mouth of the Cowlitz River. Osprey nest on the upstream end of the island. The slough behind the island, Carrolls Channel, can be used if you wish to avoid commercial shipping traffic on the main channel of the Columbia. The eastern shore of the island offers primitive camping. Carrolls Channel is not particularly scenic, however, due to the presence of Interstate 5 and the Burlington Northern Railway.

SUGGESTED DAY AND OVERNIGHT TRIPS

Cottonwood Island

DISTANCE	7 miles round-trip.
CAMPING	Cottonwood Island.

Launch at Prescott Beach and paddle north along the Oregon shore, keeping well away from the shipping lanes that lie close to Cottonwood Island. At the downstream end of Cottonwood Island, cross the main channel and return to Prescott Beach by way of Carrolls Channel.

Mouth of the Cowlitz River

DISTANCE	4 miles one way.
CAMPING	None.

Launch at Gerhart Gardens and paddle down the Cowlitz River to the Columbia. Cross the main channel of the Columbia and land at Rainier Riverfront Park.

TRAIL REACH 8

Longview to Oak Point

DISTANCE   11 miles.

MAPS   USGS Rainier, Kelso, Delena, Coal Creek, and Oak
Point 7.5-minute NOAA Charts 18524 and 18523.

This reach of the Columbia leaves the industrial landscape of Longview and Rainier behind and enters the lush landscape of the lower Columbia, which still resembles the environment seen by Lewis and Clark. It contains several islands, including, in downstream order, Dibblee, Lord, Walker, Fisher, Hump, Crims, and Gull Islands. Dibblee and Gull are both designated campsites, and the downstream tip of Walker is used as a primitive campsite.

Two miles downriver from the Lewis and Clark Bridge in Longview is Mount Coffin, located on a point on the Washington shore. Lewis and Clark noted this "remarkable Knob," which, like Coffin Rock near Prescott, was used by Indians for internment of their dead. During construction of the Port of Longview, the 240-foot landmark was quarried and leveled for its gravel. This port is now the third largest port facility in Washington State.

Near the upstream end of Crims Island stands Mayger, a former fishing village with old net sheds and a long dock but no public boat access. It was named after C. W. Mayger, a native of France who came to Oak Point, Washington, around 1865 and later settled east of Oak Point in what was to become Mayger. The post office, established in 1889, was also named for him, and Mayger was the first postmaster. On the Washington shore north of Crims Island is the tiny logging community and former mill site of Stella, devastated by fire years ago. It was named for the first postmaster's daughter, Stella Packard. A small museum is operated here by the Stella Historical Society. There is no boat access to Stella.

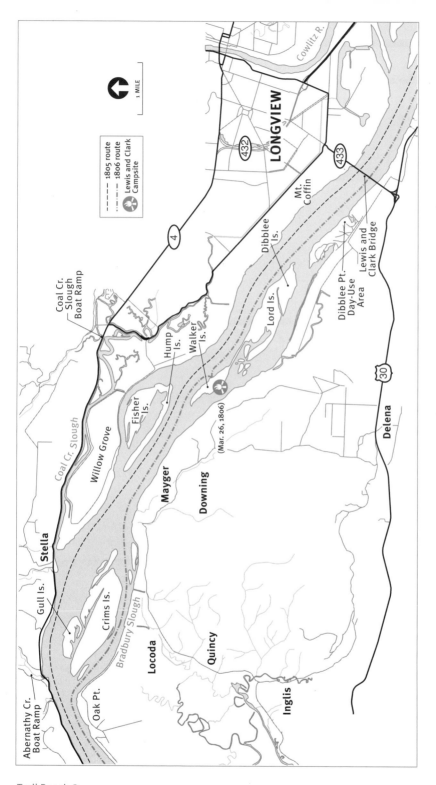

1 MILE

- – – – 1805 route
- · – · 1806 route
- Lewis and Clark Campsite

LONGVIEW

Cowlitz R.

432

433

4

30

Mt. Coffin

Dibblee Is.

Lord Is.

Walker Is.

Hump Is.

Fisher Is.

Willow Grove

Coal Cr. Slough Boat Ramp

Coal Cr. Slough

Stella

Gull Is.

Crims Is.

Bradbury Slough

Locoda

Oak Pt.

Abernathy Cr. Boat Ramp

Mayger

Downing

(Mar. 26, 1806)

Quincy

Inglis

Delena

Dibblee Pt. Day-Use Area

Lewis and Clark Bridge

Trail Reach 8

The trail reach ends at Oak Point, Oregon, just downstream from Crims and Gull Islands. Crims was named Bakers Island in 1792 by Lieutenant William Broughton for the second lieutenant of Captain Vancouver's ship. Lewis and Clark named it Fanny's Island, after Clark's younger sister Frances. Today it retains the surname (as do many islands in the river) of a pioneer homesteader, in this case James Crim. Crims Island is now owned by the Columbia Land Trust, which plans to transfer its acreage to the U.S. Fish and Wildlife Service, and by the State of Oregon.

BOATING CAUTIONS AND CONDITIONS

Frequent, strong upstream winds are often encountered from Oak Point downriver. Stay away from the numerous wing dams.

RIVER ACCESSES

Dibblee Point

FACILITIES	Beach.
ACTIVITIES	Fishing.
RESTRICTIONS	Day use only.

Formerly used by ATV and motorcycle enthusiasts, this sandy peninsula (also known as Slaughters Dike) is now largely occupied by a large industrial plant. The Dibblee Point day-use area, controlled by the Oregon Division of State Lands, is now primarily used by bank fishermen. To reach the beach from Rainier, drive north on Highway 30 for about a mile, and turn right on Rockcrest Street shortly before reaching the Lewis and Clark Bridge to Longview. Turn left on West Rainier Dike Road, following it west for about a mile, and work your way further west on a network of primitive roads to a beach.

Coal Creek Slough Boat Ramp

FACILITIES	Boat ramp, parking.
ACTIVITIES	Launching only.
RESTRICTIONS	Day use only.

This boat ramp is located at milepost 55 on Highway 4, 7 miles west of Kelso, immediately before the bridge over Ditch 6. Paddling down the Coal Creek

Slough for about 4 miles from this ramp will provide access to the Columbia. Phone 360-577-3030.

Willow Grove Park

FACILITIES	Boat ramp, long sandy beach, picnic tables, hiking trails, playground, water, toilets, parking.
ACTIVITIES	Picnicking, hiking.
RESTRICTIONS	Day use only. Fee for launching motorized boats.

This 60-acre park is located west of Longview and Kelso near the downstream ends of Fisher and Hump Islands at 7400 Willow Grove Road. To reach it from Interstate 5 exit 39 in Kelso, drive west on Highway 4 for 7 miles, turn left at milepost 55.2 on Highway 432, and follow it for three-quarters of a mile. Turn right on Willow Grove Road and follow it for 3 miles to the park. This park has been divided into two facilities with two separate entrances. The eastern portion consists of the boat ramp and a huge parking lot to accommodate the vehicles and trailers using the ramp. The western portion consists of picnic areas, lawns, and smaller parking areas. Both portions include beaches from which small craft may be hand-launched. Phone 360-577-3030.

Abernathy Creek Boat Ramp

FACILITIES	Primitive boat ramp, small beach, parking.
ACTIVITIES	Launching only.
RESTRICTIONS	Day use only.

The Washington Department of Fish and Wildlife maintains a primitive boat ramp on Abernathy Creek, just upstream from the mouth of the creek where it empties into the Columbia at Abernathy Point. At milepost 48.4 on Highway 4, about 14 miles west of Kelso, turn north on Abernathy Creek Road. Follow this road for about a tenth of a mile, then turn left and follow a primitive dirt road to the ramp. Abernathy Creek is usually not navigable at low tide. At these times, you may be able to launch on a small beach at the mouth of the creek.

OTHER FACILITIES AND POINTS OF INTEREST

Dibblee Island

FACILITIES	Campground.
ACTIVITIES	Camping.
RESTRICTIONS	None.

Dibblee Island, owned by Columbia County, is a small island at the upstream end of Lord Island. On many maps it is unnamed. The island has been officially designated with a metal sign as a campsite on the Lewis and Clark Columbia River Water Trail, and a small campground and fire ring have been built on its upstream end. The sloughs in the area of Dibblee, Lord, and Walker Islands provide a wide range of birding opportunities.

Lord Island

FACILITIES	None.
ACTIVITIES	Birding.
RESTRICTIONS	Private property.

The Weyerhaeuser Company owns the 210-acre Lord Island. Efforts are being made to preserve it as a wildlife sanctuary, possibly with camping permitted. The sloughs and marshlands around the island are great areas for birding.

Walker Island

FACILITIES	None.
ACTIVITIES	Primitive camping.
RESTRICTIONS	None.

On March 26, 1806, the wind, river current, and tidal effect had slowed the progress of the expedition up the river, and after traveling only 18 miles, the Corps made camp on today's Walker Island. Confusion as to the exact location of this campsite was not resolved until 1904, when Clark's original route maps were finally located. A primitive camping area can be found at the downstream end of the island.

Fisher and Hump Islands
FACILITIES	None.
ACTIVITIES	Birding.
RESTRICTIONS	Private property.

These islands lie just south of Coal Creek Slough. Launch from Willow Grove Park to circumnavigate them.

Gull Island
FACILITIES	None.
ACTIVITIES	Primitive camping, birding.
RESTRICTIONS	None.

Gull Island is located immediately north of Crims Island. A metal sign designates a sandy beach on the northern side of the island as a Lewis and Clark Columbia River Water Trail campsite. The southern side channels are good for birding.

SUGGESTED DAY AND OVERNIGHT TRIPS

Longview to Willow Grove Park
DISTANCE	12 miles one way.
CAMPING	Dibblee Island or Walker Island.

Launch at Gerhart Gardens in Longview (see Trail Reach 7), paddle down the Cowlitz River 2 miles to the Columbia, and head down the Columbia 10 miles to Willow Grove Park.

Dibblee, Lord, and Walker Islands
DISTANCE	6 miles round-trip.
CAMPING	Dibblee Island.

Launch at Dibblee Point and circumnavigate Dibblee, Lord, and Walker Islands. To avoid the shipping lanes, stay in the channel south of these islands rather than circumnavigating them. For a shorter trip, explore the sloughs between Lord and Dibblee Islands.

Coal Creek Slough

DISTANCE	2 to 8 miles round-trip.
CAMPING	None.

Launch at the Coal Creek Slough Boat Ramp, paddle west for about a mile, and turn south to explore the many sloughs in the Willow Grove area. This is an excellent paddle trip for beginners, as the entire trip is on protected waters.

Crims and Gull Islands

DISTANCE	6 miles round-trip.
CAMPING	Gull Island.

From Abernathy Creek Boat Ramp, cross the Columbia to the western end of Crims Island and circumnavigate both Crims and Gull Islands. Smaller nearby islands can also be explored. Camping is not permitted on Crims Island.

TRAIL REACH 9

Oak Point to Nassa Point

DISTANCE   8 miles.

MAPS   USGS Oak Point and Nassa Point 7.5-minute NOAA
           Chart 18523.

Trail Reach 9 offers a variety of open waters, islands, and backwater sloughs to explore. The areas around Wallace Island, Clatskanie, and Westport (see Trail Reach 10) are particularly noted for interesting side channels and sloughs, each accommodating a wide variety of wildlife species.

While ascending the Columbia in 1810, Nathan Winship sighted the first groves of oak trees on the river and named the prominent point on the southern shore (off the western end of today's Crims Island) Oak Point. Today, however, the name Oak Point has crossed the river to a small community on the northern shore of the river, and the original Oak Point is no longer labeled on most maps. Winship and his brothers attempted to establish the first trading post on the Columbia on the point, but abandoned the settlement because of Chinook hostilities. The Chinook controlled commerce on the river and were determined to maintain their trading power. The long dock located here was built during World War II to ship ammunition to the Pacific Theater.

Just west of Oak Point, in the early days of the twentieth century, some fifty horse-drawn seine net crews operated on the Oregon shore, along with hundreds of wooden fish traps.

On November 6, 1805, after a day paddling downstream in the cold and rain, the Corps entered the Coast Range. High mountains met the river's edge

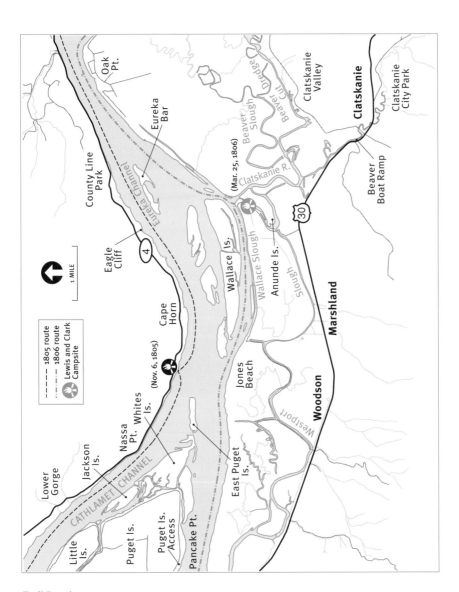

1 MILE

- - - - 1805 route
········· 1806 route
Lewis and Clark Campsite

Lower Gorge

Jackson Is.

Little Is.

Puget Is.

Nassa Pt.

Puget Is. Access

Whites Is.

CATHLAMET CHANNEL

Pancake Pt.

(Nov. 6, 1805)

Cape Horn

East Puget Is.

Jones Beach

Westport

Woodson

Eagle Cliff

4

County Line Park

Eureka Channel

Oak Pt.

Eureka Bar

Wallace Is.

Wallace Slough

Anunde Is.

Slough

Marshland

(Mar. 25, 1806)

Clatskanie R.

Beaver Slough

Beaver Cut

Dredge

Clatskanie Valley

Clatskanie

30

Beaver Boat Ramp

Clatskanie City Park

and offered few locations for a suitable campsite. After moving stones on the beach to make a level site, camp was made about a mile downstream from Cape Horn. For ten miserable days they experienced rain, high winds, cold, and dangerous waves as they continued to move slowly toward the mouth of the Columbia.

This trail reach ends at Nassa Point, near the upstream tip of Puget Island.

BOATING CAUTIONS AND CONDITIONS

The area on the Oregon side from Oak Point downriver is subject to strong winds. Be aware of tidal and ship wave action in all of these lower Columbia River areas, and take special care to tie boats securely above the high-tide line when you come ashore. The river in the Cape Horn region is especially subject to very strong winds and waves.

RIVER ACCESSES

County Line Park

FACILITIES	Beach, campsites, toilets.
ACTIVITIES	Camping, picnicking.
RESTRICTIONS	Fee for camping.

This 5.5-acre park is located a short distance east of the line between Cowlitz County and Wahkiakum County. The park is somewhat of a joint effort; the land is located in and leased to Wahkiakum County, owned by the Washington Department of Natural Resources, and maintained by the Cowlitz County Department of Public Works. It is located at milepost 45.4 on Highway 4, about 17 miles west of Kelso. A few tent campsites are situated at the western end of the park. Boats can be hand-launched from the beach. Phone 360-577-3030.

Clatskanie City Park

FACILITIES	Boat ramp, campsites, picnic area, playground, bike path, toilets, parking.
ACTIVITIES	Camping, picnicking, biking.
RESTRICTIONS	Fee for camping.

This large city park is located on the Clatskanie River in downtown Clatskanie, about half a mile upstream from Beaver Boat Ramp. The boat ramp is used much less than Beaver Boat Ramp, so it may be more desirable, even though it is located farther from the Columbia. To reach Clatskanie City Park from Highway 30 in Clatskanie, turn north on Conyers Street, drive one block, then turn right into the park and drive about a block to the boat ramp on the left. Kayak rentals are available locally.

Beaver Boat Ramp

FACILITIES	Boat ramp, dock, interpretive panels, food, supplies, toilets, parking.
ACTIVITIES	Launching only.
RESTRICTIONS	Day use only.

This Columbia County park, also known as Beaver Landing, is located at milepost 61.8 on Highway 30, immediately west of downtown Clatskanie. Phone 503-392-2353. Although the ramp is not located on the Columbia, the Columbia can be reached by paddling 2.5 miles north on the Clatskanie River. The Clatskanie River also provides access to a network of sloughs to the west that can be followed to the town of Westport, 7 miles down the Columbia (see Trail Reach 10). This route is particularly attractive to paddlers wishing to avoid the open waters of the Columbia. Several suggested trips begin at this boat ramp.

On March 25, 1806, seeking a safe harbor from the wind, the explorers found a tolerable camp along low ground for the evening. "It was with some difficulty that we could find a spot proper for an encampment," said Lewis, "the shore being a swamp for several miles back." They finally found the entrance to the Clatskanie River, which provided greater protection. Here they found a party of ten Indians who had set up a camp for fishing and hunting seals. The Indians gave them seal meat, a great improvement over their diet of "poor" elk meat.

The Clatskanie Valley was called Fanny's Bottom by Clark, who later changed the name to Fanny's Valley. Native Americans in the area used the word Tlasts-kani to describe a place in the mountains, and pioneers applied the anglicized version to the river and valley. The historic riverboat community of Clatskanie was founded as Bryantville in 1884. The 1899 Flippin Castle, now a museum, was built by an early "gypo" logger and sawmill owner. The museum is located at 620 SW Tichenor. Phone 503-728-3608.

Westport Slough

FACILITIES	Culvert.
ACTIVITIES	Launching only.
RESTRICTIONS	Day use only.

The eastern end of Westport Slough has recently been reconnected to the Clatskanie River by means of a large culvert, through which canoes and kayaks may be paddled. During times of high water, boats may be portaged. The site of the culvert is also a useful launching point, particularly for paddlers seeking ready access to the Wallace Island area of the Columbia. To reach this access point, drive northwest from Clatskanie on Highway 30. At milepost 63.7, about 2 miles northwest of Clatskanie, turn north on Point Adams Road and follow it about half a mile to the culvert at the intersection of Beeson Road and Point Adams Road.

Jones Beach

FACILITIES	Beach, picnic area.
ACTIVITIES	Picnicking, windsurfing, kiteboarding, kite-flying.
RESTRICTIONS	Day use only.

This huge sandy beach is very popular with windsurfers, kiteboarders, and kite-flyers. If you've never heard of it, there's a reason: it was recently created out of sand dredged from the shipping lanes of the Columbia. Jones Beach is located near the community of Woodson, between Clatskanie and Westport. To reach this park, turn north from Highway 30 just before milepost 68 (about 6.5 miles west of Clatskanie), drive north on Woodson Road, cross the bridge, and turn right at the sign pointing to Jones Beach. Follow the curvy Woodson Road along the dike 2.5 miles to the large beach area. The beach lies halfway between the western end of Wallace Island and the eastern end of Puget Island. Be careful driving on the beach, as it is easy to get stuck in the sand. Boats can be hand-launched.

Jones Beach is a popular spot for windsurfing, kiteboarding, and kite-flying.

OTHER FACILITIES AND POINTS OF INTEREST

Eureka Bar

FACILITIES	None.
ACTIVITIES	Primitive camping.
RESTRICTIONS	None.

Eureka Bar, also known as Quill Island, is a dredge-spoil island and an official water trail campsite. Camp on the northern side of the island for protection from ship wakes.

Wallace Island

FACILITIES	None.
ACTIVITIES	Primitive camping on small islands nearby.
RESTRICTIONS	No camping on Wallace Island.

Named Sturgeon Island by the expedition, Wallace Island is now named after Wallace Slang, an early settler. The island was purchased on March 15, 1995, by the U.S. Fish and Wildlife Service and is now part of the Julia Butler Hansen National Wildlife Refuge for the Columbian white-tailed deer. The island can be crossed midway via a channel lined with trees. A small unnamed manmade island just north of the western end of Wallace Island can be used for camping, as can two other small unnamed islands close to the Oregon shore off the southern side of Wallace Island. At low tide on Wallace Island and on the small islands north of it, you can see vertical (liquefaction) "sand dikes" cutting through a mud-cap layer of different colors caused by the earthquake of January 26, 1700.

East Puget Island

FACILITIES	None.
ACTIVITIES	Rest area for boaters.
RESTRICTIONS	Day use only. Access by boat only.

The Washington Department of Natural Resources owns this small dredge-spoil island at the eastern tip of Puget Island. Boaters use the northern shore as a rest stop.

SUGGESTED DAY AND OVERNIGHT TRIPS

Clatskanie River and Wallace Island

DISTANCE	5 to 11 miles round-trip.
CAMPING	Small islands north of Wallace Island.

The area around the mouth of the Clatskanie River is a maze of sloughs, marshes, and islands. Understandably, many of the sloughs are misnamed on some maps. Here's a quick guide: The Clatskanie River empties into Wallace Slough and the channel of the Columbia south of Wallace Island. In the bottomland east of the Clatskanie River lie Beaver Slough and Beaver Dredge Cut. The latter is connected to the Clatskanie River, but the former has been cut off by dikes. The many sloughs and channels offer several options for paddling. For a short day trip, paddle from Beaver Boat Ramp to the mouth of the Clatskanie River, about 5 miles round-trip. For a longer (11-mile) trip, extend it by circumnavigating Wallace Island, and consider camping on one of the small islands to the north. See the description of Wallace Island for more information on camping.

Clatskanie to Westport

DISTANCE	12 miles one way.
CAMPING	None.

This trip constitutes the first leg of the Columbia River Heritage Canoe Trail, a 45-mile paddle trail created in 1991 by the Oregon Historical Society. The entire trail extends from Clatskanie to the mouth of the John Day River, east of Astoria, but this leg covers the distance between the two Oregon towns of Clatskanie and Westport (see Trail Reach 10).

Anunde Island lies in the Clatskanie River near its mouth. Just west of this island is the eastern end of Westport Slough, which leads 7 miles west to Westport. Although the connection between the Clatskanie River and Westport Slough was closed in 1937, it has recently been reconnected by a 90-foot culvert, through which small boats may be paddled. This reconnection restores the historic fish passage of the Clatskanie River system. During periods of high water or high tide, boats may be portaged between the Clatskanie River and Westport Slough.

For paddlers traveling between Clatskanie and Westport, two options are available: one taking place on the open waters of the Columbia, the other taking place entirely on protected backwater sloughs. Both trips begin at Beaver Boat Ramp in Clatskanie and paddle down the Clatskanie River. For the backwater trip, turn left near the mouth of the Clatskanie River, paddle behind Anunde Island, and then portage (or paddle through the culvert) into Westport Slough, following it for several miles to the public boat ramp in Westport at the foot of Old Mill Town Road. For the open-water trip, continue out the mouth of the Clatskanie River, then turn left on Wallace Slough, the channel of the Columbia south of Wallace Island. Follow Wallace Slough to the open Columbia, which leads to the western end of Westport Slough. Paddle up the slough about a mile to the boat ramp, about a quarter of a mile upstream from the ferry landing. The ferry landing is not available for public use.

Cathlamet to County Line Park

DISTANCE	12 miles one way.
CAMPING	Wahkiakum Mooring Basin or County Line Park.

This trip takes place entirely on the open waters of the Columbia. It can be paddled in either direction, after consulting both a tide table and a wind forecast. The western end of the trip is the Elochoman Slough Marina at Cathlamet (see Trail Reach 10). The eastern end is County Line Park at milepost 45.4 on Highway 4. The route passes under the spectacular cliffs of Cape Horn (not to be confused with the Cape Horn on the Washington side of the Columbia River Gorge), which rise up out of the water, leaving few places to get out of your boat. (One small sandy beach can be found just west of Nassa Point.) Rounding this point was as perilous to the canoe fur brigades as South America's Cape Horn was to sailing ships. This mountainous promontory continues downstream along the Washington shoreline and is known locally as the Lower Gorge (see Trail Reach 10). The eastern part of the trip is exposed to the shipping lanes of the Columbia, but the west part travels north of Puget Island and is thus protected from the shipping lanes, which pass south of Puget Island.

Plate 1. *Meriwether Lewis* by Charles Willson Peale, from life, 1807. Courtesy of the Independence National Historical Park, Philadelphia.

Plate 2. *William Clark* by Charles Willson Peale, from life, 1807–1808. Courtesy of the Independence National Historical Park, Philadelphia.

Plate 3 (over). *Lewis and Clark on the Lower Columbia* by Charles M. Russell, 1905. Gouache, watercolor, and graphite on paper. Courtesy of the Amon Carter Museum, Fort Worth, Texas (1961.195).

Plate 4. Among the species described by Lewis and Clark was the great-horned owl. Courtesy of the Oregon Department of Fish and Wildlife.

Plate 5. Tundra swans were also described by the explorers.

Plate 6. The trailhead is located on Hamilton Island, 2.5 miles downstream from the Bonneville Lock and Dam Washington Shore Visitor Complex.

Plate 7. Beacon Rock, named by Lewis and Clark in 1805, is now a state park and popular boating area. Photo by Ellen Morris Bishop.

Plate 8. The tiny Phoca Rock, right, lies just upstream from Cape Horn. Photo by Ellen Morris Bishop.

Plate 9. Old pilings are all that is left of the steamboat landing at Cottonwood Beach. Passenger service between here and the Portland-Vancouver area began in 1880 and ended in 1916.

Plate 10 (opposite). Government Island and magnificent Mount Hood as seen from the Portland area. Photo by Ellen Morris Bishop.

Plate 11 (above). Mount St. Helens as seen from the wetlands just east of Portland International Airport. Photo by Ellen Morris Bishop.

Plate 12. At the northern end of Bachelor Island, boaters may hear raucous squawks as they pass one of the largest great blue heron rookeries of the Pacific Northwest. Courtesy of the Oregon Department of Fish and Wildlife.

Plate 13. St. Helens Courthouse Docks, with Sand Island in the background.

Plate 14. The Lewis and Clark Bridge at Longview, Washington.

Plate 15. The Wahkiakum County Ferry provides hourly service between Puget Island and Westport, Oregon.

Plate 16. The ghost-remains of old canneries and net barns still survive along the lower Columbia.

Plate 17. The boat ramp at Skamokawa Vista Park is located just across Skamokawa Creek and below Redmen Hall.

Plate 18. A view of Puget Island from Bradley State Park.

Plate 19. The remains of Clifton's fish-processing buildings.

Plate 20. The Astoria-Megler Bridge links Astoria to Point Ellice in Washington State.

Plate 21. The Twilight Eagle Sanctuary and its shallow waters provide fertile fishing grounds for eagles.

Plate 22. Beautiful Youngs River Falls. Photo by Ellen Morris Bishop.

Plate 23. The old Pillar Rock Cannery. Pillar Rock stands guard just offshore.

Plate 24. The lush area around Cape Disappointment, Fort Canby State Park.
Photo by Ellen Morris Bishop.

Plate 25 (over). The Cape Disappointment Lighthouse is among the oldest lighthouses on the Pacific
Coast.

TRAIL REACH 10

Nassa Point to Skamokawa

DISTANCE   10 miles.

MAPS   USGS Nassa Point, Cathlamet, and Skamokawa 7.5-
            minute NOAA Chart 18523.

This trail reach is among the most interesting to boaters for its history, varied waters, and wildlife, as well as for several public-access sites along the river and nearby sloughs. For starters, there is Puget Island, a 6-mile-long island settled and diked by Norwegian dairy farmers and fishermen, whose ancestors still attend a Lutheran church and a Norse hall on the island. For an excellent bicycle ride, try the 20-mile road around the perimeter of the island. It is flat, scenic, and nearly devoid of traffic. Lieutenant William Broughton named Puget Island in 1792 for one of Captain George Vancouver's lieutenants, Peter Puget, for whom Vancouver also named Puget Sound. Lewis and Clark called the island Sea Otter Island. It is connected to the Washington mainland by a bridge and to the Oregon mainland by a toll ferry at Westport.

Then there is the Julia Butler Hansen National Wildlife Refuge for the Columbian white-tailed deer. Located between Cathlamet and Skamokawa, this refuge offers several islands and sloughs for exploring by boat, in addition to excellent wildlife viewing. It contains 5,600 acres of wetlands, meadows, and wooded areas, and several islands. Established in 1972 as the Columbian White-Tailed Deer National Wildlife Refuge, the name was changed in 1988 to honor Julia Butler Hansen, a Cathlamet resident who became the first woman to chair an appropriations subcommittee in Congress. During the time of Lewis and Clark, the Columbian white-tailed deer ranged from The Dalles to Astoria, but its habitat has been greatly diminished. In addition to the deer, Roosevelt elk, tundra and trumpeter swans, and other wildlife take advantage

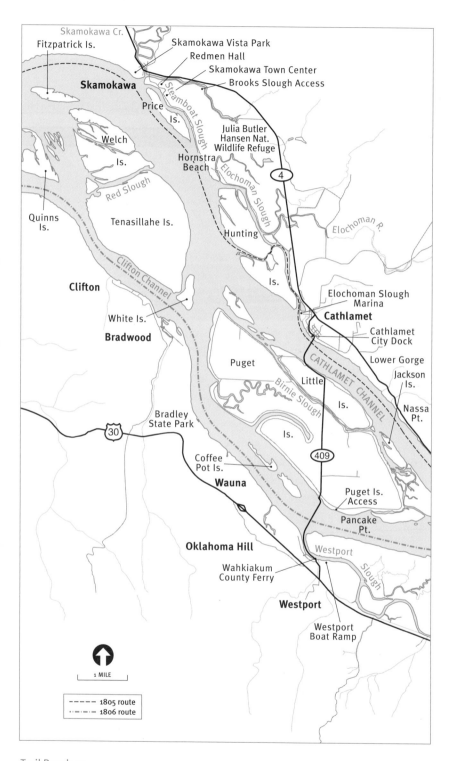

Skamokawa Cr.
Fitzpatrick Is.
Skamokawa Vista Park
Redmen Hall
Skamokawa Town Center
Brooks Slough Access
Skamokawa
Steamboat Slough
Price
Is.
Welch
Julia Butler
Hansen Nat.
Wildlife Refuge
Hornstra
Beach
Is.
Red Slough
Elochoman Slough
4
Quinns
Is.
Tenasillahe Is.
Hunting
Elochoman R.
Clifton Channel
Clifton
Is.
Elochoman Slough
Marina
White Is.
Cathlamet
Bradwood
Cathlamet
City Dock
Puget
Lower Gorge
Little
Jackson
Is.
Birnie Slough
Is.
Nassa
Pt.
Bradley
State Park
CATHLAMET CHANNEL
Is.
30
409
Coffee
Pot Is.
Wauna
Puget Is.
Access
Pancake
Pt.
Oklahoma Hill
Westport
Wahkiakum
County Ferry
Slough
Westport
Westport
Boat Ramp

1 MILE

----- 1805 route
·—·—·— 1806 route

of the secure habitat. The refuge is open daily from dawn to dusk, but no camping is allowed. Refuge headquarters are located on Steamboat Slough Road west of Cathlamet. Phone 360-795-3915.

On November 7, 1805, Lewis and Clark visited the Hunting Islands that now make up a part of the Julia Butler Hansen National Wildlife Refuge. Clark wrote of the visit:

> *After delaying at this village one hour and a half we Set out piloted by an Indian dressed in a Salors dress, to the main Chanel of the river, the tide being in we Should have found much dificuelty in passing into the main Chanel from behind those islands, without a pilot, a large marshey Island near the middle of the river near which Several Canoes Came allong Side with Skins roots, fish &c. to Sell, and had a temporory residence on this island, here we See great numbers of water fowls about those marshey Islands.*

The historic towns of Cathlamet and Skamokawa offer lodging and food in addition to their colorful pasts. Don't expect much else in the way of civilization on this stretch of the Washington shore, however. Cathlamet and Skamokawa may be small towns, but they are the largest communities in Wahkiakum County, Washington's smallest county. But though the county is small, it has its own ferry (see Plate 15). The twelve-car Wahkiakum County Ferry—the last of the ferries that once operated on the lower Columbia—travels back and forth across the Columbia between Puget Island and Westport, Oregon, leaving Westport every hour at quarter after and leaving the island every hour on the hour. There is a toll, but the leisurely trip is worth the time and small expense. Plan to arrive at the ferry landing a bit early in case more than twelve cars are already waiting.

Cathlamet, located 27 miles west of Kelso, was the site of a large Chinookan village in the early 1800s. The town takes its name from the Chinookans who called themselves Kathlamets or Kala-amat. The Kathlamets were the westernmost tribe of the Upper Chinookans. Culturally they were oriented to the river and to the salmon-fishing traditions of the Lower Chinookans. At the time of Lewis and Clark, Caltharmar was the name of their main village on the southern side of the river; the Wahkiakum village was across the river on the northern shore. The word Calamet, meaning "stone," may be the derivation for the aboriginal naming of this location on the river and subsequently of the tribe's name. In 1846 a retiring Hudson's Bay Company employee, James

Birnie, set up a trading post on the river at the location of the present town. In 1866 two brothers from Sacramento, G. W. and William Hume, established the first salmon cannery at Eagle Cliff, on the Washington shoreline 8 miles upstream from Cathlamet in Wahkiakum County. During the spring of 1867 they packed four thousand cases of forty-eight cans each (Cone and Ridlington 1996). "By 1874 there were twelve [canneries] between Astoria and Portland and by 1883 fifty-five on or near the Columbia, packing 630,000 cases of 48 one-pound cans valued at $3 million, using only chinook" (Netboy 1980). By 1887 the diminishing runs of salmon were beginning to alarm citizens. The hydroelectric dams of the 1930s did not help, and by 1950 the commercial salmon industry on the Columbia was largely a thing of the past. Today the Wahkiakum County Historical Society operates a museum at the corner of Division and River Streets in Cathlamet.

Like most small towns along the Columbia River, Skamokawa was oriented toward the river as its major mode of transportation, commerce, and communication. At the turn of the century the bustling town was called Little Venice. The houses and businesses were typically built facing the river in much the same way that structures face streets in more ordinary communities. It was not until 1917 that Skamokawa, established in 1844, was linked by a road to neighboring communities. The name of the town may be a Chinookan word meaning "smoke over the water," a reference to the frequently foggy conditions on the river. In 1841 Lieutenant Charles Wilkes recorded meeting a Chinookan chief by the name of Skumah-queah. This was Chief Skamokawa, who greeted most of the early explorers in the region, including Lewis and Clark.

The Friends of Skamokawa have restored an historic schoolhouse and turned it into Redmen Hall, which includes a museum and the River Life Interpretive Center, with exhibits on the history and prehistory of the area, native communities, first settlers, and the salmon and timber industries. The hall also includes a bookstore and the works of local artists. It is open Wednesday through Saturday and is located across Highway 4 from Skamokawa Town Center. Phone 360-795-3007.

BOATING CAUTIONS AND CONDITIONS

When coming ashore in any area of the lower Columbia River, take special care to tie boats securely above the high-tide line because of tidal and ship wave action. The river in the Cape Horn region is subject to very strong winds and waves. Elochoman Slough can be very shallow in places at low tide. Also be alert to frequent log rafts and barges in the region. Steamboat Slough provides protection from wind and ship traffic.

RIVER ACCESSES

Westport Boat Ramp

FACILITIES	Boat ramp, dock, interpretive panel, toilets, parking.
ACTIVITIES	Launching only.
RESTRICTIONS	Day use only.

This Clatsop County public boat ramp is located on Westport Slough at the foot of Old Mill Town Road in Westport, about a quarter of a mile upstream from the ferry landing. To reach it, turn north off Highway 30 in Westport at the toll-ferry sign. The road soon splits. To the left is the ferry landing, to the right the boat ramp. (The ferry landing, at the foot of Westport Ferry Road, resembles a boat ramp but is not available for public use.) Boaters leaving from the Westport Boat Ramp can either proceed downstream 1 mile to the Colum-

A concrete ramp at Westport provides boater access to Westport Slough and the Columbia.

bia or upstream 12 miles to Clatskanie, following the route described under Trail Reach 9 for the Clatskanie to Westport trip.

Puget Island Access

FACILITIES	Beach, toilets, parking.
ACTIVITIES	Launching only.
RESTRICTIONS	Day use only. Permit required. Fee.

This public-access area is located on the southern side of Puget Island, half a mile east of the ferry landing. From Cathlamet, drive 3 miles south across the island on Highway 409 to the ferry landing, then turn east and drive half a mile on Sunny Sands Road to a large gravel parking area. A Washington Stewardship Access Decal must be displayed to use this facility. Boats can be hand-launched.

Another Puget Island access ramp may soon be developed a mile downstream from the ferry landing. It will be called Svensen Park, and the ramp area will be sheltered from ship wakes by Coffee Pot Island. Again, a Washington Stewardship Access Decal will be required.

Cathlamet City Dock

FACILITIES	Dock, viewing platform.
ACTIVITIES	Launching only.
RESTRICTIONS	Day use only.

The city of Cathlamet maintains a small public dock at the foot of Broadway Street in downtown Cathlamet, from which boats may be hand-launched. The dock is a third of a mile west of the Highway 409 bridge to Puget Island.

Elochoman Slough Marina

FACILITIES	Boat ramp, docks, campground, fuel, showers, toilets, parking, nearby café.
ACTIVITIES	Camping.
RESTRICTIONS	Fee for camping and boat launching.

Wahkiakum County maintains a large mooring basin and full-service marina at the foot of Third Street on the northwest edge of Cathlamet. Short trails connect the marina to nearby Strong Park, the site of the Wahkiakum Museum, at the corner of Division Street and River Street in Cathlamet. Campsites are located on the spit between the boat basin and the river. When paddling out of the mooring basin, bear right on Elochoman Slough to paddle past the Hunting Islands toward Skamokawa, or bear left to reach the Columbia. Phone 360-795-3501.

Hornstra Beach

FACILITIES	Sandy beach.
ACTIVITIES	Launching only.
RESTRICTIONS	None.

From Cathlamet, proceed 3 miles north on Highway 4 toward Skamokawa to the bridge over the Elochoman River. Cross the bridge and turn left to follow the road 3.5 miles to the beach. This road continues through the Julia Butler Hansen National Wildlife Refuge to Skamokawa.

Brooks Slough Access

FACILITIES	Boat ramp.
ACTIVITIES	Launching only.
RESTRICTIONS	Day use only.

This unmarked public boat ramp is located at milepost 30.1 on Highway 4, 5.5 miles west of Cathlamet or 1 mile east of Skamokawa. It is located on Brooks Slough, which can be paddled west about a mile to the Columbia at Skamokawa.

Skamokawa Vista Park

FACILITIES	Boat ramp, campground, RV hookups, picnic area, group shelter, toilets.
ACTIVITIES	Full-service camping, picnicking.
RESTRICTIONS	Fee for camping.

Just west of the Skamokawa Creek Bridge on Highway 4 in Skamokawa, turn south on Pleasant Point Road and drive about a block to a boat ramp, part of Skamokawa Vista Park (see Plate 17). The campground and picnic areas are just west of the boat ramp at the foot of School Road. The park is named for the scenic view of the Columbia from the point on which the campground is locat-

The picturesque Brooks Slough near Skamokawa.

ed. It is operated by Wahkiakum County Port District 2, whose office is in a tiny building at the park entrance. The building also serves as the town library. Phone 360-795-8605. Canoes and kayaks may be rented a short distance away at the Skamokawa Town Center.

Near Skamokawa Vista Park once stood an Indian village known as Wahkiakum, occupied as early as twenty-three hundred years ago. After Lewis and Clark visited the site on November 7, 1805, Clark wrote: "This village, is at the foot of the high hills on the stard side back of 2 Small islands it contains 7 indifferent houses. . . . Here we purchased a Dog Some fish, wappato roots and I purchased 2 beaverSkins for the purpose of makeing me a roabe as the robe I have is rotten and good for nothing."

Skamokawa Town Center

FACILITIES   Dock, inn, kayak and canoe center, conference suite, restaurant, general store, boat rentals.

ACTIVITIES   Participating in guided tours, paddle clinics.

RESTRICTIONS   No camping.

Skamokawa Town Center lies opposite Redmen Hall in the heart of Skamokawa and features its own dock. Its buildings are listed on the National Register of Historic Places. Paddlers are encouraged to register their float plans here for the wildlife refuges. Phone 360-795-8300 or 1-888-920-2777. Among the guided tours available are moonlight paddles, campouts, historical and wildlife interpretive tours of the lower Columbia and its wildlife refuges, and a tour entitled "Exploring the Trail of Lewis and Clark."

OTHER FACILITIES AND POINTS OF INTEREST

Lower Gorge

FACILITIES   None.

ACTIVITIES   Touring this very scenic region.

RESTRICTIONS   None.

This stretch of the Columbia, known locally as the Lower Gorge, boasts vertical cliffs composed of fifteen-million-year-old lava flows and a series of beautiful 80-foot waterfalls, which are best seen after winter and spring rains.

Bradley State Park

FACILITIES   Viewpoint, picnic area, toilets.

ACTIVITIES   Picnicking, viewing Puget Island and the Columbia River.

RESTRICTIONS   Day use only.

This small state park is located near the summit of Clatsop Crest on the edge of a bluff above Puget Island (see Plate 18). It offers grand vistas of Puget and Coffee Pot Islands. To reach this viewpoint, turn north off Highway 30 at milepost 74.9, about 4 miles west of Westport.

Tenasillahe and White Islands

FACILITIES	Hiking trail.
ACTIVITIES	Hiking on Tenasillahe Island, primitive camping on White Island.
RESTRICTIONS	No camping on Tenasillahe Island.

Tenasillahe Island is among the largest islands of the Julia Butler Hansen National Wildlife Refuge. A dike was built around the perimeter of the island to prevent flooding when it was used for farming prior to being acquired for a refuge. The public is not allowed to enter the island except on the perimeter dike, which makes an excellent hiking path. Just upstream from Tenasillahe Island is tiny White Island, a dredge-spoil island also known as Lark Island. Because White Island is located outside the boundary of the wildlife refuge, camping is permitted.

Clark used the descriptive term Marshey Islands, rather than an applied geographic name, to describe Tenasillahe Island and the nearby smaller islands. The island's present name is composed of two Chinookan words: *tenas* ("small") and *illahe* ("land").

SUGGESTED DAY AND OVERNIGHT TRIPS

Puget Island

DISTANCE	12 miles round-trip.
CAMPING	None.

Although Puget Island is quite large, it can easily be circumnavigated in a day if the winds and tides cooperate. Launch at Puget Island Access and paddle clockwise or counterclockwise, depending on when the tide is expected to change. The southern side of the island is exposed to the shipping lanes of the Columbia, so keep an eye open for large freighters and their large wakes. Some paddlers prefer to beach their boats when a freighter appears, while others prefer to stay in the water. Keeping close to shore, where the water is shallow, is usually not a good idea, because the shallow water makes the wake even higher.

Puget Island is surrounded by several smaller islands that offer interesting sloughs to explore or use for sheltered paddling when circling the main island. Two islands off the southern shore offer some protection from ship wakes. Along the northern shore is Little Island, which is more than 2 miles long.

The slough behind this island, named Birnie Slough for Cathlamet founder James Birnie, offers an interesting alternative to the Cathlamet Channel.

If possible, time this trip so that you will be paddling around the southeastern end of Puget Island at high tide. Several islands located at that end of the island offer very narrow and shallow sloughs that can be used to avoid the open waters and main shipping lanes of the Columbia. The sloughs are complex and difficult to follow, so carry the USGS Nassa Point 7.5-minute topographic map and watch carefully for narrow openings that will allow you to complete the journey without backtracking.

Westport Slough to Puget Island

DISTANCE	5 miles round-trip (upstream route) or 15 miles round-trip (downstream route).
CAMPING	None.

Here is another interesting paddle around Puget Island. From the Westport Boat Ramp, launch into the Westport Slough and follow it east to the Columbia. Carefully cross the Columbia, watching out for strong currents. You will need to turn either left (downstream) or right (upstream). For a short trip, turn right and follow the shoreline past Pancake Point to enter Birnie Slough, at marker 6. Continue through this scenic wildlife area to Cathlamet and return.

Turning left will take you on an interesting, though far longer, trip. Proceed downriver, following the Puget Island shoreline closely past the many homes found along the beach. Camping is not allowed in this area. Many pilings jut out from the shore, so be careful as the current increases. There are several inlets to explore. As you proceed around the downstream tip of Puget Island (staying close to the shore to avoid the fast current), you will see a small inlet with a sandy beach. This is a good place to stop for lunch. Proceeding on around the tip you will encounter a small island, called Ryan Island. Either paddle around Ryan Island or cut between it and Puget Island. If the tide is low, watch for sand bars. You will now be entering Birnie Slough. Continue upstream to Little Island, which is easily identified by the bridge connecting it to Cathlamet.

At this point, if the tide is in, you can continue on Birnie Slough between Puget Island and Little Island. If the tide is low, forget it and proceed around Little Island via Cathlamet Channel, cutting inside Jackson Island, past houseboats and private moorages, to enter Birnie Slough at the upstream end of Little Island. Keep left to avoid little forks entering the channel. This is a great area for watching birds, especially waterfowl. Birnie Slough exits straight across the Columbia from the Westport Slough and the starting point of the trip.

This is a long paddle with strong currents and is not recommended as a one-day trip for beginners. There are many different ways of boating the area. Alternatively you could start from Cathlamet Marina. There are bed-and-breakfasts in Westport, on Puget Island, and in Cathlamet.

Cathlamet to Skamokawa

DISTANCE	7 miles one way.
CAMPING	Elochoman Slough Marina or Skamokawa Vista Park.

This popular trip can be paddled in either direction, depending on the winds and tide. Its popularity is largely due to the fact that most of the trip is on protected waters behind Price and Hunting Islands, which lie along the northern shore of the Columbia between the two towns. Start at Skamokawa Vista Park and paddle to the Elochoman Slough Marina, or vice versa. The route is easy: simply follow the northern shore of the Columbia, staying behind the islands. The only parts of the trip that are exposed to the open waters of the Columbia are a mile-long section in the middle and a short section just outside Skamokawa.

Brooks Slough and Skamokawa Creek

DISTANCE	Up to 9 miles round-trip.
CAMPING	Skamokawa Vista Park.

For inexperienced paddlers, or for anyone else who would like to avoid the ship traffic and wind of the open waters of the Columbia, the Skamokawa area offers two secluded sloughs: Brooks Slough and Skamokawa Creek. Both enter the Columbia at Skamokawa. Launching at Skamokawa Vista Park, paddle up one slough and then the other. Skamokawa Creek leads north from the town for about 2 miles to a small waterfall. Brooks Slough leads east for about 2.5 miles, past the Brooks Slough Boat Ramp on Highway 4. If the tide is going out, be careful that you and your boat are not left high and dry.

Tenasillahe Island

DISTANCE	2 to 5 miles round-trip.
CAMPING	White Island.

From Skamokawa Vista Park, cross the main channel of the Columbia to Tenasillahe Island, the interior of which is not open to the public. You can choose to either circumnavigate the island by boat or hike the 7-mile perimeter dike trail. Take binoculars to view a wide variety of birds and mammals, and note the diversity of plants on the island. Primitive camping is available on White Island, just off the upstream end of Tenasillahe.

Welch Island

DISTANCE	11 miles round-trip.
CAMPING	None.

This lengthy tour involves much more than Welch Island; it passes Fitzpatrick, Grassy, Quinns, Woody, Tronson, Horseshoe, Tenasillahe, and Price Islands as well (see Trail Reach 11). From the Washington shore at Skamokawa Vista Park, paddle southwest, directly across the Columbia, to Welch Island. On an ebb tide you will have to set a fairly steep ferry angle of 150 or even 120 degrees to prevent the current from carrying you past the western end of the island. An alternative would be to paddle east from Skamokawa up Steamboat Slough to the upriver end of Price Island, and cross the main channel to Welch Island. After exploring the northern shore of Welch Island, either paddle through the center of it on a narrow slough or paddle between it and Fitzpatrick Island. A word of caution, however: this passage is impossible at low tide. When an outgoing tide flows over this shallow area against a southwest wind, 3- to 4-foot waves are possible.

Continue southwest (bearing roughly 220 degrees) to pass between Grassy and Quinns Islands. Proceed on a bearing of about 250 degrees, passing between Woody and Tronson Islands, to the channel at the western end of these islands, which separates them from the eastern end of Horseshoe Island. At this point you can choose to head northwest, back out to the Columbia, and continue on to explore Horseshoe Island. Afterward return to Prairie Channel and paddle toward Tenasillahe Island. Head northeast through the channel that separates Welch Island from Tenasillahe Island. A small beach on Tenasillahe Island, just as the channel opens to the Columbia, is a good place for a rest stop. Cross the Columbia to the upriver end of Price Island and Steamboat Slough, and paddle down the slough to Skamokawa.

TRAIL REACH 11

Skamokawa to Settler Point (Southern Route)

DISTANCE   13 miles.

MAPS   USGS Skamokawa, Aldrich, Knappa, Cathlamet Bay
7.5-minute NOAA Chart 18523.

The water trail splits at Skamokawa, with the Northern Route continuing along the Washington shore past Three Tree Point, Jim Crow Point, Pillar Rock, Elliott Point, Altoona, Grays Bay, Portuguese Point, Megler, Point Ellice, and Chinook Point to Ilwaco (Trail Reaches 14, 15, and 16—about 35 miles) and the Southern Route following the Oregon shore past Aldrich Point, Knappa, Settler Point, John Day River, and around Tongue Point to Astoria (Trail Reaches 11, 12, and 13—about 29 miles). Although the river widens considerably here and the ocean influence is quite pronounced, the countless islands of the Lewis and Clark National Wildlife Refuge offer a degree of protection from the rough conditions often present on the open waters of the Columbia.

    The Southern Route of the water trail begins with Trail Reach 11 at Skamokawa, crossing the Columbia and following the Oregon shore past Aldrich Point, Knappa, and Svensen, to Settler Point. This pathway along the Oregon shoreline was followed by Lewis and Clark on their return voyage upriver in March 1806. To many paddlers this reach offers the finest paddling available anywhere along the lower Columbia. From Skamokawa, after crossing the Columbia, there are two ways to navigate around Welch Island. The shorter, downstream passage enters the channel between Fitzpatrick Island and Welch Island, proceeds upstream around Quinns Island, passes Aldrich Point,

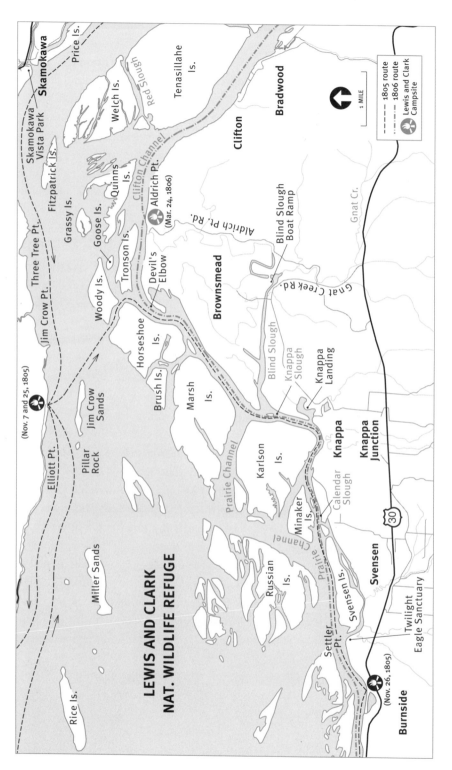

LEWIS AND CLARK
NAT. WILDLIFE REFUGE

Rice Is.

Miller Sands

Elliott Pt.

Pillar
Rock

Jim Crow
Sands

Woody Is.

(Nov. 7 and 25, 1805)

Jim Crow Pt.

Three Tree Pt.

Fitzpatrick Is.

Skamokawa
Vista Park

Skamokawa

Price Is.

Grassy Is.

Goose Is.

Welch Is.

Quinns
Is.

Red Slough

Tronson Is.

Devil's
Elbow

Clifton Channel

Aldrich Pt.
(Mar. 24, 1806)

Clifton

Tenasillahe
Is.

Horseshoe
Is.

Brush Is.

Marsh
Is.

Brownsmead

Aldrich Pt. Rd.

Blind Slough
Boat Ramp

Bradwood

Gnat Cr.

Prairie Channel

Karlson
Is.

Blind Slough

Knappa
Slough

Gnat Creek Rd.

Knappa
Landing

Russian
Is.

Minaker
Is.

Prairie Channel

Calendar
Slough

Knappa

**Knappa
Junction**

30

Settler
Pt.

Svensen Is.

Svensen

Twilight
Eagle Sanctuary

(Nov. 26, 1805)

Burnside

1 MILE

------- 1805 route
········· 1806 route
Lewis and Clark
Campsite

and follows the Oregon shoreline to Settler Point. The longer, upstream passage enters Red Slough between Welch and Tenasillahe Islands and follows the Oregon shoreline downstream. Both routes take you past Aldrich Point.

From Aldrich Point you again have two options. The first option, and the one favored by paddlers wishing to cover as much territory as possible to the west, is to follow the Oregon shoreline downstream through Devil's Elbow and Clifton Channel. Clifton Channel, as you will notice, becomes Prairie Channel when passing Horseshoe and Marsh Islands. At Karlson Island you can keep to the right and follow Prairie Channel around the northern side of Karlson Island to the west and then south down to Svensen Island, Settler Point, and the community of Burnside. Turning left at the Karlson Island junction takes you south along Knappa Slough, past the mouth of Blind Slough, to the town of Knappa. Continuing west on the southern shoreline you will enter Calendar Slough, which soon joins Prairie Channel, and follow along Svensen Island to Settler Point. At the eastern, upstream tip of Svensen Island is a narrow channel, which you can enter to access the main channel lying between the island and the mainland; this leads to Settler Point via Svensen and its houseboat community. Other access points that avoid crossing the Columbia are described under River Accesses. Skamokawa Vista Park, which is also included in this reach, is described under Trail Reach 10.

The Lewis and Clark National Wildlife Refuge is an estuarine environment that encompasses 35,000 acres of islands and tidal marshes. It provides habitat for many small and large mammals, along with more than 175 species of migratory waterfowl and other birds. Lewis and Clark traveled through the maze of these islands, which they referred to as the Seal Islands, going both east and west. Boating through the protected islands, marshes, and sloughs of the refuge in the early morning or on a moonlit evening is an unforgettable experience. You are likely to encounter six-hundred-year-old Sitka spruce trees as well as beavers, river otters, osprey, great blue herons, and nesting bald eagles. Make sure, however, that you are aware of the boating conditions in the area, and take all necessary precautions. For maps, information, and access restrictions, phone 360-795-3915 or 360-484-3482. Overnight camping is not allowed within the refuge.

BOATING CAUTIONS AND CONDITIONS

When crossing the main channel from Skamokawa, be aware that the passage between Fitzpatrick and Welch Islands should be entered with caution. When an outgoing tide flows over this shallow passage against a southwest wind, 3- to 4-foot waves are possible. Although fascinating to boat, the extensive maze of waterways within the Lewis and Clark National Wildlife Refuge makes it easy to get confused or lost, particularly in fog. Tides in this trail reach can also exert powerful influence and may cause a reversal of the river's current. The variation between high and low tide can exceed 10 feet, so do not attempt to enter shallow sloughs when the tide is receding. Most sloughs are quite accessible at high tide, and some become mudflats at low tide. Pick a day when high tide occurs sometime between noon and two o'clock, and plan to enter areas most subject to tidal fluctuation about two hours before high tide. Tide tables for the area can be found at sporting goods stores, local boating outfitters, or on the Internet (search for "Oregon Ocean Paddling Society").

Although not always possible, it is usually best to plan your paddle such that your main direction of travel is with the current, riding the ebb on the outbound leg and the flood on the return. Virtually all the islands of the lower Columbia River are marshy to some extent, though they tend to be drier in summer. Getting from your boat to "dry" land can be a very mucky business, especially in the sloughs cutting through the islands. At low tide many inland passageways are impassable. Do not attempt to paddle in shallow sloughs when the tide is receding or your boat may become stuck for twelve hours or more. If you do become stuck, do not attempt to walk on the exposed mud; oftentimes the mud will not support body weight, and you yourself may become stuck in the mud, with disastrous consequences when the tide rises. Strong winds are often present here, as they are throughout the lower Columbia. Consult a weather forecast before launching.

RIVER ACCESSES

Clifton

FACILITIES	Dock.
ACTIVITIES	Exploring what remains of this colorful old fishing village.
RESTRICTIONS	No camping. The village is mostly private property; access is by permission only.

Clifton's old, rusting iron ferry dock can be reached from Highway 30 by turning north at the sign to Clifton about a mile beyond the turnoff to Bradley State Park. Follow the winding road 3.5 miles to the old fishing settlement. Continue past several houses to a gravel road on the left, across from the old fish-processing buildings. Proceed a quarter of a mile further, crossing the rail-road tracks to the large dock on the Clifton Channel.

In contrast to other lower Columbia ethnic communities that hailed from Scandinavia, Clifton was settled by Greeks, Yugoslavs, and Italians. However, one of the first salmon canneries on the river was established here in 1873 by J. W. and V. Cook. In the 1890s it was a prosperous community of some three hundred people, with a church, two saloons, clothing and food stores, and fish-processing buildings, some of which remain on their frail pilings (see Plate 19). The post office, established in 1874, is barely standing. Some fish are still brought to Clifton for transshipment to Portland markets. A painting of the town in its heyday hangs in the Columbia River Maritime Museum in Astoria.

Paddlers at Aldrich Point prepare to explore the Lewis and Clark National Wildlife Refuge.

Aldrich Point

FACILITIES	Boat ramp, toilets, parking.
ACTIVITIES	Launching only.
RESTRICTIONS	Day use only.

Aldrich Point, the northernmost point in Oregon, offers excellent access to the myriad islands of the Lewis and Clark National Wildlife Refuge. To fully appreciate the options available, and to ensure your safe return, be sure to carry

NOAA Chart 18523. To reach Aldrich Point, turn north on Gnat Creek Road from milepost 79.3 on Highway 30 (just west of Gnat Creek), drive 1 mile, turn right on Aldrich Point Road, and follow it 4 miles to the boat ramp.

Lewis and Clark camped at Aldrich Point on March 24, 1806, during their return journey. Lewis wrote, "We continued our route along the South side of the river and encamped at an old village of nine houses opposite to the lower Wackkiacum village." As rain and wind continued, the expedition hugged the Oregon shore. Indians swarmed about them to trade. They had food to sell—roots, seal, dog, sturgeon, dried salmon—but charged prices so high that the captains frequently could not, or would not, buy. Some Indians refused to sell their food for anything but tobacco.

Aldrich Point was named for R. E. Aldrich, who once operated a store there. The Corps of Discovery applied the name Point Samuel, for Samuel Lewis, a relative of Meriwether Lewis and copyist of a map drawn by Clark in 1814.

Blind Slough Boat Ramp

FACILITIES	Boat ramp.
ACTIVITIES	Launching only.
RESTRICTIONS	Day use only.

This boat ramp, also called Autio Boat Dock, can be reached from Highway 30 by turning north at milepost 79.3 (just west of Gnat Creek) at a sign pointing to Brownsmead. Follow Gnat Creek Road 1.75 miles to this primitive boat ramp on Blind Slough, about a third of a mile east of the Barendse Road bridge south of Brownsmead. This boat ramp is privately owned by the Autio family, but they hold it open for public use.

Knappa Landing

FACILITIES	Beach.
ACTIVITIES	Launching only.
RESTRICTIONS	Day use only.

Knappa Landing provides ready access to the central portion of the Lewis and Clark National Wildlife Refuge. To reach it, turn north off Highway 30 at Knappa Junction (milepost 82) and follow Knappa Dock Road north for 1.5 miles to an old dock. To launch here you need to use the small cobble beach located between the dilapidated dock on the left and the private dock on the right. Substantial improvements are planned for this key access point.

OTHER FACILITIES AND POINTS OF INTEREST

Knappa

FACILITIES	Restaurants, nearby launch site to the Columbia.
ACTIVITIES	Sightseeing.
RESTRICTIONS	None.

The community of Knappa is the site of the "Cathlahmah" village visited by Lewis and Clark. According to the explorers, the people of this village had a custom of scaffolding the deceased in canoes, elevating them above the tidewater mark on the "Seal Islands" opposite the mainland. The village was later moved to the northern shore of the river, giving rise to the name of Cathlamet, Washington. The present town of Knappa was named after an early settler, Aaron Knapp Jr., who lived in the community for many years.

Horses were used from the 1890s to the 1920s to harvest salmon in this reach of the Columbia. The horse barns, on pilings, can be seen in the background. Courtesy of the Oregon Historical Society (49091).

Svensen

FACILITIES	Small market, gas, café.
ACTIVITIES	Visiting this historic townsite.
RESTRICTIONS	No camping.

Svensen lies 12 miles east of Astoria on Highway 30 and is another of the forgotten fishing villages, now skeletons of their vibrant past, that were based on the Columbia's "inexhaustible" salmon resources. This Finnish emigrant community derives its name from a sailor named Peter Svensen, who reportedly jumped ship in Astoria and settled in the area in 1877. It was not until 1895, however, that the name of the local post office was changed from Bear Creek to Svensen. Also named for him is Svensen Island, which lies just offshore from the town. Now a houseboat community, it is connected to the mainland by a high, arching bridge, which permitted the passage of the once busy gill-net fleet. The island is 1.5 miles long, and cattle still graze on its lush pasturelands. Settler Point juts out from the Oregon shoreline at its downstream tip.

The diary of Mary Riddle (Gault 1984), an early settler in Svensen who kept daily accounts of her life for over fifty years, describes pioneer life here, as in the entry for November 28, 1885: "Yesterday I saw our new neighbor, Mrs. Coffey, for the first time. She is a poor, homesick little woman. I feel so sorry for her to think of the change she has made from the beautiful, little town of Harland, Iowa, to this dreary, dark, drizzling, rainy, muddy, woody, unsettled, uncivilized country." Several years later, on October 29, 1893, she wrote: "We went down to the creek [Bear Creek] and caught 16 dog salmon and dragged them home. We now have 306 salmon buried in our garden for manure."

SUGGESTED DAY AND OVERNIGHT TRIPS

Lewis and Clark National Wildlife Refuge

DISTANCE	3.5 miles round-trip.
CAMPING	Aldrich Point.

Launch from Aldrich Point to explore the refuge's islands immediately north and west. There is much to see in this area, including many islands. For a short day trip, paddle north between Quinns and Tronson Islands, and then paddle northwest to tiny Goose Island and larger Woody Island. Watch for geese, bald eagles, and beavers. On the northern shore of Woody Island are a few places to pull in for a lunch stop. (Be sure to pull your boat far up on the beach in case of ship wakes or a rising tide.) Proceeding counterclockwise around Woody Island, paddle between Woody and Horseshoe Islands and then between Horseshoe and Tronson Islands before returning east to Aldrich Point. This tour requires about four hours, including a lunch break and time for leisurely wildlife viewing. If time allows, explore Horseshoe Island, Marsh Island, and the many small sloughs that penetrate the interior of those islands, but be very careful not to paddle in shallow sloughs when the tide is falling.

Paddlers take a break on Woody Island in the Lewis and Clark National Wildlife Refuge.

Blind Slough

DISTANCE	8 to 10 miles round-trip from Knappa Landing.
CAMPING	None.

Blind Slough is a fascinating 900-acre Nature Conservancy preserve dedicated to protecting a Sitka spruce swamp. It is closed to public access in February, March, July, and August. Access is available at both the western and eastern ends of the preserve, at Knappa Landing and the Blind Slough Boat Ramp. The most interesting parts of the slough are the tributary sloughs (Grizzly Slough, Warren Slough, and several smaller unnamed sloughs), which enable paddlers to penetrate deep into the Sitka spruce swamp and see a great variety of birdlife. Be very careful not to paddle up any of the smaller sloughs when the tide is falling, however, as it is easy to become stranded. Also avoid paddling under a low obstruction, such as a fallen tree, when the tide is rising, or your return route may soon become blocked.

Buried spruce stumps from the earthquake of January 26, 1700, can be seen on the eastern shore of Knappa Slough, just south of the mouth of Blind Slough. On the western side of Knappa Slough, exposed cutbanks on Karlson Island show convoluted mudbeds and dikes associated with deformed, buried wetlands from the Cascadia earthquake. Similar evidence can be seen on the northwestern shore of Karlson Island, where cutbanks reveal earthquake-induced submergence of marshlands.

Boaters prepare to enter the Blind Slough from the Blind Slough Boat Ramp.

TRAIL REACH 12

Settler Point to Astoria

DISTANCE   10 miles.

MAPS   USGS Cathlamet Bay, Olney, and Astoria 7.5-minute NOAA Chart 18521.

The Columbia achieves its widest point at Trail Reaches 12 and 15, spanning some 10 miles between Cathlamet Bay on the Oregon side to Grays Bay on the Washington side. On November 26, 1805, after the expedition decided to return to the southern shore, camp was made on the windward side of Settler Point, west of Svensen in Clatsop County, Oregon. They dined on wapato roots traded by Indians for fishhooks.

From November 27 to December 7, 1805, the Corps camped on the western side of the neck of Tongue Point, as Clark noted: "Below this point [Tongue Point] the waves becme So high we were Compelled to land unload and traw up the Canoes, here we formed a Camp on the neck of Land which joins Point William to the main at an old Indian hut." From November 29 to December 5, Lewis and five other men scouted the Youngs Bay region for a secure camp for winter. No records of the campsites used during this seven-day reconnaissance were found in the journals or expedition maps.

On March 23, 1806, during their return journey, the expedition camped on the eastern side of Tongue Point at Mill Creek. Lewis described this portion of the trip: "At 1/4 before three we had passed Meriwethers bay [Youngs Bay] and commenced coasting the difficult shore; at 1/2 after five we doubled point William [Tongue Point], and at 7 arrived in the mouth of a small creek where we found our hunters." Today, unfortunately, this campsite lies in a restricted area largely contaminated by post–World War II Liberty ship dismantling operations. Cleanup efforts are underway.

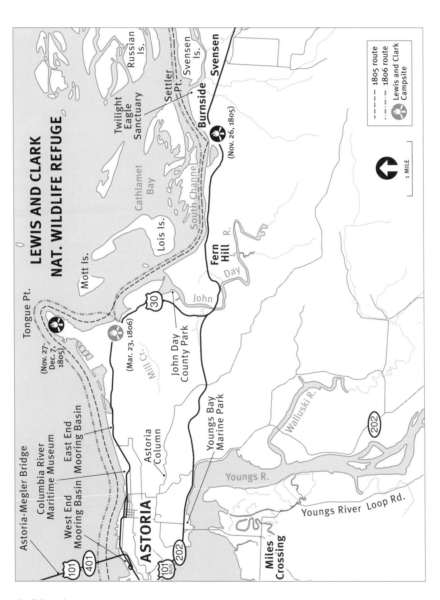

Trail Reach 12

LEWIS AND CLARK NAT. WILDLIFE REFUGE

Astoria-Megler Bridge

Columbia River Maritime Museum

Tongue Pt.

(Nov. 27 – Dec. 7, 1805)

East End Mooring Basin

West End Mooring Basin

ASTORIA

Astoria Column

(Mar. 23, 1806)

Mill Cr.

Mott Is.

Cathlamet Bay

Twilight Eagle Sanctuary

Russian Is.

Settler Pt.

Svensen Is.

Burnside

Svensen

(Nov. 26, 1805)

Lois Is.

South Channel

John Day County Park

John Day R.

Fern Hill

Youngs Bay Marine Park

Youngs R.

Walluski R.

Miles Crossing

Youngs River Loop Rd.

30

101

401

101 BUS

202

202

1 MILE

- - - - - 1805 route
- · - · - 1806 route
⚘ Lewis and Clark Campsite

Tongue Point was named by Lieutenant William Broughton in 1792 while he was exploring the Columbia River estuary for Captain George Vancouver's Northwest Expedition. The Corps of Discovery landed on "a beautiful shore of pebbles of various colors" and named it Point William, after William Clark. In 1920 a submarine base was constructed on the point. Today the U.S. Coast Guard occupies the military facilities there. The tip of Tongue Point is part of the Lewis and Clark National Wildlife Refuge; camping is not permitted.

Astoria, the first commercial American settlement on the Pacific Coast, was founded by the Pacific Fur Company in 1811 as the first fur-trading post in Oregon Country. The post was named for the owner of the American Fur Company, John Jacob Astor, one of America's richest businessmen. The settlement was not called a fort until it was surrendered to the British in 1813, a result of the British-American conflict in the War of 1812. The British rechristened the trading post and built a fort, naming it Fort George to honor the king of England. (A small park at Fifteenth and Exchange Streets in Astoria contains a partial replica of Astor's 1811 stockade on the original site.) The British name was gradually replaced with Astoria after Americans reclaimed the settlement five years later. In 1825, continuing to protect their claims to the Pacific North-

Hundreds of gill nets were dried and repaired at the Union Fishermen's Cooperative Packing Company in Astoria. Courtesy of the Oregon Historical Society (28323).

west, the British moved the headquarters for their fur-trading enterprise to Fort Vancouver. In 1847 Astoria became the first U.S. post office on the Pacific Coast.

At the heart of Astoria is its working waterfront, which can be traversed by a paved riverwalk that extends from Sixth to Seventeenth Streets. The Sixth Street Pier, located at the foot of Sixth Street about half a mile east of the Astoria-Megler Bridge, offers a viewing platform where several expedition sites can be seen on the Washington side of the river, including Grays Point, Point Ellice, Chinook Point, Baker Bay, and Cape Disappointment. Likewise the Astoria Column on Coxcomb Hill provides a magnificent view of the Columbia River estuary and shoalwater inlet, Youngs Bay. From May 12 to October 6, the downtown Astoria Sunday Market offers a variety of food, fun, and crafts. For a grand tour of this fascinating and historic city, take a ride on the Astoria Riverfront Trolley. "Old 300" is a beautifully restored 1913 streetcar that carries passengers from the Port of Astoria to the East End Mooring Basin. One of its stops is the Columbia River Maritime Museum.

The 4.5-mile-long Astoria-Megler Bridge, which crosses the Columbia River at the western end of Astoria, connects Oregon and Washington (see Plate 20). It was completed in 1966 and is the longest continuous-truss bridge in North America.

Inside the packing company, seen here in 1941, workers dressed salmon for shipments to local markets and canneries. Courtesy of the Oregon Historical Society (76312).

BOATING CAUTIONS AND CONDITIONS

Extreme caution is recommended when passing Tongue Point due to strong winds, currents, and tidal action. Stay close to the shoreline when negotiating this well-known, precarious point. Hazardous boating conditions and severe weather, due to wind against tide, can also prevail when boating around the Astoria waterfront with its many structures and pilings. Tug traffic can be heavy as bar and river pilots come and go from the waterfront.

RIVER ACCESSES

Twilight Eagle Sanctuary

FACILITIES	Viewing platform, interpretive panels.
ACTIVITIES	Wildlife viewing.
RESTRICTIONS	Day use only.

This wildlife sanctuary for nesting eagles is located along a 1.5-mile section of old Highway 30 that runs through Burnside between Svensen and Fern Hill (see Plate 21). The only improvement is a modest viewing platform along the old highway. Canoes and kayaks may be carried down a short steep trail to the railroad tracks and a short distance to the west, where they may be launched in a marshy bay of the Columbia. To reach the sanctuary, turn north off Highway 30 at milepost 87.8, about 8 miles east of Astoria, and drive half a mile to the viewing platform.

John Day County Park

FACILITIES	Boat ramps, dock, toilets, large parking area.
ACTIVITIES	Launching only.
RESTRICTIONS	Day use only. Fee.

Clatsop County maintains a boat ramp just inside the mouth of the John Day River, about 4 miles east of Astoria at milepost 93.5 of Highway 30. When driving from Portland, turn right to the boat ramp about a mile after crossing the bridge over the John Day River.

The John Day River empties into Cathlamet Bay east of Tongue Point. It is one of two rivers in Oregon named for a member of William Price Hunt's Astoria overland brigade of 1811–1812 who went insane and died in the Pacific Northwest. The river was named Ke-ke-mar-que Creek by the Corps of Dis-

The boat ramp at John Day County Park offers easy access to the Columbia.

covery in an attempt to apply its Chinookan name. When naming rivers the explorers often applied words they heard Indians use, not realizing that western Indians actually named descriptive points on rivers rather than giving the entire river a name.

East End Mooring Basin

FACILITIES	Boat ramp, docks, toilets, parking.
ACTIVITIES	Launching only.
RESTRICTIONS	Day use only.

This boat basin and boat ramp are located just off Highway 30 (Leif Erickson Drive) at the foot of Thirty-sixth Street on the eastern side of Astoria. Use the small dock just upstream from the main dock. The dock and ramp are maintained by the Port of Astoria. Phone 503-325-8279.

Columbia River Maritime Museum

FACILITIES	Tie-up dock, museum, gift shop, parking.
ACTIVITIES	Viewing museum exhibits, shopping.
RESTRICTIONS	Day use only.

This large and recently expanded maritime museum includes extensive sections on the colorful history of the Columbia River and is nationally recognized as having one of the finest collections of nautical artifacts in the United

States. It is located on the eastern side of Astoria on Highway 30 (Marine Drive) at the foot of Eighteenth Street. Among other things, you can learn the story of how the Columbia River bar came to be known as the Graveyard of the Pacific: since 1792 some two thousand vessels, including two hundred large ships, have gone down there, killing more than seven hundred people. The museum, a must-see, is open from 9:30 A.M. to 5:00 P.M. Phone 503-325-2323. The city also maintains an adjacent public dock at the foot of Seventeenth Street where visitors can explore the *Lightship Columbia*. Phone 503-325-5821, extension 24. Boaters can use the temporary tie-up dock adjacent to the *Lightship*.

West End Mooring Basin

FACILITIES	Docks, toilets, parking.
ACTIVITIES	Launching only.
RESTRICTIONS	Day use only.

This mooring basin is essentially surrounded by the Red Lion Motel complex just off Highway 30 in downtown Astoria. The western side is at the foot of Portway Street, the eastern side at the foot of Basin Street. There is no boat ramp, but boats may be hand-launched in a quiet bay at the foot of Basin Street. Phone 503-325-8279.

Youngs Bay Marine Park

FACILITIES	Boat ramp, toilets, parking.
ACTIVITIES	Launching only.
RESTRICTIONS	Day use only.

This public boat ramp is located at the Astoria Yacht Club. From downtown Astoria, drive south on Highway 101 to Youngs Bay. Turn east on Business Highway 101 (West Maritime Drive) and follow it toward the northern end of the Youngs Bay Bridge. About two blocks before the northern end of the bridge, turn left and follow signs to the yacht club. The boat ramp is located on Youngs Bay, the bay immediately south of Astoria into which the Youngs River and the Lewis and Clark River flow from the south. Phone 503-325-7275.

Lewis and Clark attempted to apply the aboriginal name Kihow-a-nah-kle to the Youngs River, but both Youngs Bay and Youngs River had already been discovered, explored, and named by Lieutenant Broughton on October 22, 1792. Broughton named Youngs River for Sir George Young of the royal navy, who was knighted in 1781 and became an admiral in 1799. Youngs Bay was

Old pilings at Youngs Bay, with Saddle Mountain in the distance. Photo by Ellen Morris Bishop.

named Meriwethers Bay by Clark in honor of Lewis, and Tongue Point was named Point William by Lewis in honor of Clark; but neither name replaced in history the names provided by Broughton. This proved true for numerous other geographical features, including Baker Bay and Mount Hood.

OTHER FACILITIES AND POINTS OF INTEREST

Astoria Column

FACILITIES	Viewing platform, concession booth, toilets.
ACTIVITIES	Viewing the mouth of the Columbia and Youngs Bay.
RESTRICTIONS	Annual parking fee.

The 125-foot column on Coxcomb Hill was built in 1926 as a monument to the arrival of the railroad in the Northwest. It is covered in winding, colorful artwork that chronicles the history of the area, beginning with Indian settlements and moving on to the arrival of Lewis and Clark and subsequent migration of white settlers. The column is open daily from dawn to dusk. To reach the viewing platform at the top, you must climb 164 steps. It's worth the effort! Phone 503-325-2963 for more details. This is a must-see.

SUGGESTED DAY AND OVERNIGHT TRIPS

John Day to Tongue Point
DISTANCE	4 miles round-trip.
CAMPING	None.

Paddle downstream from the ramp at the John Day County Park, and follow the shoreline north to the old shipyards where World War II Liberty ships were dismantled after the war. On the way, you will pass a low bluff enclosed with floating booms to contain contaminants. This is the site of the first camp made by Lewis and Clark on their return voyage, March 23, 1806. Do not attempt to continue around Tongue Point unless you are an experienced paddler and both wind and tide conditions are favorable.

John Day to Settler Point and Svensen
DISTANCE	8 miles round-trip.
CAMPING	None.

From the ramp at the John Day County Park, paddle downstream to South Channel and proceed up the channel to Settler Point and on to the houseboat community at Svensen. Return the same route. This is a safe, easy, interesting day trip.

John Day to Mott and Lois Islands
DISTANCE	7 miles round-trip.
CAMPING	None.

Launch at the John Day County Park ramp and proceed downstream under the railroad drawbridge to enter Cathlamet Bay. This is a huge area of open water and is subject to strong upstream winds, so quickly head east toward Lois Island and follow its shoreline to the northern end. At the northern tip you will find a sandy beach for lunch. Both Lois and Mott Islands are marine bird sanctuaries, so bring your binoculars and bird guide. In addition to waterbirds, Lois Island also boasts a small population of Columbian black-tailed deer. As with all islands in the lower Columbia, be sure to tie your boat well above the high-tide mark. Continue around Lois Island, heading south toward South Channel, and follow the channel west to return to John Day.

Youngs River

DISTANCE	9 miles one way.
CAMPING	None.

This day trip requires a 9-mile shuttle. Leave your vehicle at the Youngs Bay Marine Park and return to the Alternate Highway 101 and Highway 202 junction. Turn right and continue south on Highway 202 for 8 miles to Olney. Turn right onto Youngs River Loop Road, cross the bridge over the Klaskanie River, and put in at the launch site. Paddle down 1.5 miles to Youngs River and continue downstream through forested shorelines before entering the open, scenic, often windy pasturelands to Youngs Bay. Follow the bay shoreline back to the Youngs Bay Marine Park. Since the river is subject to tidal fluctuations, you'll want to launch at high tide, following it out as you cruise downriver. Plan to arrive before high tide, and take a short side trip by continuing 3 miles beyond your put-in site and taking the road on the left (just beyond the bridge over Youngs River) to the majestic Youngs River Falls (see Plate 22). This small park, with its beautiful 65-foot-high cataract, was visited by members of the expedition while hunting during their stay at Fort Clatsop.

Walluski River

DISTANCE	6 miles round-trip.
CAMPING	None.

This short, easy day trip begins at the Youngs Bay Marine Park and follows the shoreline 3 miles up Youngs River to its confluence with the Walluski River. Paddle up the Walluski to the Walluski Loop Road and return. The Walluski is a very scenic river with open grasslands and mostly private land along the shoreline.

TRAIL REACH 13

Astoria to Fort Clatsop

DISTANCE   8 miles.

MAPS   USGS Astoria and Warrenton 7.5-minute NOAA Chart 18521.

This final trail reach—and the end of the Lewis and Clark Columbia River Water Trail on the Oregon shore—embraces the very mouth of the Columbia and contains a rich array of maritime activity, beautiful beaches, dense forests, pastoral rivers and wetlands, and the historical landmarks of Fort Clatsop and Fort Stevens.

The western extremity of Astoria has had several names since Lieutenant William Broughton named it Point George in honor of the king of England. Lewis and Clark named it Point Meriwether, the Astorians named it Point Astoria (after which the Nor'westers renamed it Point George), and the Wilkes Expedition named it Youngs Point. The current name, Smith Point, is derived from pioneer Samuel Smith, who took up a donation land claim on the point. Today the Youngs Bay Bridge leads from Smith Point to the Warrenton area.

The town of Warrenton was platted as Lexington in 1848 and later named for D. K. Warren, an early settler. Members of the expedition, on hunting forays from Fort Clatsop, often passed through the area hunting for elk along the Skipanon River. The Skipanon River was named Skip-a-nor-win by Lewis and Clark after a name of Indian origin (though the Chinookan name was applied only to the mouth of the river). It was an important trade route for Indians along the coast.

The most northwestern city in Oregon is Hammond, named for Andrew Hammond, who built the Astoria and Columbia River Railroad. It is home to the U.S. Coast Guard Station at Point Adams, which was named in 1792 by

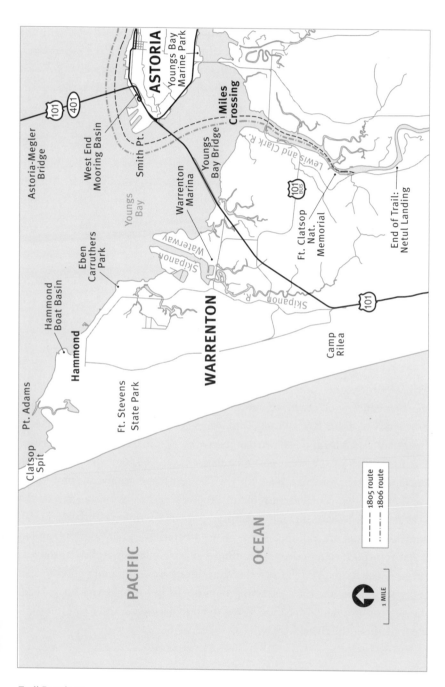

PACIFIC

OCEAN

ASTORIA

WARRENTON

Hammond

Astoria-Megler Bridge

West End Mooring Basin

Smith Pt.

Youngs Bay Marine Park

Miles Crossing

Youngs Bay Bridge

Warrenton Marina

Youngs Bay

Hammond Boat Basin

Eben Carruthers Park

Skipanon Waterway

Ft. Clatsop Nat. Memorial

End of Trail: Netul Landing

Lewis and Clark R.

Skipanon R.

Camp Rilea

Pt. Adams

Clatsop Spit

Ft. Stevens State Park

101

401

101
1805

101

1 MILE

- - - - 1805 route
- · - · 1806 route

Captain Robert Gray to honor President John Adams. Gray named the northern cape on the mouth of the river Cape Hancock (now Cape Disappointment), presumably for John Hancock, and the low sandy peninsula on the Oregon side Point Adams in an attempt to closely identify "Columbia's River" with the United States. Clatsop Spit was formed after construction of the South Jetty, and Point Adams no longer marks the mouth of the Columbia.

BOATING CAUTIONS AND CONDITIONS

Strong currents, tides, and winds should be anticipated at the entrance to Youngs Bay and the Lewis and Clark River, approaching Fort Clatsop. Youngs Bay is very shallow, and at low tide much of it becomes mudflats. Crossing through this area must be done at high tide.

RIVER ACCESSES

Netul Landing

FACILITIES	Modern dock and boat ramp, toilets, parking.
ACTIVITIES	Exploring Fort Clatsop and the Lewis and Clark River.
RESTRICTIONS	Day use only.

This boat landing on the Lewis and Clark River is the official end of the Lewis and Clark Columbia River Water Trail in Oregon. It is part of the Fort Clatsop River Day-Use Area and is located on Fort Clatsop Loop Road about a quarter of a mile south of the main entrance to the fort. The location was used by Willamette Industries as a dock for their logging operations, and numerous steel and wooden pilings still remain. Proposed additions to the area by the National Park Service include a trailhead for canoe and kayak access; toilets; picnicking areas, including a group picnic shelter; large parking lots; multimodal transportation options, including a shuttle bus stop linked to the fort and regional tourism sites and venues; an interpretive-program staging area for school groups; and bicyclist tour groups on the Lewis and Clark Loop Road. The day-use area will also be connected to Fort Clatsop via a wetland interpretive trail along the river.

Warrenton Marina

FACILITIES	Boat ramp, fuel, groceries, café, laundry, toilets.
ACTIVITIES	Nearby camping.
RESTRICTIONS	Fee.

The city of Warrenton maintains a marina on the Skipanon River. From the marina the Columbia can be reached by paddling about 1.5 miles north on the Skipanon Waterway. To reach this boat ramp, drive west from Astoria on Highway 101. After crossing Youngs Bay, turn right on Harbor Drive and follow it about a mile to Warrenton. Just before the bridge over the Skipanon River, turn left on Ensign Street. Phone 503-861-3822.

The extensive Warrenton Marina on the Skipanon River.

Hammond Boat Basin

FACILITIES	Boat ramp, dock, small beaches, fuel, groceries, laundry, showers, toilets.
ACTIVITIES	Nearby camping.
RESTRICTIONS	Day use only. Fee for boat launching.

The city of Hammond maintains a large boat basin and public park just east of Point Adams. To reach it, turn north on Lake Drive at the four-way stop in

Hammond. Launch either from the ramp at the southern end of the basin or from one of two small beaches at the northern end of the park. This boat ramp is the westernmost public ramp on the Oregon shore of the Columbia River. Phone 503-861-1461.

OTHER FACILITIES AND POINTS OF INTEREST

Fort Clatsop National Memorial

FACILITIES	Visitor center, replica of the fort, canoe landing.
ACTIVITIES	Participating in living-history programs.
RESTRICTIONS	Day use only. Fee.

The first U.S. military establishment to be built in the Pacific Northwest was winter quarters for the Corps of Discovery from December 7, 1805, to March 23, 1806. It rained all but 12 of the 106 days spent at the fort—the rainiest period ever recorded. The 50-foot-square fort was built around seven cabins on what was then called the Netul River, after the Chinookan name, but which received its present name as the Lewis and Clark River in 1925. The fort was named to honor the Clatsop Indians living in the area.

Fort Clatsop National Memorial.

Today the site is a national memorial maintained by the National Park Service. The replica fort was built in 1955 by citizens and organizations of Clatsop County to mark the sesquicentennial of the nation's most successful overland expedition. The facility offers living-history interpretive programs that allow you to travel back in time to experience the living quarters, people, and neighbors of the Corps, all functioning as they did during that time. Among the other sites to visit are Chinook and Clatsop Indian villages, a tribal longhouse, and the salt works at Seaside, Oregon. A greenway trail corridor used by the explorers, connecting Fort Clatsop with the Pacific Coast, offers visitors a firsthand opportunity to walk through forests and beach terrain, encountering plants and animals noted by the captains in their journals. The fort is open year-round except for Christmas Day.

Eben Carruthers Park

FACILITIES	Picnic area, toilets.
ACTIVITIES	Picnicking, viewing the Columbia.
RESTRICTIONS	Day use only.

The Columbia River Walkway near Warrenton provides Lewis and Clark interpretive signs and views of expedition sites at Tongue Point and Youngs Bay in Oregon, and at Point Ellice and Cape Disappointment in Washington.

Fort Stevens State Park

FACILITIES	Year-round full-service campground, RV hookups, yurts, boat ramp, museum, trails.
ACTIVITIES	Hiking, biking, wildlife viewing, picnicking, participating in guided tours.
RESTRICTIONS	Historical area open from 10:00 a.m. to 6:00 p.m., May through September.

Named for Isaac Stevens, the first governor of Washington Territory (1853–1857), the Fort Stevens Military Reservation guarded the southern shore of the Columbia River from the Civil War through World War II. With Fort Canby guarding the northern shore along with Fort Columbia, a triangular defense was established at the mouth of the river. On June 21, 1942, the fort was shelled by a Japanese submarine, but no damage was done and no fire was returned.

After the U.S. Army Coast Artillery abandoned the facilities, the area was converted to the state's largest park. Here you can explore the old gun batteries and visit the park's excellent museum. Numerous trails (including over 5 miles of hiking trails and 7 miles of scenic bike paths) lead to miles of sand dunes and to what is left of the British vessel *Peter Iredale*, wrecked in 1906. The Oregon Coast Trail begins at the South Jetty and incorporates part of the trail that Captain Clark used to explore the Oregon Coast. An underground tour is also an option, as is a tour of the park in a 2.5-ton army truck. Fort Stevens State Park includes full-service camping facilities, and the small towns of Warrenton and Hammond offer accommodations such as bed-and-breakfasts. Phone 503-861-2000.

SUGGESTED DAY AND OVERNIGHT TRIPS

Lewis and Clark River

DISTANCE	6 or 8 miles round-trip, 9 miles one way.
CAMPING	None.

This small but beautiful river gently flows north, fed by its numerous tributaries in the Coast Range extending south and east as far as Saddle Mountain State Park. In the last 5 to 6 miles it meanders through open pastureland dotted with farms and grazing cattle, reminiscent of the lush, green dairy lands of Tillamook, Oregon, to the south.

The lower river is tidal, and you should launch at high tide. For a short paddle without a shuttle, take Alternate Highway 101 from Astoria, cross Youngs Bay Bridge, turn right at Miles Crossing, and cross the bridge over Lewis and Clark River. Continue on 1 mile to a sign pointing to Fort Clatsop and turn left onto Fort Clatsop Road, proceeding through the national memorial. Drive on 2.5 miles to a bridge over the river. Launch at the ramp on the eastern side of the bridge, paddle down to Fort Clatsop, and return—a distance of about 6 miles.

For a longer paddle, continue south past the first bridge (here the road takes on a new name: Lewis and Clark Road) for another 2.5 miles to its intersection with Logan Road on the left. Follow Logan Road a quarter of a mile to the bridge, and put in. Round-trip, this is about 8 miles.

Another option involves a 9-mile shuttle. Leave one car at the Youngs Bay Marine Park, drive across the bridge to Miles Crossing, and follow the direc-

The picturesque Lewis and Clark River, south of Fort Clatsop.

tions given for the shorter trips. This shuttle option involves entering Youngs Bay. Inclement weather dictates paddling close to the shoreline back to the marine park.

Skipanon River

DISTANCE	1 to 4 miles round-trip.
CAMPING	None.

Two options are suggested for a trip through this quiet river. For the first, put in at the Warrenton Marina and paddle upriver 2 miles. This involves a short portage around a tide gate on the river. (The gate is in the process of being revamped.) This small stream winds slowly through residential areas, under a bridge, and continues into forested reaches on public land. You can actually paddle all the way to Cullaby Lake, 8 miles south. Alternatively, put in at the Warrenton Marina and paddle down to the mouth of the river (1 to 2 miles), passing sea lions loitering on the west bank docks about halfway down, and return.

TRAIL REACH 14

Skamokawa to Deep River (Northern Route)

DISTANCE   14 miles.

MAPS   USGS Skamokawa, Cathlamet, Grays River, Knappa, Rosburg, and Cathlamet Bay 7.5-minute NOAA Chart 18523.

The Northern Route of the water trail begins at Skamokawa and proceeds downriver along the Washington shoreline, keeping well away from the ship channel, which runs close to the Washington shore. You will pass several small pocket beaches and Three Tree Point before reaching Jim Crow Point (a distance of about 6 miles). Watch for tidal fluctuations. From Jim Crow Point, continue downstream past Pillar Rock, Elliott Point, Altoona, and Harrington Point to Grays Bay. This trail reach is for experienced open-water paddlers only. It is subject to strong winds and ship wakes; no protected bays or sloughs can be found along it. There are also no recommended road access points to the Columbia and few campsites along this entire stretch of river, as the shoreline is all under private ownership above ordinary high tide. The nearest campsites are at Elliott Point and Deep River. At Grays Bay it is prudent to follow the shoreline around Pigeon Bluff and north to the mouth of Grays River and Miller Point to Deep River and the Oneida Access area. The distance from Altoona to Deep River is 3.5 miles.

For fascinating side trips, explore Grays River and Deep River. Both rivers are placid, flowing gently through beautiful open bottomlands with forested shorelines. Both fluctuate with the tide as well, and though boating on Deep River is not affected by this, the narrow channel approaching Grays River is

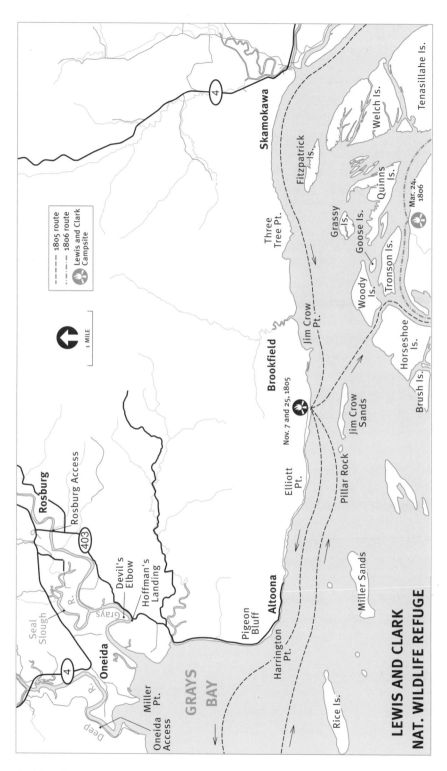

LEWIS AND CLARK
NAT. WILDLIFE REFUGE

1805 route
1806 route
Lewis and Clark
Campsite

1 MILE

Trail Reach 14

shallow at low tide (1 to 2 feet) and surrounded by extensive mudflats and pilings often exposed by the tide.

History fills this reach of the Columbia. Grays Bay was named by British Captain George Vancouver to honor American Captain Robert Gray, who crossed the treacherous Columbia bar and entered the mouth of the river in 1792, later naming it after his ship. England's claim to the Pacific Northwest was blunted when Vancouver anchored in Puget Sound at the time Gray entered the Great River of the West and claimed it for America.

BOATING CAUTIONS AND CONDITIONS

When following the Washington shoreline downstream, be aware that tides in this unprotected stretch exert powerful influence and cause reversal of the river's current. Thus this reach of the Columbia can be very hazardous, especially considering its exposure to the windy 4-mile-wide Grays Bay, with its shallows, mudflats, snags, and numerous pilings. Although the crossing from Altoona to Rocky Point (see Trail Reach 15) can be relatively easy on a calm day, you will be safer following the shoreline, as the expedition did. This safer route will also allow you to explore the two rivers that enter the bay.

RIVER ACCESSES

Elliott Point

FACILITIES	Small dock, bed-and-breakfast, beach.
ACTIVITIES	Camping.
RESTRICTIONS	Private property beyond beach.

A small dock is planned for this site, which will also include a bed-and-breakfast called the Dahlia House, a large, white Victorian home built in the 1890s and overlooking Elliott Point. Phone 360-795-3420.

Rosburg Access

FACILITIES	Boat ramp.
ACTIVITIES	Launching only.
RESTRICTIONS	None.

This launch site to Grays River is located half a mile south of the town of Rosburg, Washington, on Highway 403 (Altoona-Pillar Rock Road). Turn right before the bridge and park near the Rosburg Community Hall. The boat ramp is 50 yards southwest of the hall.

Hoffman's Landing

FACILITIES	Primitive boat dock, gangplank from road to dock.
ACTIVITIES	Launching only.
RESTRICTIONS	None.

Hoffman's Landing is at Devil's Elbow, located at rivermile 1 on the Grays River (and not to be confused with the Devil's Elbow near Aldrich Point). This tiny launch site is on Highway 403 (Altoona-Pillar Rock Road) 2.5 miles south of Rosburg. Caution is recommended when launching from the rickety wooden dock. There are other small private docks on the Grays River in this area, but you will need to ask permission prior to launching.

Oneida Access

FACILITIES	Dock, asphalt boat ramp, primitive campground, toilet.
ACTIVITIES	Camping.
RESTRICTIONS	Fee.

This privately owned boat ramp and primitive campground are located on Deep River, about a quarter of a mile upstream from where the river empties into Grays Bay. To reach the ramp, turn south on Oneida Road from Highway 4 at milepost 10.8, just west of the Deep River Bridge, then follow Oneida Road south for 2 miles to the ramp. A sign at the house on the left indicates "pay boat fee here."

OTHER FACILITIES AND POINTS OF INTEREST

Jim Crow Point

FACILITIES	None.
ACTIVITIES	None.
RESTRICTIONS	Private property. No camping.

Jim Crow Point is named for James DeSaule, a cook for the Wilkes Expedition who deserted the U.S. Navy vessel *Peacock* in 1841 when it ran aground and broke up. DeSaule was a Peruvian black man, giving rise to the name for the point on which he decided to settle rather than continuing his mariner ways.

Pillar Rock

FACILITIES	None.
ACTIVITIES	None.
RESTRICTIONS	Private property. No camping.

Pillar Rock, which stands in the river north of Marsh Island, was named by Lieutenant William Broughton in October of 1792. This Miocene basalt rock once rose 75 to 100 feet above the water, depending on the tide. Unfortunately, since its top was removed for installation of navigational marker 17 and a light, it now stands only about 25 feet high. The rock is best viewed from the water, but a shoreline road extends east from Altoona and dead-ends at the old community of Pillar Rock. Here a portion of the old Pillar Rock Cannery, built in 1877, still stands on the site of a Hudson's Bay Company fish saltery (see Plate 23). The famous rock lies directly offshore about 300 yards. According to a Wahkiakum myth (of which there are three versions) the rock was named Taluaptea, after a chief who displeased the spirits and was turned to stone.

The Corps camped twice on the Washington shore opposite Pillar Rock. The first camp was on November 7, 1805, when traveling downriver, and the second was on November 25, 1805, when returning upriver to cross the Columbia and avoid its wide, hazardous estuary. On November 7, Clark wrote the following in his journal: "Great joy in camp we are in View of the Ocian, this great Pacific Octean which we been So long anxious to See. And the roreing or noise made by the waves brakeing on the rockey Shores (as I Suppose) may be heard disticly." They had mistaken the Columbia River estuary for the open ocean, which was some 25 miles distant. It would take them another week to reach their destination

Altoona

FACILITIES	None.
ACTIVITIES	Exploring this old fishing village.
RESTRICTIONS	Private property. No camping.

The community of Altoona was founded in 1903 as a fish cannery called the Altoona Mercantile and Fish Company. Hans Peterson named it after a major fish-processing city on Germany's Elbe River. The site was used in the 1830s by the Hudson's Bay Company as a fish receiving station and saltery, in direct competition with Nathaniel Wyeth's American establishment on the southern shore of the Columbia. To reach Altoona, turn south off Highway 4 at Rosburg (milepost 15) and follow Highway 403 (Altoona-Pillar Rock Road) 7 miles. All

The Pillar Rock Cannery as it looked in 1905. Courtesy of the Oregon Historical Society (73544).

that remains of the salmon industry are pilings now used by bald eagles looking for a salmon meal.

SUGGESTED DAY AND OVERNIGHT TRIPS

Grays River and Seal Slough

DISTANCE	4 miles round-trip.
CAMPING	None.

Note the Boating Cautions and Conditions described for Trail Reach 14 before
attempting this day trip, which must be undertaken at high tide. The historic
and scenic Grays River is a good spot for birding. You can paddle it upstream
for 10 miles, through farmlands and forested shorelines robust with blackberries and dogwoods, before it becomes very shallow and narrow. Rosburg Access,
half a mile south of Rosburg, includes a good boat ramp. From this put-in site,
depending upon the tide, you can paddle upstream to Washington's only covered bridge and exit (a distance of about 5 miles), or continue upstream an
additional mile and exit at the Grays River Bridge on Highway 4, at the junction of Klints Creek and Grays River off Sauterland Road. Rosburg Access and
the two other access points described for this trail reach can be used in order to

Pilings mark the location of the once busy fishing village of Altoona.

paddle downstream and exit at Devil's Elbow. One mile before reaching Devil's Elbow, Seal Slough enters the river from the west. This is an interesting 2-mile stretch to explore—note the exposed snags of red cedar trees buried in the earthquake of January 26, 1700. Many paddlers put in at Devil's Elbow (after leaving a shuttle vehicle at one of the upstream access points) and paddle upstream.

Deep River
DISTANCE	6 miles.
CAMPING	Oneida.

Deep River is located 2 miles west of the mouth of Grays River and 1 mile west of Miller Point. The channel approaching the river is deep (7 to 9 feet) and is marked on the eastern side by red buoys and on the western side by pilings. Oneida Access is on the left half a mile upstream. The lower stretch, like Grays River, is lined with private homes, docks, and fishing shacks. Sitka spruce trees and blackberries line the shores, and a variety of waterfowl are encountered at nearly every turn. Three miles up this scenic river, after passing Svensen's landing area on the left, Highway 4 crosses the river. You can take-out there and return to Oneida, or continue upstream 1.5 miles to the old townsite of Deep

The scenic Deep River near Highway 4.

River, on the left. There is a private Oneida campground on Deep River; a fee is required.

The community of Deep River, located about 4.5 miles upstream (outside the boundaries of this trail reach), was first settled around 1875 by Finnish emigrants. By the 1890s it was a thriving logging settlement with its own steamboat landing, post office, stores, and school. Like similar "turn-of-the-century" river towns, such as Clifton, Altoona, and Knappton, only broken river pilings remain—a sad testament to dwindling fish and timber resources, and the modern highways and huge ships that bypass them today.

For more specific details on paddling Grays and Deep Rivers, see *Paddle Routes of Western Washington* (Huser 2000), and for fascinating short histories of the bygone fishing communities along the lower Columbia, take a look at *Reach of Tide, Ring of History: A Columbia River Voyage* (McKinney 1987).

TRAIL REACH 15

Deep River to Chinook Point

DISTANCE   14 miles.

MAPS   USGS maps Rosburg, Knappton, and Chinook 7.5-
            minute NOAA Chart 18521.

From Deep River, the route in this trail reach continues south along Grays Bay, passes the small Brix Bay, rounds Rocky Point, Portuguese Point, and Grays Point, and continues past Knappton, Knappton Cove, Cliff Point, Hungry Harbor, Megler, and Point Ellice (beneath the Astoria-Megler Bridge) to end up at Chinook Point, part of Fort Columbia State Park.

When the Corps of Discovery attempted to cross Grays Bay on November 8 and 9, 1805, they called it Shallow Bay. Rain and wind continued all during the first day, forcing them to follow the shoreline. Several Corpsmen and Sacagawea became seasick from the high waves, and the Corps was forced to seek shelter at Portuguese Point, which they named Cape Swells. The exact location on the point for their two-day camp cannot be precisely determined from Clark's journal entries or maps. On November 9, high winds and rain forced the party to postpone challenging the waves with their open dugouts. That night, a high tide and large drift logs threatened to crush their canoes. Conditions became critical. (For a detailed account of this and other expedition events in Trail Reaches 15 and 16, see Ziak 2002.)

About 3 miles south of Grays Bay, in the middle of the Columbia, lies Rice Island, a dredge-spoil island created between 1962 and 1964 by the Army Corps of Engineers. Most of Rice Island is owned by the Oregon Division of State Lands. The eastern tip, however, is owned by the Washington Department of Natural Resources. The island was once host to the largest Caspian tern nesting colony on earth, accommodating twenty thousand birds, but a

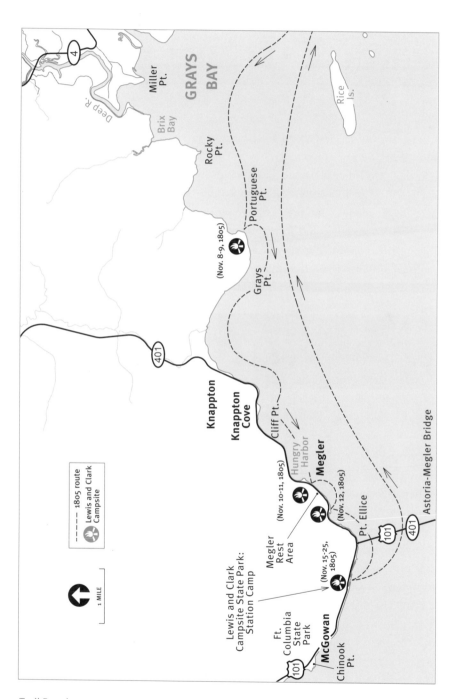

GRAYS BAY

Miller Pt.

Deep R.

Brix Bay

Rocky Pt.

Portuguese Pt.

(Nov. 8–9, 1805)

Grays Pt.

Rice Is.

4

401

Knappton

Knappton Cove

Cliff Pt.

Hungry Harbor

Megler

(Nov. 10–11, 1805)

(Nov. 12, 1805)

Pt. Ellice

Astoria-Megler Bridge

Lewis and Clark Campsite State Park: Station Camp

Megler Rest Area

(Nov. 15–25, 1805)

Ft. Columbia State Park

McGowan

Chinook Pt.

101

401

------ 1805 route
Lewis and Clark Campsite

1 MILE

relocation effort moved the colony to East Sand Island near the mouth of the river.

BOATING CAUTIONS AND CONDITIONS

Just west of the mouth of Deep River is Brix Bay, with its exposed shoals. When passing Rocky Point and Portuguese Point, be aware of strong currents, waves, and wind; and when following the coastline past Grays Point and Knappton, be wary of extensive mudflats, hazardous pilings, and backwater eddies. Point Ellice is known for its wind, current, and occasional 6- to 7-foot waves. Pilings and wing dams are dangerous on the ebb at Point Ellice, McGowan, and off Chinook Point. Ebb tides in the main channel in this area can reach 10 knots (12 miles per hour). After passing Point Ellice, continue following the shoreline 2 miles to Chinook Point and Fort Columbia State Park (neither provides access to the river).

RIVER ACCESSES

Knappton

FACILITIES	None.
ACTIVITIES	Fishing.
RESTRICTIONS	Day use only.

Knappton was founded in 1867 as Cementville by Jabez Knapp, who had hopes of producing cement for construction along the Columbia. When the raw materials gave out, Knapp built a sawmill to supply lumber for building. Eventually the townsite grew and the name was changed to honor its founder. Old pilings and a stone monument on the riverbank are all that remain of this townsite. From here Grays Point and Portuguese Point can be viewed from a roadside pullout located at milepost 4 on Highway 401, 4 miles east of the bridge to Astoria. Boats may be hand-launched from this site.

A sport-fishing boat maneuvers through pilings at Knappton, Washington.

Knappton Cove

FACILITIES	Museum, rental apartment.
ACTIVITIES	Touring the site.
RESTRICTIONS	Day use only.

Old pilings close to shore are the remnants of Joseph Hume's salmon cannery, built in 1876. The outer piling field (including four dolphins) marks the site of the old Columbia River Quarantine Station, which operated from 1899 to 1938. Most original buildings from the station remain onshore, three-quarters of a mile west of the stone marker at milepost 4 on Highway 401. The federal quarantine facility fumigated incoming vessels and quarantined thousands of immigrants at this port of entry. The entire site is listed on the National Register of Historic Places.

The Lazaretto quarantine hospital building on Highway 401 is now the privately owned Knappton Cove Heritage Center. It houses a museum showcasing the old Columbia River Quarantine Station, "the Ellis Island of the Pacific Northwest." For further information contact the manager at home, north of the quarantine station, or phone 503-738-5206. A two-bedroom year-round vacation rental apartment is also located here. There is no ramp, but boats can be hand-launched at the shore.

The Knappton Cove Heritage Center, formerly a quarantine hospital building, houses an interesting museum and a rental apartment.

OTHER FACILITIES AND POINTS OF INTEREST

Megler Rest Area

FACILITIES	Information booth, toilets.
ACTIVITIES	Rest area for drivers.
RESTRICTIONS	Day use only.

Megler was named for pioneer Washington legislator Joseph Megler, who owned the salmon cannery on the leeward side of Point Ellice. The Astoria-Megler Bridge crosses the Columbia River near this point. The Megler Rest Area on Highway 401, 1 mile east of the bridge, offers a spectacular view of the Columbia River estuary. This was the landing site for the old ferry between Astoria and Megler before the bridge was constructed.

The Corps of Discovery camped near Megler from November 10 to November 14, 1805. Attempting to round Point Ellice, the party was pinned down for five days by rain, wind, waves, rolling logs, and tidal swells. Clark noted their troubles:

> *Saw great numbers of Sea Guls, the wind rose from the N.W. and the waves became So high that we were compelled to return about 2 miles to a place we Could unload our Canoes, which we did in a Small nitch at the mouth of a*

Small run on a pile of drift logs where we Continued untill low water, when the river appeared calm we loaded and set out, but was obliged to return finding the waves too high for our Canoes to ride, we again unloaded the Canoes, and Stoed the loading on a rock above the tide water. . . . Every man as wet as water could make them and nothing to eate but pounded fish.

The first campsite of November 10 and 11, 1805, was located just east of Megler. On November 12 the camp was moved half a mile west in order to obtain fresh water and salmon from a brook. This second camp is believed to be the place Clark described as "this dismal nitich where we have been confined for 6 days passed, without the possibility of proceeding on, returning to a better Situation, or get out to hunt, Scerce of Provisions, and torents of rain poreing on us all the time." By November 15 the rain had finally stopped, the wind had settled down, and they were able to round Point Ellice.

Point Ellice, a large mountainous point that projects into the Columbia, was named by the British Northwest Fur Company to honor Edward Ellice, an agent of the London company. The point's Chinookan name was Kah-eese. Captain Clark called it both Point Distress and Blustering Point.

A miserable camp was endured by the explorers at this cove, which Clark appropriately called the "dismal nitich."

Lewis and Clark Campsite State Park (Station Camp)
FACILITIES   Picnic tables, interpretive panels.
ACTIVITIES   Picnicking.
RESTRICTIONS   Day use only.

The famous Lewis and Clark campsite used from November 15 to November 25, 1805, called Station Camp, is now a small state park in the community of McGowan, 1.75 miles west of the northern end of the Astoria-Megler Bridge. This is the location from which the expedition first viewed the Pacific Ocean, and it was the final Washington shore campsite on their westward journey. It was established on a sandy beach on the western side of Point Ellice, near a stream and west of an abandoned Chinookan village. For ten days this camp was used as a base for exploration and documentation. The actual site is now under water.

Lewis, with four members of the party, explored Cape Disappointment first and assigned November 14, 1805, as the date the expedition reached the mouth of the Columbia River. Clark traced Lewis's exploration route on one of his maps, but no records exist showing the location of Lewis's three campsites. Clark also drew a map of the northern shore of the mouth of the Columbia with compass bearings to verify the exact location of the base camp. His calculations put the total mileage between the mouth of the Columbia and the mouth of the Missouri River at 4,162 miles (which proved to be accurate within 40 miles). Clark, with ten men, explored the cape and surrounding countryside.

The Lewis and Clark Campsite State Park commemorates the location where each member of the expedition was polled for a location for winter camp—the first recorded "vote" of any kind by a female or black person in American history. The Fort Clatsop area on the southern side of the river was chosen for its abundance of game and wapato and for its protection from winter weather. The location also afforded an opportunity to meet trading vessels sailing along the Pacific Coast. There are plans to enlarge Station Camp and make it a National Park Service unit in conjunction with Fort Clatsop, as well as to add a canoe landing site. An 18-mile Lewis and Clark Discovery Trail is also planned and will stretch from Station Camp to Ilwaco.

The nearby community of McGowan began in 1848 when Father Louis Linnet claimed 320 acres for a Roman Catholic mission on the windward side of Point Ellice. Patrick McGowan purchased the claim in 1852 and started a salmon saltery, later building a cannery at the town already named in his honor. In 1904 McGowan donated land for St. Mary's Church and financed its construction. The church stands beside Highway 101, a few feet east of Station Camp. McGowan's heirs donated the land for the small park.

Fort Columbia State Park

FACILITIES	Picnic area, exhibits, youth hostel, toilets.
ACTIVITIES	Picnicking, touring historic military buildings and fortifications.
RESTRICTIONS	Open mid-April to September 30.

Fort Columbia was built between 1885 and 1905, one of several forts designed to protect the mouth of the Columbia from entry by hostile ships. It is located on Chinook Point, a rocky headland jutting into the Columbia 2.5 miles west of the Astoria-Megler Bridge (Lewis and Clark called it Point Open Slope). The entrance to the park is just north of the Highway 101 tunnel under the headland. Steep cliffs prevent boat access to the Columbia.

The Chinook Point Military Reservation was first established at the mouth of the Columbia in 1864 because of strained Anglo-American relations and the Civil War. The first troops were sent to Fort Columbia in 1898 to construct facilities to mine the river and build modern housing. The fort was completed by 1904. As the third point of a "triangle of defense," it guarded the mouth of the Columbia, remaining in operation until after World War II. It is now a state park with a youth hostel and an interpretive center for the U.S. Army Coast Artillery and Chinook Indians. The restored facilities include batteries, barracks, and officers' quarters. In 1805 Clark reported a Chinookan village east of here with thirty-six longhouses "deserted by the Indians and in full possession of the flees."

SUGGESTED DAY AND OVERNIGHT TRIPS

Knappton to Deep River

DISTANCE	14 miles round-trip.
CAMPING	Oneida.

Overnight paddling trips are common from Knappton to Deep River, but exposed shoals, pilings, strong currents, wind, and waves must always be expected. Play it safe and stay close to the shoreline. This trip is recommended for summer paddling. A fee is required at the private Oneida campground on Deep River.

TRAIL REACH 16

Chinook Point to Fort Canby

DISTANCE   8 miles.

MAPS   USGS Chinook and Cape Disappointment 7.5-minute
NOAA Chart 18521.

This final reach of the water trail on the Washington shore crosses Baker Bay,
named by Lieutenant William Broughton for a British merchant, Captain
James Baker of the vessel *Jenny*. *Jenny* was anchored inside the mouth of the
Columbia when Broughton explored the river for Captain Vancouver in 1792.
Trade with Native Americans for sea otter skins led to commerce on the river,
but the secretive merchants did not always record their trade routes. Territorial sovereignty would be left to explorers with vested nationalistic interests. To
Lewis and Clark, Baker Bay was Haley's Bay, named for the Indians' favorite
white trader, who had anchored in the bay.

The Chinook River, which enters the Columbia at Baker Bay, retains the
name Clark gave it in 1805 (though he spelled it "Chinnook"). The name originates from *Tsinuk*, the Chehalis (Salish) Indian name for the Chinook nation
and villages that occupied the lower banks of the Columbia River. Two and a
half miles west of the mouth of the Chinook River, the Wallacut River enters
the bay. On November 19, 1805, Clark and eleven men camped on the eastern
side of the Wallacut after returning from an exploration of Cape Disappointment and Long Beach. The present name for the river comes from the Indian
Walihut ("place of stones"). Lewis and Clark called it White Brant Creek.

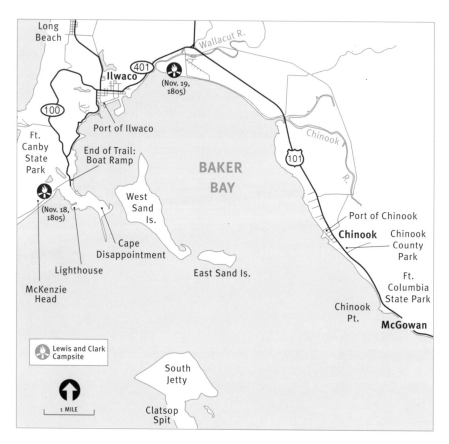

Long
Beach

Wallacut R.

401

Ilwaco

(Nov. 19,
1805)

100

Ft.
Canby
State
Park

Port of Ilwaco

End of Trail:
Boat Ramp

Chinook

101

**BAKER
BAY**

(Nov. 18,
1805)

West
Sand
Is.

Port of Chinook

Chinook   Chinook
County
Park

Cape
Disappointment

Lighthouse

East Sand Is.

Ft.
Columbia
State Park

McKenzie
Head

Chinook
Pt.

McGowan

Lewis and Clark
Campsite

South
Jetty

1 MILE

Clatsop
Spit

Trail Reach 16

BOATING CAUTIONS AND CONDITIONS

This reach is subject to the direct influence of the ocean. It should be undertaken only if you are very experienced with saltwater paddling in open waters under rough conditions. The shallow area off the town of Chinook should be crossed only at high tide. Be especially aware of the three very dangerous, lengthy wing dams lying off of Chinook Point. The long, dredged Chinook Channel leads to a launch ramp, moorage, fuel, and supplies. The Port of Ilwaco is 4 miles further down the Baker Bay shoreline and is reached by another long dredged channel. Restaurants, motels, a grocery store, and laundry services are within a short walking distance. Continue on down the shoreline to Fort Canby State Park, the official end of the Lewis and Clark Columbia River Water Trail in Washington. Do not attempt to reach the other end of the water trail near Fort Clatsop in Oregon by crossing the Columbia here. Instead, return upriver (as the expedition did) to the Jim Crow Point area before crossing the river. From this point, steer south between Woody and Horseshoe Islands and head down Devil's Elbow to Prairie Channel.

RIVER ACCESSES

Chinook County Park

FACILITIES	Boat ramp, picnic area, water, toilets.
ACTIVITIES	Picnicking.
RESTRICTIONS	Day use only.

This well-maintained county park is located on the Columbia just east of the town of Chinook at milepost 3.8 on Highway 101, about a mile west of Fort Columbia State Park. To reach it, turn off Highway 101 at Chinook Park Road. The park is long and narrow and offers a boat ramp (best used at high tide) and a panoramic view of Baker Bay and the Sand Islands.

Port of Chinook

FACILITIES	Boat ramps, docks, moorage, fuel, toilets.
ACTIVITIES	Launching only.
RESTRICTIONS	Day use only. Fee.

This port is located at milepost 4 on Highway 101, 3.5 miles northwest of the Astoria-Megler Bridge. The mooring basin and boat ramps are at the foot of

Portland Street. The harbor is protected by a long rock jetty. Fresh seafood is also for sale here. Phone 360-777-8797.

Port of Ilwaco

FACILITIES	Boat ramps, docks, showers, toilets, restaurants, shops, seafood markets.
ACTIVITIES	Shopping.
RESTRICTIONS	Day use only. Fee for boat launching.

Ilwaco is about 11 miles west of the Astoria-Megler Bridge. To reach the port facility from Highway 101 (Spruce Street) in Ilwaco, turn toward the river on Elizabeth Street and follow it to the ramp at the end of the spit that forms the mooring basin. This safe harbor, with its many facilities and services, is accessible twenty-four hours a day, seven days a week. Phone 360-642-3143.

Port of Ilwaco.

On the beach near here Clark saw a California condor feeding on a whale carcass. The bird was shot and one of its large wings taken back and given to President Jefferson. The Ilwaco Heritage Museum, 115 SE Lake Street, includes Lewis and Clark exhibits and features four thematic galleries and outdoor displays. It is open from 9:00 A.M. to 5:00 P.M. Monday through Saturday and from 12:00 P.M. to 4:00 P.M. Sunday. The Ilwaco area also offers many bed-and-breakfasts and other accommodations. The city was founded in 1868 and has a colorful history. For example, conflicts that took place here between gill netters and fish trappers in the late 1890s required armed intervention.

Fort Canby State Park

FACILITIES	Boat ramp, interpretive center, lighthouse, large camp ground, picnic areas, hiking trails, toilets.
ACTIVITIES	Camping, hiking, picnicking, touring interpretive center and lighthouse.
RESTRICTIONS	Fee for boat launching.

This 1,884-acre park is located 3 miles southwest of Ilwaco off Highway 101 and includes 250 campsites. To reach it, drive west on Highway 101 (Spruce Street) through Ilwaco. When the highway turns north, continue west on Robert Gray Drive to the park. The boat ramp is located on the eastern side of the park on Baker Bay. You can also hand-launch your craft in the park at "Waikiki Beach" on the western side of Cape Disappointment. Continue past the park entrance on North Jetty Road for 200 yards to a parking lot on the left. There is no ramp here, but there is a sandy beach for launching just west of the parking lot. This day-use area includes toilets, picnic tables, and barbecue grills, and a camping area is across the road. Tours of the historic Cape Disappointment Lighthouse are also available (see Plate 25). Four trails lead to the scenic headlands of the park. Phone 360-642-3078. This park marks the official end of the water trail in Washington.

Fort Canby was first called Fort Cape Disappointment and later Fort Canby Reservation. In 1852 Congress authorized this military post to be placed at the mouth of the Columbia River. Completed in 1865, it was named in 1875 to honor Brevet Major General Edward Canby, killed in the Modoc Indian War. After World War II the fort was converted to a state park, and in 1976 the Lewis and Clark Interpretive Center was constructed near the underground batteries of the old army fort. The center has received a multimillion-dollar remodeling and now provides a comprehensive story of the expedition, history of the river, and grand views of the mouth of the Columbia. Exhibits portray the medical treatment, food, entertainment, and discipline involved in the expedition (including sketches of expedition members) and important contributions made by the many Indian tribes.

On November 18, 1805, Clark, along with eleven men, explored Cape Disappointment and camped near the base of McKenzie Head in what is now

Fort Canby. Photo by Ellen Morris Bishop.

Fort Canby State Park. Washington State plans to build a replica campsite here, with outdoor interpretive panels. This once beachfront campsite has changed since the time of Lewis and Clark, however, and is now surrounded by an alder forest. After exploring for 19 miles, Clark climbed McKenzie Head for the view, then walked along the beach and even carved his name on a tree in the Long Beach area. Earlier Lewis had climbed Cape Disappointment and carved his name on a tree, which Clark later located.

Cape Disappointment, whose name is among the oldest geographical names in Washington State, was called No-wehl-kai-ilse by the Chinooks. Its present name was bestowed in 1788 by British sea captain and fur trader John Meares. Meares was looking for the Columbia River, and though he had found it, he later concluded that the mouth of the river was only an entrance to a bay. In his discouragement at missing the river, he named the nearby headland Cape Disappointment. The treacherous river bar and high waves created what early seamen called the Graveyard of the Pacific. The cape is crowned by an 1856 lighthouse 220 feet above the water.

A hiking trail at Cape Disappointment. Photo by Ellen Morris Bishop.

OTHER FACILITIES AND POINTS OF INTEREST

Long Beach
FACILITIES   Stores, beaches, motels, restaurants.
ACTIVITIES   Beachcombing.
RESTRICTIONS   None.

It was here, on November 19, 1805, that Clark carved his name and the date on the trunk of a small pine tree. The event is commemorated by a small city park at the northern end of what is called the Discovery Trail. A bronze pine tree designates the most northwestern point achieved by the Corps of Discovery.

Twenty-eight miles long and aptly named, Long Beach is the nation's longest natural beach. The many hiking and nature trails around Cape Disappointment and in the nearby Willapa National Wildlife Refuge and Leadbetter Point State Park (both of which are north of this trail reach) offer the opportunity to view the natural history of the peninsula, its estuaries, and its thousand-year-old western red cedars. The Discovery Trail retraces the expedition's route from the Ilwaco area, over the headlands, and up the Long Beach Peninsula to the city of Long Beach.

SUGGESTED DAY AND OVERNIGHT TRIPS

Ilwaco to West Sand and East Sand Islands
DISTANCE   4 miles round-trip.
CAMPING   West Sand Island.

The Sand Islands are dredge-spoil islands created by the Army Corps of Engineers and will be turned over to Bureau of Land Management jurisdiction. Be careful of wind and waves in this area, especially on the southern side of West Sand Island, which offers excellent birding but has no facilities. Primitive camping is available on this island.

East Sand Island is now a federal refuge for colonial nesting seabirds, including some thirteen thousand Caspian terns, several thousand pairs of gulls, six to seven thousand double-crested cormorants, and at least four thousand brown pelicans. Needless to say, visitors are not allowed on any portion of this small island. Boating around it is permissible, however, and observing this incredible number and variety of birds from the water is an unforgettable experience.

The Caspian tern population on East Sand Island was relocated from Rice Island, where the birds were consuming more than ten million young salmon a year. At the new nesting grounds, salmon smolt constitute only 33 percent of the birds' diet, compared with a previous 75 to 90 percent. This is due to the variety of other species in the area, such as herring, anchovies, and sardines. Caspian terns arrive in April from Mexico and leave in October.

Conversion Tables

INCHES	CENTIMETERS		MILES	KILOMETERS
$^1/_4$	0.60		$^1/_4$	0.40
$^1/_2$	1.25		$^1/_2$	0.80
$^3/_4$	1.90		$^3/_4$	1.20
1	2.50		1	1.60
2	5.00		2	3.20
3	7.50		3	4.80
4	10.00		4	6.40
5	12.50		5	8.00
6	15.00		6	9.60
7	17.50		7	11.20
8	20.00		8	12.80
9	22.50		9	14.40
10	25.00		10	16.00
			20	32.00
			30	48.00
FEET	METERS		40	64.00
$^1/_4$	0.08		50	80.00
$^1/_2$	0.15		60	96.00
$^3/_4$	0.23		70	112.00
1	0.30		80	128.00
2	0.60		90	144.00
3	0.90		100	160.00
4	1.20		500	800.00
5	1.50		1,000	1,600.00
6	1.80		10,000	16,000.00
7	2.10			
8	2.40			
9	2.70			
10	3.00			
20	6.00			
30	9.00			
40	12.00			
50	15.00			

$$^\circ C = {}^5/_9 \times (^\circ F - 32)$$
$$^\circ F = (^9/_5 \times {}^\circ C) + 32$$

Lower Columbia River Water Trail Committee

To address the lack of safe and accessible campsites and the maintenance of an environmentally sensitive water trail, a bistate coalition, representing broad interests, has formed the Lower Columbia River Water Trail Committee. This group, composed of individuals, organizations, businesses, and government agencies from Oregon and Washington, works as an ad hoc committee of the Lower Columbia River Estuary Partnership in cooperation with the National Park Service's Rivers and Trails Program. All interested parties are invited to join. Phone 503-226-1565.

The goals of the committee are to promote the water trail as a valuable resource for recreation, education, and stewardship; increase and improve launch, landing, and camping sites for small, nonmotorized watercraft; promote places of historical, cultural, and recreational interest along the river; and to connect people physically, intellectually, and spiritually with the lower Columbia.

Lewis and Clark
Discovery Greenway

The Lewis and Clark Discovery Greenway is among the most unique and innovative bistate projects to have come out of the Lewis and Clark Bicentennial. As the expedition paddled their way through what is now the Portland-Vancouver metropolitan region, they stopped to camp or explore at fourteen sites. These locations, from Rooster Rock to the Ridgefield National Wildlife Refuge, constitute a rich historical, cultural, and ecological resource for the bistate region. Protecting, restoring, and connecting the sites represents a 75-mile spine of commemorative improvements linked by roads and hiking, biking, and water trails. Such linkage provides a connectivity among the locations and enhances the ability of residents and visitors to experience, firsthand, via different modes of travel, the educational, environmental, and historical meaning of the expedition's passage through the area.

The project also creates regional partnerships with individuals, groups, and agencies to develop useful, functional, and permanent installations and images that will help define the region's identity and explain its rich historical riverine heritage for residents and tourists alike for decades to come.

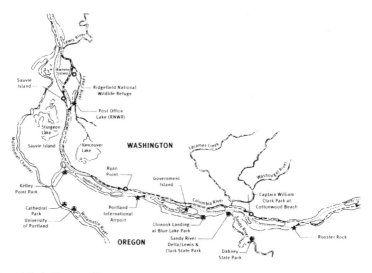

The Lewis and Clark Discovery Greenway.

Geographical Features
Named by Lewis and Clark

The following list includes the names of geographical features covered in this book. Names given by Lewis and Clark are provided with their contemporary equivalents and are organized geographically east to west.

NAME GIVEN BY LEWIS AND CLARK	CURRENT NAME
Brant Island	Bradford Island, Oreg.
Strawberry Island	Hamilton Island, Wash.
Beaton Rock Creek	Woodward Creek, Wash.
Broad Brook	Hamilton Creek, Wash.
Beaton Rock, Beacon Rock	Beacon Rock, Wash.
Phoca, Seal Rock	Phoca Rock, Oreg.
Quick Sand River	Sandy River, Oreg.
Seal River, Sea Calf River	Washougal River, Wash.
White Brant Island, Island of Fowl	Lady Island, Wash.
Diamond Island	Government Island, Oreg.
White Goose Island, Twin Island	Lemon Island, Oreg.
Image Canoe Island	Hayden Island, Oreg.
Tomahawk Island	Tomahawk Island, Oreg.
Mount Jefferson	Mount Jefferson, Oreg.
Multnomah River	Willamette River, Oreg.
Wappato Island	Sauvie Island, Oreg.
Wap-pa-too Valley, Columbia Valley	Portland-Vancouver area, Oreg.
Green Bryor Island, Cathlapotle Island	Bachelor Island, Wash.
E-lal-lar Island, Deer Island	Deer Island, Oreg.
Cah-wah-na-hi-ooks River	Lewis River, Wash.
Cath-la-haws Creek	Kalama River, Wash.
Cow-e-lis-kee River	Cowlitz River, Wash.
Knob	Mount Coffin, Wash.
Fanny's Island	Crims Island, Oreg.
Fanny's Bottom, Fanny's Valley	Clatskanie Valley, Oreg.
Sturgeon Island	Wallace Island, Oreg.
Sea Otter Island	Puget Island, Wash.

NAME GIVEN BY LEWIS AND CLARK	CURRENT NAME
Marshey Islands	Tenasillahe Island, Oreg.
Rock	Pillar Rock, Wash.
Seal Islands	Woody, Horseshoe, Karlson, and Marsh Islands, Oreg.
Shallow Bay	Grays Bay, Wash.
Cape Swells	Portuguese Point, Wash.
Harbor Point	Cliff Point, Wash.
Point Distress, Blustering Point	Point Ellice, Wash.
Station Camp, Camp Point	McGowan, Wash.
Point Open Slope	Chinook Point, Wash.
Haley's Bay	Baker Bay, Wash.
Cape Disappointment	Cape Disappointment, Wash.
Point Adams	Point Adams, Oreg.
White Brant Creek	Wallacut River, Wash.
Chinook River	Chinook River, Wash.
Point Lewis	Leadbetter Point, Wash.
Point Samuel	Aldrich Point, Oreg.
Ke-ke-mar-que Creek	John Day River, Oreg.
Point William	Tongue Point, Oreg.
Point Meriwether	Smith Point, Oreg.
Meriwethers Bay	Youngs Bay, Oreg.
Kihow-a-nah-kle River, Wo-lump-ked River	Youngs River, Oreg.
Netul River, Fort River	Lewis and Clark River, Oreg.
Skip-a-nor-win River	Skipanon River, Oreg.

Animals and Plants Described by Lewis and Clark

President Jefferson instructed Lewis and Clark to take note of the animals and plants along their route. Although they were not expert zoologists or botanists, the expedition leaders described in great detail many mammals, birds, reptiles and amphibians, fish, trees, shrubs, and herbs that had never before been identified. Along with animal skins, they collected roots, bulbs, seeds, cuttings for propagation, and dried and pressed plants. Their collection was extensive while they were on the eastern side of the Rocky Mountains, but as they moved west it dwindled. At times in the mountains they were much more interested in collecting animals for food than collecting specimens for the president.

The difficulties of collecting animals and plants, preserving them, and transporting them back to civilization were magnified many times by the distance, rough terrain, and weather. The numerous plants collected up the Missouri River to Fort Mandan in North Dakota during the summer and fall of 1804, together with notations on their virtues and properties when known, were sent back to St. Louis in the spring of 1805. Specimens encountered beyond Fort Mandan, however, were not as readily conveyed back to civilization. For example, the exciting collection of new forms from the high prairies and Rocky Mountain foothills, tucked away for safekeeping in a bearskin cache at the Great Falls of the Missouri, were, by return-trip time, flood-soaked beyond recovery. As the journey became more arduous over the western mountains, Lewis and Clark, of necessity, showed less perseverance in animal and plant collecting. The return trip from the Pacific added little more. However, while at Fort Clatsop near the mouth of the Columbia, the expedition leaders found time to complete their journals, including lengthy descriptions of animals and plants in the Northwestern rainforest (Beidleman 1966). By the end of their journey they had described 178 plants and 122 animals previously unrecorded for science.

The following lists include the animals and plants Lewis and Clark identified from near the Columbia River below the present location of the Bonneville Dam. These lists have been excerpted from a comprehensive list compiled by Oregon botanists Jerry and Mike Igo in 1999 and from *Lewis and Clark: Pioneering Naturalists* (Cutright 1969). Along with the scientific and common name of each species, these lists include the date that species was recorded by Lewis and Clark and the location in which it was found. The Oregon grape, which is Oregon's state flower, is not included; although present along the lower Columbia, Lewis collected it upstream from Bonneville Dam. Current endangered and threatened species of the lower Columbia include the American peregrine falcon, lower Columbia River steelhead, Bradshaw's lomatium, Western snowy plover, Snake River sockeye salmon, brown pelican, marbled murrelet, water howellia, Aleutian Canada goose, Northern spotted owl, bald eagle, and Snake River chinook salmon.

FISH

SCIENTIFIC NAME	COMMON NAME	DATE	LOCATION
Acipenser transmontanus	white sturgeon	Nov. 11, 1805	Pacific City, Wash.
Platichthys stellatus	starry flounder	Mar. 13, 1806	Fort Clatsop, Oreg.
Salmo gairdneri	rainbow trout (steelhead)	Mar. 13, 1806	Fort Clatsop, Oreg.
Thaleichthys pacificus	eulachon	Feb. 24, 1806	Fort Clatsop, Oreg.

REPTILES AND AMPHIBIANS

SCIENTIFIC NAME	COMMON NAME	DATE	LOCATION
Taricha granulosa	rough-skinned newt	Mar. 11, 1806	Fort Clatsop, Oreg.
Thamnophis ordinoides	northwest garter snake	Mar. 28, 1806	Deer Island above Cowlitz, Wash.

BIRDS

SCIENTIFIC NAME	COMMON NAME	DATE	LOCATION
Aechmorphoris occidentalis	western grebe	Mar. 7, 1806	Fort Clatsop, Oreg.
Anser albifrons	white-fronted goose	Mar. 15, 1806	Fort Clatsop, Oreg.
Aythya collaris	ring-necked duck	Mar. 28, 1806	Fort Clatsop, Oreg.
Branta canadensis minima	lesser Canada goose	Mar. 8, 1806	Fort Clatsop, Oreg.
Bubo virginianus saturatus	dusky great-horned owl	Mar. 6, 1806	Fort Clatsop, Oreg.
Corvus brachyrhynchos	American crow	Nov. 29, 1805	Tongue Point, Oreg.
Corvus caurinus	northwestern crow	Mar. 3, 1806	Fort Clatsop, Oreg.
Corvus corax	common raven	Mar. 3, 1806	Fort Clatsop, Oreg.
Cygnus columbianus	tundra swan	Mar. 9, 1806	Fort Clatsop, Oreg.

SCIENTIFIC NAME	COMMON NAME	DATE	LOCATION
Dryocopus pileatus	pileated woodpecker	Mar. 4, 1806	Fort Clatsop, Oreg.
Fulmarus glacialis	northern fulmar	Mar. 7, 1806	Fort Clatsop, Oreg.
Gavia pacifica	Pacific loon	Mar. 7, 1806	Fort Clatsop, Oreg.
Gymnogyps californianus	California condor	Nov. 18, 1805	Mouth of the Columbia River
Larus glaucescens	glaucous-winged gull	Mar. 7, 1806	Fort Clatsop, Oreg.
Larus occidentalis	western gull	Mar. 7, 1806	Fort Clatsop, Oreg.
Larus philadelphia	Bonaparte's gull	Mar. 7, 1806	Fort Clatsop, Oreg.
Oreortyx pictus	mountain quail	Apr. 7, 1806	Washougal, Wash.
Perisoreus canadensis	gray jay	Jan. 3, 1806	Fort Clatsop, Oreg.
Picoides villosus	hairy woodpecker	Apr. 5, 1806	Mouth of the Willamette River, Oreg.
Podiceps grisegena	redneck grebe	Mar. 10, 1806	Fort Clatsop, Oreg.
Troglodytes pacificus	western winter wren	Mar. 4, 1806	Fort Clatsop, Oreg.
Tympanuchus phasianellus	Columbia sharp-tail grouse	Mar. 1, 1806	Fort Clatsop, Oreg.

MAMMALS

SCIENTIFIC NAME	COMMON NAME	DATE	LOCATION
Aplodontia rufa	mountain beaver	Feb. 26, 1806	Fort Clatsop, Oreg.
Cervus canadensis	Roosevelt elk	Dec. 2, 1805	Mouth of the Columbia River
Enhydra lutris	sea otter	Nov. 20, 1805	[furs collected from Columbia River Indians]
Eutamias townsendi	Townsend's chipmunk	Feb. 25, 1806	Fort Clatsop, Oreg.
Felisrufus fasciatus	Oregon bobcat	Feb. 21, 1806	Fort Clatsop, Oreg.
Odocoileus hemionus subsp.	Columbian black-tailed deer	Nov. 19, 1805	Mouth of the Columbia River
columbianus Phoca vitulina	harbor seal	Oct. 23, 1805	Below Celilo Falls, Oreg.
Procyon lotor	raccoon	Feb. 25, 1806	Fort Clatsop, Oreg.
Scapanus townsendi	Townsend's mole	Feb. 26, 1806	Fort Clatsop, Oreg.
Tamiasciurus douglasi	chickaree	Feb. 25, 1806	Fort Clatsop, Oreg.
Taxidea taxus	western badger	Feb. 26, 1806	Fort Clatsop, Oreg.
Vulpes fulva	western red fox	Feb. 21, 1806	Fort Clatsop, Oreg.

PLANTS

SCIENTIFIC NAME	COMMON NAME	DATE	LOCATION
Abies grandis	grand fir	Feb. 6, 1806	Fort Clatsop, Oreg.
Alnus rubra	red alder	Mar. 26, 1806	Near Cowlitz River, Wash.
Argentina anserina	cinquefoil	Mar. 13, 1806	Fort Clatsop, Oreg.
Blechnum spicant	deer fern	Jan. 20, 1806	Fort Clatsop, Oreg.
Cardamine nuttallii	slender toothwort	Apr. 1, 1806	Mouth of the Sandy River, Oreg.
Cirsium edule	edible thistle	Mar. 13, 1806	Fort Clatsop, Oreg.
Claytonia parviflora	small-flowered montia	Mar. 26, 1806	Cowlitz River, Wash.
Claytonia sibirica	candyflower	Apr. 8, 1806	Beacon Rock, Wash.
Cornus nuttallii	Pacific dogwood	Apr. 5, 1806	Mouth of the Sandy River, Oreg.
Dryopteris austriaca	mountain woodfern	Jan. 20, 1806	Fort Clatsop, Oreg.
Equisetum spp.	horsetail	Jan. 22, 1806	Fort Clatsop, Oreg.
Fraxinus latifolia	Oregon ash	Nov. 30, 1805	Astoria, Oreg.
Fritillaria affinis	chocolate lily	Apr. 10, 1806	Bradford Island, Oreg.
Gaultheria shallon	salal	Jan. 20, 1806	Fort Clatsop, Oreg.
Hordeum jubatum	foxtail barley	Mar. 13, 1806	Fort Clatsop, Oreg.
Leymus mollis	American dune grass	Nov. 18, 1805	Cape Disappointment, Wash.
Lupinus littoralis	seashore lupine	Jan. 24, 1806	Fort Clatsop, Oreg.
Malus fusca	western crabapple	Jan. 28, 1806	Fort Clatsop, Oreg.
Oxalis oregana	redwood sorrel	Mar. 15, 1806	Fort Clatsop, Oreg.
Paxistima myrsinites	Oregon boxwood	Nov. 16, 1805	Baker Bay, Wash.
Physocarpus capitatus	ninebark	Mar. 25, 1806	Lower Columbia River
Picea sitchensis	Sitka spruce	Feb. 4, 1806	Fort Clatsop, Oreg.
Pinus monticola	white pine	Feb. 2, 1806	Fort Clatsop, Oreg.
Polysttichum munitum	sword fern	Feb. 13, 1806	Fort Clatsop, Oreg.
Pseudotsuga menziesii	Douglas fir	Feb. 6, 1806	Fort Clatsop, Oreg.
Pteridium aquilinum	bracken fern	Jan. 22, 1806	Fort Clatsop, Oreg.
Quercus garryana	Oregon white oak	Mar. 26, 1806	Below Cowlitz River, Wash.
Ribes divaricatum	straggly gooseberry	Mar. 25, 1806	Puget Island, Wash.

SCIENTIFIC NAME	COMMON NAME	DATE	LOCATION
Ribes sanguineum	red-flowering currant	Mar. 27, 1806	Mouth of the Cowlitz River, Wash.
Rubus spectabilis	salmonberry	Mar. 27, 1806	Mouth of the Cowlitz River, Wash.
Rubus ursinus	trailing blackberry	Mar. 25, 1806	Puget Island, Wash.
Sagittaria latifolia	wappato	Mar. 30, 1806	Sauvie Island, Oreg.
Sambucus caerulea	blue elderberry	Feb. 2, 1806	Fort Clatsop, Oreg.
Thuja plicata	western redcedar	Nov. 6, 1805	Puget Island, Wash.
Trillium ovatum	trillium	Apr. 10, 1806	Bradford Island, Oreg.
Tsuga heterophylla	western hemlock	Feb. 5, 1806	Fort Clatsop, Oreg.
Typha latifolia	cattail	Nov. 6, 1805	Puget Island, Wash.
Urtica dioica	stinging nettle	Mar. 25, 1806	Puget Island, Wash.
Vaccinium membranaceum	square-twig bilberry	Feb. 7, 1806	Fort Clatsop, Oreg.
Vaccinium ovatum	coast huckleberry	Jan. 27, 1806	Fort Clatsop, Oreg.

GPS Navigation
of the Water Trail

Navigation along the Lewis and Clark Trail consisted of Clark using a compass and dead reckoning to determine heading and distances traveled day by day. Astronomical observations were made by the captains at periodic intervals to establish latitude position along the trail. Obtaining accurate positioning required precise celestial observations and complex calculations to be made in the field under very difficult circumstances. In spite of these limitations, Clark created maps of the expedition's route that amaze and impress cartographers to this day.

The completion of the Global Positioning System (GPS) in the early 1990s revolutionized global navigation. GPS relies on twenty-four low-earth-orbiting satellites in combination with inexpensive ground-based receivers to provide a precise position anywhere on the globe. In addition to position information, GPS data includes distance traveled, duration of travel, direction of travel, average speed, and other useful information.

Before setting out, make sure you understand when to use the GPS and when to use a chart and compass. Familiarize yourself with the tools of navigation and how they work together. GPS devices are very complex handheld computers that take time and effort to master and use. It is equally important to understand more "old-fashioned" navigation methods. GPS receivers can fail; batteries can go dead. GPS is not a substitute for understanding how to correctly use a chart and compass; it is simply a tool that can add to the safety and enjoyment of an outing.

Use current maps and charts, including this water guide, to select your route and plan your trip. Several very good sources for digital maps and navigation applications can be loaded onto a personal computer to make this very easy and enjoyable. These maps and applications can be found at most outdoor stores or where GPS receivers are sold. Once you know where you want to go, you can use a personal computer to create waypoints along your intended route. These digital "bread crumbs" can then be uploaded to the GPS receiver and linked together to create a map of your intended route, from the trailhead to the desired destination.

On the water trail use the GPS receiver to establish a new waypoint or position at the trailhead. This will be very useful when navigating back to the starting point. Know where you are on your map and verify it against the new waypoint. If the collected waypoint does not match the previously stored waypoint for the trailhead, make sure you understand why before you rely on the routes and waypoints you have stored in your GPS. Make sure you have extra batteries, maps, and a compass. Once on the trail, collect and store GPS waypoint information at important junctions, turns, and landmarks. This will be very useful information if you need to retrace your route or if you get lost. It will also allow you to plot your exploration on a map at a later time. Monitor the data from your GPS receiver to provide valuable information about your trip. How far is it to the campsite? What is your average speed? How long will it take to return to the trailhead? This information may save you from having to find camp or the trailhead in the dark.

If you wish to try your hand at locating Lewis and Clark campsite areas, use the following list, which includes latitude and longitude coordinates on all twenty-five 1805 and 1806 campsites from Bonneville Dam to the coast:

CAMPSITE AREA	LATITUDE	LONGITUDE	DATE
Fort Rains, Wash.	45 39.216	121 54.857	Nov. 1, 1805
Rooster Rock, Oreg.	45 32.465	122 16.224	Nov. 2, 1805
Government Island, Oreg.	45 34.823	122 30.343	Nov. 3, 1805
Post Office Lake, Wash.	45 44.303	122 45.123	Nov. 4, 1805
Prescott Beach County Park, Oreg.	46 3.410	122 53.777	Nov. 5, 1805
Wallace Island/ Cape Horn, Wash.	46 9.086	123 16.471	Nov. 6, 1805
Opposite Pillar Rock, in Wash.	46 15.653	123 35.236	Nov. 7, 1805
Portuguese Point, Wash.	46 16.897	123 45.253	Nov. 8–Nov. 9, 1805
Point Ellice, Wash.	46 14.922	123 52.016	Nov. 10–Nov. 14, 1805
Station Camp, Wash.	46 15.052	123 55.003	Nov. 15–Nov. 25, 1805
Opposite Pillar Rock, in Wash.	46 15.652	123 35.144	Nov. 25, 1805
Settler Point, Oreg.	46 10.023	123 41.545	Nov. 26, 1805
Tongue Point, Oreg.	46 12.320	123 45.904	Nov. 27–Dec. 7
Fort Clatsop, Oreg.	46 8.041	123 52.756	Dec. 7, 1805– Mar. 23, 1806

CAMPSITE AREA	LATITUDE	LONGITUDE	DATE
Mill Creek/ Tongue Point, Oreg.	46 11.594	123 45.714	Mar. 23, 1806
Aldrich Point, Oreg.	46 14.113	123 30.788	Mar. 24, 1806
Clatskanie River, Oreg.	46 8.264	123 13.931	Mar. 25, 1806
Walker Island, Oreg.	46 8.7671	123 2.846	Mar. 26, 1806
Goble, Oreg.	46 0.905	122 52.451	Mar. 27, 1806
Deer Island, Oreg.	45 59.005	122 50.887	Mar. 28, 1806
Bachelor Island/ Wapato Portage, Wash.	45 49.9981	122 45.624	Mar. 29, 1806
Vancouver, Wash.	45 36.896	122 39.058	Mar. 30, 1806
Cottonwood Beach, Wash.	45 34.615	122 21.491	Mar. 31–Apr. 6, 1806
Shepperd's Dell State Park, Oreg.	45 32.658	122 13.364	Apr. 6–Apr. 8, 1806
Bradford Island, Oreg.	45 38.210	121 56.866	Apr. 9, 1806
Fort Rains, Wash.	45 39.216	121 54.857	Apr. 10–Apr. 11, 1806

River Safety

There are many potential hazards involved in paddling, and for this reason it is essential to familiarize yourself with safety procedures. Before undertaking any boating trip, make certain you know what to do should anything go wrong. The Lewis and Clark Columbia River Water Trail includes its own particular dangers; see the Boating Cautions and Conditions entry included for each trail reach for descriptions of specific things to watch out for.

FLOAT PLAN

Before Lewis and Clark first departed for their voyage, they did what all good boaters do: they left a float plan. So should you. The explorers left their plan with President Jefferson, and you should leave yours with your own reliable friend. A float plan is a simple note to leave with someone who can notify the proper authorities if you do not return as scheduled. It should include name, age, address, and phone number of all members of your party; place, time, and date of departure; place, time, and date of expected return; type of boat, car, and trailer, including color, hull, and tag numbers; destination of trip and route; and survival equipment aboard, including cell phone, distress signals, whistle, mirror, flares, glow sticks, and so on. From a safety standpoint it is always prudent to boat with others in case you need assistance. Despite how rewarding it might be, solo boating is not recommended; but if you must do it, keep to stretches of water you are familiar with, and do not hesitate to seek refuge if weather conditions change.

WEATHER AND BOATING CONDITIONS

This is not an instruction manual on how to boat. All boaters assume responsibility for their own safety when out on the water. The Columbia is a powerful river, embracing many conditions that may not apply to other water recreation areas. Every boater should be aware of these conditions.

The wind on the Columbia can whip up huge waves, which can be downright dangerous for small boats, especially when the combination of river currents and fluctuating tides are added to the equation. Small-craft travelers should plan to start their day early, as the sun is the great wind generator. Some areas have more intense wind than is average for the area, typically as a result of wind bouncing off a high bluff. The upstream tip of Puget Island is a good example, and this is why it is so popular with sail boarders.

In summer you can expect sea breezes that vary, plus or minus 10 knots. Once started they usually last until sunset. Wind and water conditions can rapidly change from a glassy calm to 1- to 2-foot whitecaps. Wind blowing against the current builds steeper, higher waves than otherwise occurs. This condition can be used to detect areas where the current is fastest and can cause conditions to be roughest in the middle of the shipping channel. Some areas— Skamokawa, for example—have long fetches where the wind tends to blow onshore or from the southwest. This can result in waves that break on the beach and make for very difficult paddling or boating conditions. Along the Columbia River corridor, wind typically blows from the east (downriver) in winter and from the west (upriver) in summer.

When preparing for a trip, check weather conditions on local radio, Coast Guard radio, or the National Weather Service VHF/FM. Many boaters carry weather radios, which are relatively inexpensive and very useful. Concentrate on listening for wind directions and speeds. Wind means weather to the small boat skipper and can change with the turn of the river or the hour of the day. It can rain anytime of the year, and it rarely gets very hot on the Columbia. Water temperature in winter is below 50°F, so wetsuits or drysuits are recommended; in summer, water can be near 70°F. Check for storm-warning flags at Coast Guard stations, marinas, public docks, and yacht clubs.

Fog is another longtime river hazard, even more dangerous now than it was for the Corps of Discovery, since river traffic has increased so dramatically. If you are caught in a dense fog, it is best to wait until visibility improves—or at least proceed slowly so as to avoid other boats, shallows, rocky shoals, narrow side channels, snags, floating debris, sunken logs, pilings, and wing dams. All of these dangers are present even when visibility is good.

Tidal action affects water level almost up to the water trailhead at Bonneville. Below Portland the tidal elevation change can be nearly 7 feet, and at the river's mouth up to 12 feet. The tide changes direction every six hours. With a rising (flood) tide, the water mass moves inland and effectively "dams" or slows down the outflow of the river. When the tide reverses to the ebb tide, the river level begins to drop rapidly and there is an increase in the speed of the downriver current. These six-hour tide shifts can be used to enhance your ease of travel by coordinating your movements with the rise and fall of the river. Traveling with the current, you can often double your speed. This is essential information when selecting campsites, timing trips, or planning routes. With an incoming tide, the currents everywhere, except in the main channel, typically reverse direction and flow upstream. The reversal affects the estuaries of tributary streams and can reach as far inland as St. Helens. In the main channel, current direction changes more dramatically during periods of low water. Tide tables are available at most marine- and sporting-goods stores.

Paddling in shallow areas when the tide is going out can be very dangerous. The deep mud that remains will not support body weight, and you can become very stuck and potentially drown when the tide returns. Two experienced paddlers recently spent two days stranded on Welch Island for this reason. They arrived on the higher high tide, and the high tide that arrived twelve hours later was the lower high tide—not enough to paddle back out.

Some wing dams extend great distances into the river, and it is common for them to be submerged in spring and early summer, although there is usually a taller tripod of pilings (dolphin) at the end. Most are shown on marine charts, and many also carry channel markers. These wing dams, when you are traveling downstream, constitute "strainers," and a small boat, especially a paddle craft, can easily be caught on the upstream side and trapped against the dam or even rolled. The force of the current can pin a boat inextricably against the pilings. The current tends to be quite turbulent near the end of these dams and is a potential spilling zone. Try to avoid traveling between any offshore piling or dolphin and the shore. Stay alert to avoid these dangers.

Floating timber is a hazard, and even the most proficient boaters have lost their lives in collisions with logs. Some paddlers use an unofficial "log signal" in which a paddle is held horizontally in one hand above the head to warn others of a hazard.

BOAT TRAFFIC AND RULES OF THE ROAD

The Columbia River is a very busy marine highway for the many oceangoing tankers, cargo ships, and U.S. Navy and Coast Guard vessels that pass up and down it. Smaller vessels such as tugboats, barges, commercial and recreational fishing boats, and work boats come and go as well, as do water-skiers and jet-skiers. During the commercial fishing season, gill nets are strung across parts of the river. Avoid them by going around the ends.

Like highways, rivers have rules that govern the right-of-way. These rules, called the Rules of the Road, have the force of both state and federal law. To help avoid collisions when two boats are on crossing pathways, the boat on the right (the stand-on boat) has the right-of-way. It must hold course and speed. The boat on the left (the give-way boat) keeps clear and passes behind the stand-on boat. A boat being overtaken has the right-of-way. It must also hold course and speed. The passing boat must keep a sufficient distance to avoid colliding with the other boat or endangering it with its wake. When two boats approach each other head-on, each must alter course to the right to avoid collision. By law, large boats (those over 65 feet long) have the right-of-way where they have no room to maneuver or where they would be put in jeopardy by changing course to avoid a smaller boat. So, watch out for the big ones! They move much faster than they appear to and cannot stop or swerve to miss you even if they do see you. A simple and temporary change of your course to the right will avoid risk.

Pleasure boaters should make every effort to stay out of the shipping channels. Never cross the main channel unless you have a clear view of the channel in both directions. Always be aware of traffic on the shipping channel. The surge or wake from passing ships can swamp the shoreline, pulling improperly secured boats into the river. At every rest stop or camping spot, place your boat 10 to 15 feet above the apparent high-tide line.

In addition to the danger of direct collision with a large vessel is the danger caused by its wake, especially in shallow water where the wake breaks into a surf wave. After reaching the shore such waves may rebound and send a wave back that can create turbulence. Large oceangoing vessels often give the appearance of not leaving a wake. Such illusions can be hazardous, as these huge ships usually form a large roller-coaster series of waves. Wakes from large yachts are much steeper, even in deep water, and unloaded tugboats generate the steepest waves of all. To safely meet these waves, a small craft should turn to meet them head-on or at a quartering angle.

NAVIGATIONAL AIDS

Navigational aids are similar to highway traffic signs, helping you locate your position and steer clear of dangerous places or restricted areas. They may include moored floating buoys, signs attached to pilings, or painted informational signs mounted on towers. For example, range markers have been erected to help boaters navigate within channels. They are painted international orange with a black stripe. A safe course can be steered by lining up two range markers and staying within that alignment. Some navigational aids are lighted, and some include whistles, bells, or gongs. When moving downstream, green channel markers with odd numbers establish the right (starboard) edge of the channel, and red channel markers with even numbers show where the left (port) edge of the navigation channel is located. All of these navigational aids are shown on nautical charts.

CHARTS AND MAPS

The USGS topographical maps do not contain the information necessary for any kind of boating. To follow the Lewis and Clark Columbia River Water Trail, obtain and carry the NOAA nautical charts appropriate for the trail reaches you intend to boat. These include water depths, locations, and descriptions of aids to navigation (lights, buoys, and so on), hazards to navigation (for example, wing dams), and location of the shipping channel. Many areas become mudflats at low tide; these are clearly marked on nautical charts, but not on topographical maps. NOAA nautical charts from the trailhead to the coast include Chart 18531 The Dalles to Vancouver, Chart 18525 Vancouver to St. Helens, Chart 18524 St. Helens to Crims Island, Chart 18523 Crims Island to Harrington Point, and Chart 18521 Harrington Point to the Pacific Ocean. NOAA nautical charts are available from nautical and boating supply stores or may be obtained free of charge on the Internet. Check out Maptech's MAPSERVER at www.maptech.com or phone 1-888-433-8500, extension 209.

ANCHORING

When anchored in shallow water or pulled up on a beach, a small boat can take a beating from the breaking surf of a ship's wake. Proper anchoring involves an understanding of river currents and the effects of the tide. First select a well-protected area, preferably with a flat bottom. Head the boat into the wind or current and approach your spot slowly. Stop the boat and slowly lower the anchor to the bottom. The anchor line should be attached to the bow, made of nylon, and seven to ten times as long as the depth of water. The use of a float on the line is also recommended. This allows you to throw your anchor line overboard if a large ship or debris is coming, and then pick it up later. Check your position frequently with landmarks so as to detect drifting. To pull the anchor, move into the current until the line is vertical, then pull straight up. Tides result in great changes of water level, so it is very dangerous to tie your boat to a stationary object.

READING THE RIVER

Reading the river is an important skill to learn. With it you can recognize what's happening ahead in the river current. Anticipating events while boating is similar to driving on the freeway. Look ahead. Notice where the current is flowing in relation to the shoreline, islands, wing dams, and sand bars. The deep water is not always in the center of the river. On a bend it moves to the outside of the curve, with shallow, slow-moving water on the inside. You will find shallow water wherever the current slows down: near the shoreline, below islands, and at entrances to side sloughs.

RUNNING AGROUND

The Columbia is relatively shallow in many areas and filled with sandbars and mudbanks. If you should run aground—and it is easy to do—don't panic. Depending on the state of the tide, your grounding may or may not be serious. If the tide is rising, just be patient. The water will rise enough to float your boat again. If the tide is falling, try rocking or poling the boat to loosen the bottom. Be wary of getting out of the boat to push it off: you could quickly sink to your knees in the mud. In a powerboat you may have the option of churning a channel in the bottom with your prop. The only danger would be if you were to get sand into your water-cooling intake. Hail another boater for assistance, or as a last resort—and only if a real danger or emergency is present—call the Coast Guard. They monitor UHF Marine Channel 16 for emergency and distress calls.

SAFETY EQUIPMENT

All boats must carry U.S. Coast Guard—approved life jackets, or personal flotation devices (PFDs), in serviceable condition and readily available for every person aboard. Youths twelve and under *must* wear a life jacket when underway. Manually propelled boats are also required to have ready at hand a flashlight or lighted lantern showing a white light between sunset and sunrise and during periods of restricted visibility. Motorboats have some additional requirements, depending on their length and whether they are inboard or outboard. If you boat at night or in periods when visibility is limited, running lights are required.

CAPSIZING

If your boat swamps, do not panic. If you are not wearing your life jacket, grab it and hang on to it, or find some other floating object. Stay with the boat. In a fast-moving current, move to the upstream side so you will not be crushed if the boat hangs up on a rock or other projection. Do not swim for shore unless there is absolutely no chance of rescue and you are certain you can make it. To lessen the problem of hypothermia, keep your head out of the water and do not remove clothes or shoes. If possible, get in the boat to get as far out of the water as possible. If you are alone, assume a fetal position to help preserve body heat. If there are others in the water, huddle close in a circle.

MAN OVERBOARD

Throw a life jacket, cushion, or some other floating object to anyone who has fallen overboard, even if they can swim. If underway, slow the boat and keep the person in view. If it is nighttime, direct the best possible light onto them. Try to approach the victim from downwind. Assess what other help is available. If the person is injured and someone aboard is capable, a rescuer with a life jacket and safety line may enter the water to assist. Always turn off your boat motor when alongside someone in the water. Help the person board the boat. If they are hurt or cold, assistance may be required. Depending on the size and construction of the boat, they should be brought in over the stern. Keep them as warm as possible with any available dry clothes.

PERSONAL AQUATIC SAFETY

Wearing a life jacket is the best precaution against drowning. Eighty percent of boating-fatality victims were not wearing a life jacket. Learning to float is another good precaution. Knowing how to do this with little effort will help you stay alive, even if you do not know how to swim. With your face out of the water, lean back and lift your legs as much as possible toward a horizontal position, arms out to the side. Relax, saving as much energy as you can.

If you go into the water without a life jacket or other floating object, treading water will keep your head above the surface and retard the onset of hypothermia. Treading water involves slow, steady movements of both the arms and legs. Put your arms in front of you, palms down. Move your hands and arms apart, palms out; then bring them back together, palms in. Put one leg forward, the other back. Reverse your leg positions and keep moving them as if you are walking in the water. While treading water or floating in cold water, do not discard clothing: the air trapped inside will help you stay afloat and retain body heat.

HYPOTHERMIA

Hypothermia results when the body loses heat faster than it can produce it, causing a dangerous reduction of its inner core temperature. The consequence of exposure to wind, cold temperatures, and wetness, it is a deadly and far too common problem on Oregon's waterways. When entering cold water, people experience a sudden cold-water shock reflex. This causes them to immediately gasp for air, which can result in water entering the lungs. Victims of hypothermia often turn blue-gray, and violent shivering develops that can give way to muscle spasms and even loss of the use of arms or legs. They may also exhibit confusion or behave as though intoxicated. When water temperature is 32.5°F, the expected time of survival is about fifteen to thirty minutes; when it is 32.5°F to 40°F, survival extends to thirty to forty minutes.

PADDLER'S CHOICE OF CRAFT

Paddling opportunities on the lower Columbia River vary from the main channel, with frequent strong winds and breaking waves, to the protected side channels, sloughs, and connecting lakes. Sea kayaks are the best choice for the main channel. Open canoes and recreation kayaks are fine for cruising around the many islands and exploring the shallower, quieter waters. Pay attention to the tide table, though: many a boater has become stranded on the mud as the tide recedes from those shallows. If this happens to you, it is best to wait for the tide to change, as it is impossible to walk to shore in deep, clinging mud, and swimming to shore is often not an option. Consider using additional flotation, make sure all your gear is securely stowed, and know how to reenter your craft, with or without help, in case of a capsize.

BOATING CHECKLISTS

Whether you are paddling or powerboating, take the following steps before launching: file a float plan with a reliable person, check your boat and equipment, check weather conditions, make sure everyone aboard has a life jacket, know how to read navigational aids, and acquire an annual Access Stewardship Decal to use the boat ramps maintained by the Washington Department of Fish and Wildlife.

If you are a powerboater, there are several items you will need to make sure you have on board, including boat registration, a throwable flotation device, navigation lights, sound-signaling device (horn or whistle), fire extinguisher, carburetor or flame arrester, muffler, ventilation system, bilge pump, and anchor and mooring line. Also make sure you brief passengers on emergency procedures before launching.

Once underway, both paddlers and powerboaters should strictly abide by the Rules of the Road and be considerate of other boaters at all times. To be safe, keep a low center of gravity, avoid consuming alcohol, pay strict attention to navigational aids, be aware of large vessels in the shipping channel, keep a lantern handy at night, and know how to signal for distress.

Several items should be brought along on your trip, among them a first-aid kit, extra paddle or oar, bailing bucket, rain gear, drinking water, pocket knife, flashlight, waterproof matches, sun and wind protection, nautical charts, compass, seat pads, extra water, repair and tool kit, cellular phone, VHF marine radio, snacks, and extra insulated clothing. If you are planning to camp, bring a stove, stove fuel, survival kit, tent, rain fly, extra food, cooking and eating utensils, waterproof bags, nylon cord, sleeping bag, sleeping pad, change of clothing, toilet articles, and any medicines you might need.

INVASIVE SPECIES

Our global economy today, with its increasing international trade, provides increased, unintentional hitchhiking of various plants and animals. This globetrotting of uninvited species began hundreds of years ago when foreign ships began arriving on our shores, bringing such species as the now common Norway rat, English sparrow, and European starling. The relocation of nonnative species to new ecosystems often results in severe economic and ecological impacts, including habitat destruction, disruption of local food chains, and even the extinction of native species. Some scientists consider this problem to be the primary cause of biodiversity loss throughout the world. The economic impact, by clogging filters, pipes, pumps, motors, and municipal and industrial water systems, causes millions of dollars of damage annually. The problem has become especially acute with invasive freshwater aquatic species. New Zealand mudsnails, zebra mussels, Eurasian watermilfoil, mitten crabs, and hydrilla are just a few of the species that boaters can spread if they are not careful. Mudsnails and zebra mussels are top-of-the-list threats and were introduced mainly through the discharge of ballast water by oceangoing vessels. Once here, they are spread when boaters move their crafts to new rivers or lakes.

A native of New Zealand, the mudsnail has now invaded Europe, Asia, and Australia. In the late 1980s it was discovered in the Snake River in Idaho, and today it is found in the headwaters of the Missouri and Columbia Rivers and in the waters of Yellowstone and Grand Teton National Parks. Mudsnails were recently found in California and at the mouth of the Columbia. Though tiny (about an eighth of an inch long), their threat is mighty, and they have an awesome reproductive potential. All mudsnails are female and reproduce asexually, capable of producing fifty offspring six times throughout the year. More than half a million mudsnails per square meter have been reported in rivers in Montana.

If you are bringing your boat to the Columbia from east of the 100th meridian (generally this means Oklahoma and states east of there), you could easily introduce the zebra mussel into the waters of Oregon and Washington, causing serious problems in the process. The mussels were accidentally introduced to the Great Lakes in 1986 after oceangoing ships discarded their ballast water. The mussels have now spread throughout the Great Lakes and the St. Lawrence, Ohio, and Mississippi Rivers, and every effort is being made to prevent their spread into western waterways.

To stop the spread of these exotic species, follow a few simple steps. First, inspect your boat hull and remove any plants or animals before leaving any body of water. Drain your live well, motor, and bilge before leaving a lake or river. Empty your bait bucket on land. Never release live bait into the water. (Use of live bait is prohibited in most Oregon waters.) Wash and scrub your boat and equipment with high-pressure hot water. A garden hose will do if no other option is available. Air-dry your boat and equipment for as long as possible; five days would be ideal.

Trail Etiquette

Lewis and Clark had to practice a careful code of etiquette with the different Indian nations they encountered, as their very survival depended on establishing good relationships. The Indians were so numerous that, if they had wanted to or had been provoked, they could have overwhelmed the Corps of Discovery and terminated the expedition. The explorers also needed food, guidance, and geographical information, which in many places only Indians could provide. The explorers had no choice but to be good neighbors.

While being a good neighbor may not be quite as critical today, it remains important for boaters to live in harmony. Boating etiquette begins at the boat ramp, where consideration means not blocking access with vehicles, boats, or gear while others are waiting to land or launch. It continues on the water, where the Rules Of The Road are meant to reduce conflict and dangerous situations. Besides following these rules, always be alert for downed water-skiers, swimmers, slow boats, and fishermen. If your boat produces a large wake, slow down to protect people and property when operating near docks, floating homes, and moorages. You are legally responsible for damage caused by your wake.

RESTRICTED-ACCESS PROPERTY

If you will be camping, be aware of restrictions. Obtain permission from landowners prior to landing or camping on private property. In addition, some public lands are devoted to the protection of wildlife, such as the Lewis and Clark National Wildlife Refuge, Julia Butler Hansen National Wildlife Refuge, and the Ridgefield National Wildlife Refuge. Portions of these refuges are open for day use only. All are closed to overnight camping.

LOW-IMPACT CAMPING

Few camping areas are available on either shoreline from Skamokawa downriver. Much of the area is a national wildlife refuge, making camping illegal; and even if camping were legal it wouldn't make much of a difference since many of the islands are really marshes and offer no solid ground. All public and private campgrounds are shown on the sixteen trail reach maps included in this book. If you choose to camp elsewhere, please do your best to protect the soils, plants, and animals in the area from human impact.

The concept of low-impact camping has been accepted by most Americans and is the mark of a responsible camper. It really is possible to camp in such a way that you leave virtually no trace. This involves being aware of how your actions in setting up and occupying a site affect the environment and making sure you do the least damage to that environment. For example, avoid washing dishes with liquid detergent or soap unless there is plenty of pure water for rinsing, and do not wash them in the river. Try to avoid riverbank erosion at your landing site. Place your tent where it will do the least damage to the riparian vegetation. When you leave, simply take an extra minute to restore your site to its natural state. The next visitor will appreciate your thoughtfulness. Always remember to carry out whatever you have carried in.

FIRES

It is best to carry a small backpacking stove rather than build a fire. However, if you are allowed to build a fire and choose to do so, please follow some simple rules. Select a spot away from driftwood piles, grass, brush, or trees. Use a fire pan elevated on rocks or a fire ring on sand. Use only dead wood. Have water handy for dousing the coals to make sure the fire is out, and in case nearby vegetation catches fire. Dispose of ashes, charcoal, and partially burned wood in the river, and leave the fire site clean.

Water trail use is heaviest during summer and fall, the region's driest period. Thus, fire danger is especially high while the need for warmth is virtually nonexistent. Landowners cite fire danger as the primary reason for not wanting people to camp on or even near their property.

BEHAVIOR PROBLEMS

Most of us have experienced behavior problems in public campgrounds, such as noisy, drunken, all-night parties, boom boxes, and roaring car engines. These are difficult situations that can become dangerous if you, personally, try to make the slobs behave. Call a law enforcement officer, park host, or ranger if that is an option; if not, move your camp. Along the lower Columbia River shore campgrounds and marinas there have been numerous instances of people stealing personal property from sleeping boaters. Be aware of this and protect your property as well as possible by keeping it in your tent or close by at night. High-decibel noise and spray from jet-skis can also disturb wildlife, especially nesting birds.

TRASH

Do not throw any trash overboard! As the saying goes, "If you boat it in, boat it out." All rubbish (plastic, glass, metals, and so on) should be returned to shoreline facilities for proper disposal. This helps prevent littered beaches, dead fish, and birds strangled by plastic can-holders. A heavyweight garbage bag or two should be standard equipment.

HUMAN WASTE

Three types of onboard marine sanitation devices are available. Two of these macerate and treat sewage by chemical and/or biological decomposition. The treated waste can then be legally discharged overboard. A third (and more environmentally acceptable) device is a holding tank with formaldehyde and deodorizers. This must be emptied in onshore pump-out stations. If you have none of the above, a Porta-Potty will do the job until you get to a shoreside facility. Carry toilet paper off with other waste.

There are six pump-out stations for sewage disposal on the Washington shoreline, including stations at Beacon Rock State Park, Port of Camas and Washougal, Steamboat Landing (Vancouver), Kalama Marina, Elochoman Slough (Cathlamet), and Port of Ilwaco. In Oregon there are three sewage disposal sites: Chinook Landing (opposite the eastern end of Government Island), M. James Gleason Memorial Boat Ramp (downstream from the western end of Lemon Island), and West End Mooring Basin (Astoria).

Recreational boating that involves camping has increased so much in popularity that disposal of human waste has become a serious health and aesthetic problem. On many popular rivers that have come under government regulation it is mandatory to contain human waste during the trip and dispose of it at a waste facility on shore. The requirements in the Grand Canyon along the Colorado River are typical: before a party is permitted to launch, it must be shown that their equipment includes containers for all human waste expected during the entire trip, with the exception of urine. Boaters are advised that urine is best eliminated in the river. One reason for this is that urine does not break down or disappear, especially in dry climates, instead accumulating and creating a foul odor. Another reason is that collective devices are not large enough for both solid and liquid human wastes generated on a long trip. Your cooperation in adhering to a carry-off method is critical.

Some reliable options for handling waste include using a biodegradable bag containing kitty litter (forcing the air out, sealing the bag, and placing it in a closed container), a 3- to 5-gallon bucket with a tight-fitting lid (using lime to minimize odors), or a waterproof canister with a garbage bag liner (again using lime).

HAZARDOUS WASTE

Hazardous wastes are the byproducts of boat fueling and hull maintenance. Paints, paint thinners, paint strippers, brush cleaners, lacquers, wood preservatives, and turpentine should be disposed of properly, not in the river. Some of these chemicals are toxic to humans and other animals, and some are suspected carcinogens. Oil and gasoline are also toxic if released into the environment. To operate your boat cleanly and efficiently, tune your engine regularly and inspect fuel lines for leaks, cracks, and loose connections. When changing oil and transmission fluid, use a spill-proof or vacuum pump, slip a bag over the oil filter before removal, and wipe up oil drips with an absorption pad. Keep fluids separate so you can recycle them according to local regulations.

WATER

Lewis and Clark felt free to drink almost anywhere until they reached the last few miles in the salty Columbia estuary. Nowadays it would be foolish to drink from any free-flowing stream, because of pollution and disease organisms. The parasitic disease *Giardia lamblia* is found in lakes, creeks, rivers, and springs throughout the Northwest. Also avoid washing fruits, vegetables, dishes, or hands in untreated water. Boil water for five minutes to kill the *Giardia lamblia* parasite and any other living contaminants. Always carry an adequate supply of good drinking water while boating the Columbia.

PETS

You will do yourself and others a big favor by leaving your pets at home. Pets and wildlife do not mix. If dogs are along, keep them on a short leash.

Boat Rentals and Tours

Alder Creek Kayak and Canoe (rentals, guided tours)
250 NE Tomahawk Island Drive
Portland, Oregon 97217
503-285-0464
www.aldercreek.com

Ebb and Flow PaddleSports
(rentals, lessons, supplies)
604 SW Nebraska Street
Portland, Oregon 97201
503-245-1756

NW Discoveries
(lessons, guided tours)
P.O. Box 23171
Tigard, Oregon 97281
503-524-9192
www.nwdiscoveries.com

Pacific Wave
(lessons, rentals, guided tours, supplies)
21 Highway 101
Warrenton, Oregon 97146
503-861-0866 or 1-888-223-9794
www.pacwave.net

Portland River Company
(rentals, guided tours)
315 SW Montgomery, Suite 330
Portland, Oregon 97201
503-229-0551 or 1-888-238-2059
www.portlandrivercompany.com

Scappoose Bay Kayaking
(rentals, guided tours)
57420 Old Portland Road
Warren, Oregon 97053
503-397-2161
www.scappoosebaykayaking.com

Skamokawa Town Center
(rentals, lessons, guided tours)
1391 West State Route 4
Skamokawa, Washington 98647
360-795-8300 or 1-888-920-2777
www.skamokawakayak.com

Useful Contacts

Columbia River Journeys
P.O. Box 26
Richland, Washington 99352
509-734-9941
www.columbiariverjourneys.com

Lewis and Clark National
Wildlife Refuge
c/o Julia Butler Hansen National
Wildlife Refuge
P.O. Box 566
Cathlamet, Washington 98612
360-795-3915 or 360-484-3482

Lower Columbia River Canoe Club
P.O. Box 40210
Portland, Oregon 97240

Lower Columbia River Estuary
Partnership
811 SW Naito Parkway, Suite 120
Portland, Oregon 97204
503-226-1565
www.lcrep.org

National Weather Service
Forecast Office
5241 NE 122nd Avenue
Portland, Oregon 97230
503-261-9246
www.wrh.noaa.gov/Portland

Northwest Discovery Water Trail
Army Corps of Engineers
P.O. Box 2946
Portland, Oregon 97208
503-808-4306

Notice to Mariners
U.S. Coast Guard
915 Second Avenue
Jackson Federal Building
Seattle, Washington 98174
206-220-7280

Oregon Kayak and Canoe Club
P.O. Box 692
Portland, Oregon 97207
www.okcc.org

Oregon Ocean Paddling Society
P.O. Box 69641
Portland, Oregon 97201
http://home.teleport.com/~orops

Oregon Parks and Recreation Dept.
1115 Commercial Street NE
Salem, Oregon 97301
503-378-6305
www.oregonstateparks.org

Oregon State Marine Board
435 NE Commercial Street
Salem, Oregon 97310
503-378-8587
www.boatoregon.com

Ridgefield National Wildlife Refuge
P.O. Box 457
Ridgefield, Washington 98642
360-887-4106
http://pacific.fws.gov/ridgefield

Southwest Washington Canoe Club
P.O. Box 714
Kelso, Washington 98626

U.S. Coast Guard
6767 North Basin Avenue
Portland, Oregon 97117
503-240-9311 (day)
503-240-9301 (evening)
503-861-6105 (Astoria)
503-861-6211 (search and rescue)
360-642-2381 (emergency)
1-800-368-5647 (boating safety
hotline)
www.uscg.mil/USCG.shtm

U.S. Fish and Wildlife Service
Pacific Regional Office
911 NE Eleventh Avenue
Portland, Oregon 97232
503-872-2728
http://pacific.fws.gov

Washington Interagency Committee
for Outdoor Recreation
1111 Washington Street SE
P.O. Box 40917
Olympia, Washington 98504
360-902-3000
www.boat.iac.wa.gov

Washington Kayak Club
P.O. Box 24264
Seattle, Washington 98124
206-433-1983
www.wakayakclub.com

Washington Parks and Recreation
Department
P.O. Box 42650
Olympia, Washington 98504
360-902-8844
www.parks.wa.gov

Washington Water Trails Association
4649 Sunnyside Avenue North, Room
305
Seattle, Washington 98103
206-545-9161
www.wwta.org

Useful Web Sites

Discovering Lewis and Clark. www.lewis-clark.org
Fort Clatsop National Memorial. www.nps.gov/focl
Lewis and Clark: The Journey of the Corps of Discovery.
    www.pbs.org/lewisandclark
Lewis and Clark National Historic Trail. www.nps.gov/lecl
Lewis and Clark Trail. www.lewisandclarktrail.com
Lewis and Clark Trail Heritage Foundation. www.lewisandclark.org
Lewis and Clark Trail Heritage Foundation, Oregon Chapter.
    www.lcarchive.org/or_lcthf.html
Oregon Historical Society. www.ohs.org
Washington State Historical Society. www.wshs.org

Bibliography and Recommended Reading

Agee, James. 1992. *Fire Ecology of Pacific Northwest Forests*. Covelo, California: Island Press.

Allen, John E., and Marjorie Burns. 1986. *Cataclysms on the Columbia*. Portland, Oregon: Timber Press.

Ambrose, Stephen E. 1996. *Undaunted Courage*. New York: Simon and Schuster.

Atwater, Brian. 1996. "Coastal Evidence for Great Earthquakes in Western Washington." U.S. Geological Survey Professional Paper 1560.

Auerbach, Paul S. 1991. *Medicine for the Outdoors: A Guide to Emergency Medical Procedures and First Aid*. Boston: Little, Brown.

Beidleman, Richard G. 1966. "Lewis and Clark: Plant Collectors for a President." *Horticulture* (April).

Biddle, Henry J. December 20 and December 27, 1924. "The Story of Beacon Rock." *Spectator Newspaper* 26 (18 and 19).

Botkin, Daniel. 1995. *Our Natural History: The Lessons of Lewis and Clark*. New York: Putnam.

Brinckman, Jonathan. December 3, 2002. "Salmon Count Hits Record." *The Oregonian*.

Cody, Robin. 1995. *Voyage of a Summer Sun: Canoeing the Columbia River*. New York: Alfred A. Knopf.

Cone, Joseph, and Sandy Ridlington, eds. 1996. *The Northwest Salmon Crisis: A Documentary History*. Corvallis, Oregon: Oregon State University Press.

Cutright, Paul R. 1969. *Lewis and Clark: Pioneering Naturalists*. Lincoln, Nebraska: University of Nebraska Press.

DeVoto, Bernard. 1953. *The Journals of Lewis and Clark*. Boston: Houghton Mifflin.

Evergreen Pacific Publishing. 1991. *Evergreen Pacific River Cruising Atlas: Columbia, Snake, Willamette*. Seattle, Washington: Romar Books.

Gault, Vera Whitney. 1984. "The Diary of Mary Riddle of Svensen." *Clatsop County Historical Society Quarterly* 4 (3).

Hawthorne, Clay. 1992. "Save Our Salmon, Save Our Soul." *The Nation* 254.

Houck, Michael C., and Mary Jane Cody., eds. 2000. *Wild in the City.* Portland, Oregon: Oregon Historical Society Press.

Huser, Verne. 2000. *Paddle Routes of Western Washington: Fifty Flatwater Trips for Canoe and Kayak.* 2d ed. Seattle, Washington: Mountaineers.

Jones, Landon, ed. 2000. *The Essential Lewis and Clark.* New York: Ecco Press.

Jones, Philip N., ed. 1992. *Columbia River Gorge: A Complete Guide.* Seattle, Washington: Mountaineers.

Jones, Philip N. 1997. *Canoe and Kayak Routes of Northwest Oregon.* Seattle, Washington: Mountaineers.

Kirk, Ruth, and Carmela Alexander. 1990. *Exploring Washington's Past: A Road Guide to History.* Seattle, Washington: University of Washington Press.

Lancaster, Samuel. 1916. *The Columbia: America's Great Highway through the Cascade Mountains to the Sea.* 2d ed. Portland, Oregon: Samuel Lancaster.

Lang, William L., and Robert C. Carriker. 1999. *Great River of the West.* Seattle, Washington: University of Washington Press.

Lavender, David. 1988. *The Way to the Western Sea: Lewis and Clark across the Continent.* New York: Harper and Row.

Mack, Lois. 1999. *One Place Across Time.* Vancouver, Washington: Vancouver National Historic Reserve Trust.

McKinney, Sam. 1987. *Reach of Tide, Ring of History: A Columbia River Voyage.* Portland, Oregon: Oregon Historical Society Press.

McKinney, Sam. 1992. *Boating Guide to the Lower Columbia and Willamette Rivers.* Salem, Oregon: Oregon State Marine Board.

Metropolitan Regional Services. 1992. *Metropolitan Greenspaces: Master Plan.* Portland, Oregon: Metro.

Moulton, Gary E., ed. 1989. *The Journals of the Lewis & Clark Expedition.* Vol. 5, July 28–November 1, 1805. Lincoln, Nebraska: University of Nebraska Press.

Moulton, Gary E., ed. 1990. *The Journals of the Lewis & Clark Expedition*. Vol. 6, November 2, 1805–March 22, 1806. Lincoln, Nebraska: University of Nebraska Press.

Moulton, Gary E., ed. 1991. *The Journals of the Lewis & Clark Expedition*. 1991. Vol. 7, March 23–June 9, 1806. Lincoln, Nebraska: University of Nebraska Press.

Netboy, Anthony. 1980. *The Columbia River Salmon and Steelhead Trout: Their Fight for Survival*. Seattle, Washington: University of Washington Press.

Oregon State Marine Board. 1997. *Oregon Boating Facilities Guide*. Salem, Oregon: Oregon State Marine Board.

Oregon State Marine Board. 2001. *Oregon Marina Guide*. Salem, Oregon: Oregon State Marine Board.

Peterson, Curt, and Ian Madin. 1997. "Coseismic Paleoliquefaction Evidence in the Central Cascadia Margin, U.S.A." *Oregon Geology* 59 (3).

Plamondon II, Martin. 2002. *Lewis and Clark Trail Maps: A Cartographic Reconstruction*. Vol. 3. Pullman, Washington: Washington State University Press.

Ramenofsky, Ann. 1987. *Vectors of Death: The Archeology of European Contact*. Albuquerque, New Mexico: University of New Mexico Press.

Ronda, James P. 1984. *Lewis and Clark Among the Indians*. Lincoln, Nebraska: University of Nebraska Press.

Ruby, Robert H., and John A. Brown. 1993. *Indian Slavery in the Pacific Northwest*. Spokane, Washington: Arthur H. Clark Company.

Strong, Emory, and Ruth Strong. 1995. *Seeking Western Waters: The Lewis and Clark Trail from the Rockies to the Pacific*. Portland, Oregon: Oregon Historical Society Press.

Wells, Gail, and Dawn Anzinger. 2001. *Lewis and Clark Meet Oregon's Forests: Lessons from Dynamic Nature*. Corvallis, Oregon: Oregon State University Press.

Ziak, Rex. 2002. *In Full View: A True and Accurate Account of Lewis and Clark's Arrival at the Pacific Ocean, and Their Search for a Winter Camp along the Lower Columbia River*. Astoria, Oregon: Moffitt House Press.

Index

About the Author

Keith G. Hay has been an avid outdoorsman and kayaker throughout his long career in wildlife ecology and conservation, which has included, among other things, serving as deputy director of public affairs for the U.S. Fish and Wildlife Service. His interest in the Lewis and Clark expedition began in 1963 when he joined the U.S. Bureau of Outdoor Recreation and worked with the first national Lewis and Clark Trail Commission. In 1966 he received the commission's Jefferson Peace Medal for his two-year study of the expedition's route, and co-authored *The Lewis and Clark Trail: A Proposal for Development*, which recommended a plan for creating and preserving a "recreational ribbon" along the eleven-state trail. Keith is a founder and past president of the Oregon Chapter of the Lewis and Clark Trail Heritage Foundation, vice-president of the Lewis and Clark Bicentennial in Oregon, and a founder and national advocate for the American Greenways Program.

Photo by Jennifer Hay Preston.